BUILDING HOPE

BUILDING HOPE

Leadership in the Nonprofit World

John Bateson

PRAEGER

Westport, Connecticut
London

Library of Congress Cataloging-in-Publication Data

Bateson, John, 1951–
    Building hope : leadership in the nonprofit world / John Bateson.
        p.   cm.
    Includes bibliographical references and index.
    ISBN-13: 978–0–313–34851–8 (alk. paper)
    1. Nonprofit organizations—Management.   I. Title.
    HD62.6.B387   2008
    658′.048—dc22   2007035289

British Library Cataloguing in Publication Data is available.

Library of Congress Catalog Card Number: 2007035289
ISBN-13: 978–0–313–34851–8

First published in 2008

Praeger Publishers, 88 Post Road West, Westport, CT 06881
An imprint of Greenwood Publishing Group, Inc.
www.praeger.com

Printed in the United States of America

The paper used in this book complies with the
Permanent Paper Standard issued by the National
Information Standards Organization (Z39.48–1984).

10 9 8 7 6 5 4 3 2 1

To Suzan,
who has her own stories to tell

Contents

Preface

A fair number of people have asked me what it's like to lead and manage a nonprofit agency. Some are friends and acquaintances who are merely curious. Others are recent college graduates considering nonprofit careers, or established professionals in a variety of fields who want to transition into something that they'll find meaningful. Still others work in the nonprofit sector already and aim to move into management positions, or are new nonprofit executives who feel overwhelmed by all of the things that they think they're supposed to know and don't.

In this book, I share many of my experiences over the last twenty-seven years directing nonprofit agencies. In particular, I focus on the past eleven years in which I've led a busy, twenty-four-hour crisis center in northern California. Most of my experiences have been positive, although some didn't seem so at the time. I also describe blunders I've made for which there was no remedy except to admit my mistake and try to learn from it. My goal is to help other nonprofit leaders and managers become even better at their jobs, as well as to inform the general public about the complexities of running a nonprofit agency.

Some of what I've learned, particularly in the areas of board development, volunteer management, and fundraising, constitutes a harried yet fairly typical rite of passage for a nonprofit executive. Other things, though, especially those concerning cultural competency, advocacy, and major gift solicitation, have been unexpected, eye-opening, and, at times, soul-searching.

Dozens of books have been written about various aspects of nonprofit management. The majority are "how-to" books. More often than not they start out as a presentation given at a conference, include lots of sample forms and tip sheets, and are excerpted on Web sites. Although they have much to offer, not all of the information in them is accurate. Moreover, the books themselves can be pretty dry.

A few are more expansive. Authors like Peter Drucker have written authoritatively, with considerable wisdom. At the same time, they've never worked at a nonprofit agency. They can only describe what they see and hear, which has value yet lacks the emotional intensity of someone who's affected directly. It's one thing to say that you need to develop a diverse funding base so as not to be reliant on any single income source, yet it's another thing altogether to lie awake at night worrying about whether you're going to have to lay off staff and shut down programs because donations to your agency are lagging.

In a few instances, someone has written a book about his or her personal experiences at a nonprofit agency. The best one, in my mind, is *A Slender Thread*, by Diane Ackerman. She writes eloquently and with great insight about being a hotline volunteer at a small crisis center in New England. Unfortunately, as a volunteer she wasn't in a position to explore other facets of the agency.

I wrote this book to offer a different perspective. While it includes lots of tips—the best of what I've learned, compiled in one place—it's not intended as an instruction manual. There aren't any forms, and I don't lecture anyone. In fact, I fought against including an index, believing that one was unnecessary (the chapter titles indicate to readers the general content, after all, plus few memoirs have them and I consider this something of a memoir). My publisher insisted, though, with good reason I think now.

Mostly, what I do is tell stories. In a few instances, the names of people have been changed to protect their privacy, although usually real names are used, with permission. The stories illustrate the challenges and frustrations, but most of all the joys, of leading a nonprofit agency today.

In terms of credentials, I've been recruited to nonprofit boards of directors and recruited people to serve on my agency's board. I've been hired as an executive director, program manager, and fundraiser, and I've hired others for these positions. I've been a volunteer and I've supervised other volunteers, evaluated grant requests for funders and submitted grant requests to funders, provided direct services as a nonprofit employee and received direct services as a nonprofit client. I was a social worker the first sixteen years of my nonprofit career, and now I supervise licensed clinicians and other highly skilled people who provide crisis intervention and mental health services twenty-four hours a day, 365 days a year.

As I'm writing this, I have in front of me an *Associated Press* article that appeared earlier in the week. It says that Americans gave $295 billion to charitable causes in 2006, up from $283 billion in 2005. Individual giving constituted 75 percent of the total and, if bequests are included, the number is 83 percent. About 65 percent of households with incomes under $100,000 give to charity. The result is that the United States continues to rank first in philanthropic giving as a percentage of gross domestic product at 1.7 percent. Britain is a distant second at 0.7 percent.

What this means is that the nonprofit sector is more important than ever. People in this country give an increasing amount of money and much of their time to nonprofit agencies because they care about their communities and the fabric of services that holds them together. It's a special relationship, one built on trust, need, compassion, and hope.

I'm in the middle of it. Reading this book, you will be, too.

Acknowledgments

Over the years, it has been my good fortune to work alongside many talented, dedicated, and caring people. I want to extend a heartfelt thank you to the following individuals who continue to make the world a better place:

To Larry Sly, who launched my career—although I didn't know it at the time—by hiring me in my first nonprofit job, and who taught me, by example, what it means to put your ego aside and focus on the task at hand.

To other executive directors who've been colleagues in the field and a source of inspiration and wise counsel: Tanir Ami, Rick Aubry, Paula Barber, Angie Baur, Barbara Bernstein, Jim Bouquin, Barbara Bysiek, Liz Callahan, Carol Carrillo, Pat Coleman, Rick Crispino, Kate Ertz-Berger, Nancy Findeisen, Jane Garcia, Janet Gorewitz, Karen Grimsich, Margaret Hallett, Rhonda James, John Jones, Beatrice Lee, Barbara Maizie, Barbara McCullough, Stu McCullough, Arlette Merritt, Eve Meyer, Mariana Moore, Gina Moreland, Tim O'Keefe, Elaine Prendergast, Nancy Salamy, Gloria Sandoval, Rita Schank, Ed Schoenberger, Vi Smith, Alan Stein, Ron Tauber, and Anne Warner-Reitz.

To current members of the board of trustees of the Contra Costa Crisis Center, whose leadership, vision, and support I cherish: Nancy Bann, Shiva Berman, Alan Brast, Pete Caldwell, Marty Gonzalez, Deedee Hickerson, John Jenks, James Lee, Faye Lefebvre, Dane McCoy, Patty Owens, Mike Rekasis, Mitch Tarkoff, and Greg Thomas.

To crisis center staff, current and past, who produce miracles every day and don't see their name in print nearly often enough: Roberto Almanzán, Sidney Baird, Minerva Blaine, Mary Clark, Edith Cordone, Liezl Dizon, Brooks Elliott, Gail Fitzgerald, George Evans, Lesley Garcia, Alella Gipson, Bria James, Ann Mabee, Jim Matyas, Faye Mettler, Walt Middleton, Rico Millan, Susan Moore, Rhonda Otway, Rocio Polanco de Collazos, Judi Hampshire, the late Judy Guthrie, Cindy Rasicot, Eva Romero, Joan Stern, Brian Sugrue, Josie Trujillo, LaShonda Taylor, and Barbara Woodburn.

To three people who, along with Roberto Almanzán, have done more to increase the cultural competency of the crisis center and improve the lives of diverse populations in my community than anyone I know: Brenda Blasingame, Chia-Chia Chien, and José Martín.

To all of the volunteers at the crisis center, many more than I can possibly name, who answer our twenty-four-hour hotlines, counsel children and adults in grief, run our Leftovers Thrift Shop, and organize our annual fundraising gala. Your generosity, kindness, and devotion are unrivaled and are the main reasons why the crisis center is able to exist and enjoys the reputation that it does.

To my wife, Suzan, an extraordinary executive director in her own right, who sets such a high standard that, even on my best days, I can only aspire to it.

To our college-age children—Cassidy, Chloé, Sara, and Trevor. I love you and I'm proud of you.

And, finally, to Jeff Olson, my editor at Praeger Publishers, who first saw the value of this book and shepherded it every step of the way.

CHAPTER ONE

Starting Out: The Answer Is Near at Hand

I met once with board members from another agency. The agency had financial problems that only could be solved, it seemed, if a foundation approved a large grant.

"I don't feel good putting all of our eggs in one basket," the executive director said, "but we don't have a choice. Let's hope it works."

Hearing that, a board member replied, "We may not have a choice, but hope is not a strategy." He was a senior manager at a Fortune 500 company who said that hope had no place in strategic planning.

He was right. Hope is not a strategy, at least not a viable strategy for businesses that aim to be successful. Being hopeful means being powerless, at the mercy of others.

Yet most nonprofit agencies today are built on hope. We hope that the community values our services and funds us generously. We hope that the government enacts legislation reducing our workload rather than adding to it. We hope that our staffs remain dedicated to the cause despite long hours and relatively low wages.

We also hope that our volunteers continue to be here when they could be caring for themselves. We hope that the media find our work newsworthy. We hope that our clients get the help they need when we refer them elsewhere.

These things are largely outside our control, which is why we hope. Hope plays a bigger role in nonprofit management today than ever before.

Traditional funding sources such as corporations and United Way are drying up. Government funding is tighter. There's more competition for individual donations (just ask anyone at a local charity how his or her fundraising did immediately after 9/11 or Hurricane Katrina). Meanwhile, operating costs keep rising. How can we go on?

Ironically, this is the question that my agency, the Contra Costa Crisis Center, in Contra Costa County, California, hears every day from people who call our twenty-four-hour crisis lines. A teenage girl grieves the death of her mother. The family breadwinner loses his job. A senior citizen can't pay for health care. Now what?

We don't have answers. We listen, though, and help people sort through problems. We validate feelings, suggest options, and—most importantly—offer hope. Hope may not be an effective business strategy, but it's a powerful tonic for individuals. With hope, anything is possible.

Sometimes nonprofit agencies need hope, too. I don't think it makes us less businesslike, just more like the people we serve.

In 1974, when I graduated from college, no one I knew was planning a career in the nonprofit sector. Certainly I wasn't. A nonprofit job meant working long hours for minimum pay—if you were lucky enough to be paid. It also meant answering the same question again and again from family members and friends: "When are you going to get a real job?" By "real" they meant a job that led somewhere, where you had a future if you proved yourself, and where you had to dress up every day—or at least every day except, maybe, Fridays.

Today, working for a nonprofit organization still means long hours, though no longer than the hours of people in many other professions. And the pay remains low, at least compared with similar jobs in the for-profit world. What's changed is that nonprofit work has become fashionable. Helping others and making your community a better place to live now has status. A job at a community clinic or battered women's shelter doesn't need to lead anywhere to be socially accepted; it's an end in itself.

What's also changed is that jobs in the for-profit sector—especially at the biggest companies—aren't as secure as they once were. Mergers, layoffs, and bankruptcies are commonplace these days, leaving people who intended to build their careers and their fortunes in large companies feeling angry and betrayed. Who would have thought a few years ago that someone who worked in a local youth center would have more job security than someone who worked at Enron, Arthur Anderson, WorldCom, or Webvan?

It's not surprising that relatively few people today end up in nonprofit jobs by accident, the way I did. Nowadays, it's a conscious decision made by recent college graduates who want to dedicate themselves to a cause, and by a growing number of people in corporate positions who want to feel good about the work they're doing, where the bottom line isn't measured in dollars earned but in people served.

Working for a nonprofit organization can be rewarding, exciting, and personally satisfying. I know; I've done it for more than twenty-five years. It also can be tiring, frustrating, and emotionally draining. Often it's both, simultaneously.

For several years after graduating from Berkeley with a degree in sociology and English, I held jobs as a general laborer on a construction site, shipping clerk in a fifty-two-story office building, tennis instructor, bookseller, and freelance editor. After a brief stint of graduate school in France, I ended up with my first nonprofit position. It wasn't what I was looking for (at the time I pictured myself only a step or two away from being managing editor of a major publishing company), but

I needed a change and this job provided it. I was a truck driver, warehouseman, inventory clerk, bookkeeper, and program administrator at a food bank. There was a lot of variety to what I did, and I liked that. The job combined physical and mental challenges, and I liked that too.

I expected to stay several months. Instead, the months turned into years. My responsibilities increased as the agency grew. I hired and managed staff who drove the trucks and ran the warehouse as I had done. I wrote grant proposals and created direct mail appeals to raise money for new programs and a new building. I developed contacts with the media, with county officials, with influential legislators.

I wrote a quarterly newsletter that was mailed to 20,000 donors and excerpted in numerous publications, including *The New York Times*. I wrote portions of three state bills (all passed the California Legislature but, alas, were vetoed by Governor George Deukmejian). I chaired a countywide task force on hunger whose report received national media coverage and was read into the *Congressional Record*.

I also met my wife, Suzan, who is now executive director of another food bank, the Alameda County Community Food Bank in Oakland, California. We sometimes joke that we ruined a great professional relationship by having a personal one, and that neither one of us will ever work quite as well with anyone else as we did with each other. Still, we're both fortunate to have jobs we love.

My job since 1996 has been executive director of the Contra Costa Crisis Center, a nonprofit organization in the San Francisco Bay Area. The agency operates twenty-four-hour crisis, suicide, grief, homeless, child abuse, and elder abuse hotlines, as well as a school violence tipline (eighteen lines altogether). We also run one of the largest grief counseling programs in California, provide an array of services for homeless people, operate a heralded youth violence program, play a lead role in our county's disaster response and recovery efforts, and maintain a countywide online resource database with up-to-date information on 2,500 local services. Funding comes from a variety of sources including individual donations, corporate and foundation grants, government contracts, and proceeds from a thrift store operated entirely by agency volunteers.

I'd never supervised mental health professionals before coming to the crisis center. I hadn't dealt constantly with people in life-threatening situations either, or managed an agency that never closes. All of these were reasons why I accepted the position. I was sure I would learn a lot, and I have.

The greater challenge today, though, is managing any kind of nonprofit agency. There are 1.3 million nonprofit organizations in the United States right now, not counting religious groups, schools, government agencies, and some hospitals, which qualify under Internal Revenue Service codes but aren't what most people think of as nonprofit agencies. New organizations are founded every day, while others disappear. Those that survive have staked out turf—or in the jargon of corporate America, have found a niche—defined by geographic boundaries, population served, and kind of service provided.

One challenge for all of these nonprofit organizations is to coexist, to develop partnerships and collaborate in such a way that they're able to provide services efficiently and effectively. No one likes to fund duplicating services, so nonprofits have to demonstrate a willingness to work cooperatively with one another. This isn't always easy.

Another challenge is greater competition for financial support. Many individuals and companies today are amassing enormous fortunes; however, with a few notable exceptions (Bill Gates, Warren Buffett), this wealth isn't translating into increased giving, except to universities and the arts. Donations to soup kitchens, homeless shelters, child care centers, literacy programs, health care clinics, family counseling services, independent living centers, and many other kinds of agencies have remained largely unchanged, even though the demand for many of these services has skyrocketed and may grow even more in the future. Soliciting financial support, which includes cultivating relationships with major donors, hosting special events, and personally acknowledging generous gifts, is occupying an increasingly larger percentage of every nonprofit manager's time.

A third challenge is the need to be more accountable. It used to be that if people gave your agency money, whether they were individuals or institutions, you sent them a thank you note and that was pretty much it. The donation was entered into the organization's book-keeping system, which was maintained manually, and the money was spent as the donor specified, which usually was "to further the good work of the organization," meaning it wasn't restricted at all.

Today, though, to keep donors interested you have to thank them often and well. In addition, funders expect a detailed accounting of their money and sometimes restrict gifts to specific purposes. This isn't necessarily a bad thing, but it's one of the reasons why local charities have to spend more time raising money now and employ more people tracking it.

When I started at the food bank in 1980, the organization was 100 percent county funded. I was a county employee, worked in a county-owned building, and used county trucks, print services, phones, and supplies. Today, the county pays only 5 percent of the agency's operating budget. Most people would consider this a positive development. The food bank has developed a broad funding base and isn't dependent on any one source. Moreover, since government funding is uncertain, having greater private support means an organization's finances are more secure.

All of this is true; however, what many people don't realize is that when the food bank was 100 percent county funded, staff submitted only one funding request and one written report per year—to the county. The rest of our time was devoted to collecting and distributing food. When I left, the organization received financial support from dozens of businesses and foundations, as well as from other government entities (city, state, and Federal). Not only did staff have to submit detailed reports to each funding source, but every report was different because every funder had a different grant period and different geographic area of interest, and each gave money for a different program or service. Whereas in the beginning there was no reason to hire a bookkeeper because the executive director could handle the recordkeeping, today the organization needs a full-time accountant, two full-time finance assistants, and two part-time assistants, as well as an outside auditor. Some board members regard the addition of staff positions that aren't directly related to service as a sign that the agency is becoming too bureaucratic. It's true; however, the agency has no choice. Funders demand it.

Nonprofit organizations today also face the challenge of finding, training, and maintaining a workforce of volunteers. Every nonprofit agency depends to some extent on volunteer labor to keep costs down, yet this is more difficult today than it was twenty years ago. For one thing, more people—especially more women—work today and have less time to volunteer. Also schools, both public and private, are asking parents to help out more in the classroom to make up for cuts in government funding. The spirit of volunteerism is still strong—in fact, overall more people are volunteering now in America than ever before—but the amount of time people have to give seems to be declining. Moreover, everyone wants what few hours they can volunteer to be meaningful, to be focused on helping people directly, and this isn't always possible, particularly if special training is required and someone doesn't volunteer regularly.

INCREASED PROFESSIONALISM

When I started in 1980, most nonprofit leaders were unprofessional in the sense that we knew little about budgeting, money management, fundraising, strategic planning, program evaluation, or marketing. Some people were visionaries committed to a cause who founded and led their agencies. Others, like me, gravitated to the sector by chance. In both cases, our management skills were unpolished. Individuals saw a need in the community, a service that was missing, and worked to provide it. Over time, if the agency was successful, we developed expertise in administration, fund development, program operations, and public relations; however, rarely did we begin with it.

Today, all that's changing. There's increased professionalism in the field. One reason why is because a growing number of business and graduate schools are offering entire programs and degrees in nonprofit management. When organizations have openings at the executive director and senior management level now, the pool of candidates almost always includes applicants with academic training far greater than the previous person in the position had.

A second reason is because many people are transitioning from the for-profit to the nonprofit world. In doing so they bring a wealth of operational experience that can't help but make the whole field stronger. These professionals come in knowing how to read financial statements, draft budgets, manage resources, supervise diverse staff, and develop strategic plans. Many are savvy marketers. They probably lack fundraising experience, which is a serious shortcoming, and are unfamiliar with regulatory issues specific to nonprofits; however, their business acumen is valuable, especially to agencies that historically have been poorly managed.

The main reason why nonprofit managers are becoming more professional, though, is because they have to. Providing an important service no longer is enough. *Every* service is important today and every service is vying for

funding, space, multicultural staff, volunteers, and public recognition. Whatever
your agency's mission, you have to be efficient and effective in the way you operate. Much of this responsibility falls on the chief executive. More than anything
else, his or her leadership and management skills determine the agency's success.
A good executive director grows an agency; a mediocre one withers it.

So, what makes a good executive director? One of the most important characteristics is a positive attitude. Nonprofit leaders must be positive about the future.
They don't have to be charismatic; however, they need to believe passionately that
people can make a difference and be able to inspire, enable, and challenge others
by sharing their vision. Being persistent when confronting obstacles and resilient
in the face of disappointment and rejection are offshoots of this. A positive attitude
is infectious; it rubs off on and motivates others.

Another important characteristic is flexibility. Nonprofit executives need to be
able to perform a variety of tasks simultaneously, to adjust quickly to circumstances
that are difficult to predict, and to deal effectively with people of varying styles.

Nonprofit directors also have to be adept at building consensus. Successful
nonprofit executives make decisions in partnership with staff and board members,
and sometimes in consultation with donors, volunteers, clients, and the community
at large. The process can take much longer than in the for-profit world and include
many more people. New executive directors who come from a corporate environment can be frustrated by this culture of consensus building. Shared governance
is at the heart of every nonprofit organization, though, and individuals who can't
adjust to it don't last long.

Being able to communicate effectively is important, too. You don't have to be
an outstanding speaker or writer to lead a nonprofit agency, but you'd better be
pretty good at both. An executive director who's able to communicate simply and
directly from the heart—free of jargon, acronyms, flowery words, empty phrases,
and unnecessary statistics—is coveted for the simple reason that he or she will
connect with people and develop strong support for the agency.

It almost goes without saying, but I'll say it: you have to have good judgment.
This may seem true about most jobs; however, the ability to exercise good judgment
is critical for executive directors. Understanding the short-term and long-term
consequences of a decision, obtaining as much information as possible before
making a decision, making quick decisions when necessary, and knowing which
decisions can be made alone and which require consultation are all part of the
job. Mistakes in judgment are less forgivable than any other kind of mistake, and
nothing shakes the confidence of a board of directors more than to learn that its
chief executive acted rashly.

DIFFERENT NEEDS AT DIFFERENT TIMES

That said, every nonprofit organization needs different qualities in an executive director at different times in its history. The visionary with grassroots organizing skills who brings people together to start an agency may not have the

administrative expertise or interest to take the agency to the next level. Someone who thrives during organizational crises, when funding is threatened, equipment is failing, and people are quitting, may be bored when everything is static and programs are in maintenance mode. Every organization wants an executive director with fundraising experience; however, if the organization has never done much fundraising it needs someone who can start and build a fundraising program, not someone with advanced skills that will be wasted right now.

Boards looking for an executive director should ask what the agency needs at this point in time. By honestly assessing challenges the agency is facing, boards can find candidates whose skills and experience offer a good match rather than candidates who fit general ideals such as "good administrator," "strong leader," or "strategic thinker."

All too often, when boards consider candidates for executive director they look for individuals who are strong in areas where the previous executive director was weak. If the former executive director was charismatic, for example, but did a poor job managing employees and morale, as a result, is low, boards look for executives with a history of developing good relations with staff. If the former director was a good administrator but ineffective in promoting the agency, boards tend to be most impressed by candidates with strong marketing skills. If the former executive director was innovative but also critical of the board when it failed to embrace his or her ideas, boards look for someone they feel will be easy to work with.

None of this is bad, exactly, and in a backward way it can even work. It's just the wrong approach. Instead of comparing candidates with someone previously in the position, boards should compare them with current needs of the agency. The last executive director may have been too low-key for some people, but is a dynamic leader what's needed? Maybe it is if the agency wants to garner political support for a program or issue. If the biggest need is to improve the quality or variety of an agency's services, however, it's less important.

To understand the importance of going through this process, I'll share an experience I had. A number of years ago I applied to be executive director of an agency that provided legal assistance to poor people. I knew next to nothing about welfare codes, fair housing laws, or patients' rights; nevertheless, I figured that I could learn whatever I needed to know. The staff attorney and board member who met with me were particularly interested in my fundraising experience. At the time I thought that the agency either had financial problems that threatened its work or expansion plans that it didn't know how to fund.

It turned out to be the latter. The previous year the agency had opened two satellite offices and now the board wanted to open a third office but didn't know how to pay for it. The offices were situated in low-income communities and were critical in making the agency's services more accessible to people who couldn't afford legal representation.

A week after my initial interview I was called back for a second interview. This time the setting was much different. I was ushered into a small conference room that was filled with board members, management staff, agency attorneys, and support personnel. They stood against the walls and sat crammed around a table. There was one empty chair, clearly for me.

The board president, a vivacious woman who was an attorney in a public-interest law firm, asked the first few questions, then others followed. A common thread again was what success I'd had raising money. Since I was more expert in this than in legal issues, I was happy to focus the conversation on a subject I knew.

The interview was scheduled to last thirty minutes. After an hour, someone said that the other candidate was waiting. There were a few embarrassed looks, then I was excused.

Ultimately, the other candidate was hired. It turned out that he'd been executive director of a legal aide group in Harlem and the agency couldn't believe its luck in attracting someone so qualified. My interview was merely a warmup for the main show.

Unfortunately, whatever talents the other candidate had, fundraising wasn't among them. The third satellite office never opened, and within a year the other two offices closed. Only the central office remained and its staffing was cut to save expenses. Shortly thereafter, the executive director moved on.

It's conceivable that I or another candidate, if hired, would have fared no better. Still, people in the agency knew what they needed at the time yet chose someone who didn't fit those needs. The agency still hasn't recovered.

WHEN IT WORKS

Contrast that with another experience I had. Around the same time, I applied to be executive director of an environmental education institute. Here I actually knew something: I had volunteered with two environmental organizations, published articles in several environmental publications, and edited a California state environmental education guide used in 1,000 public schools.

The hiring process included six separate interviews over the course of a month—first with a national headhunter who was responsible for coordinating the search, then with the president who founded the agency, followed by senior agency staff, the executive directors of two sister agencies, several board members, and finally a group of five other staff. In between there was a half-day field trip in which I accompanied two instructors and a class of twenty-five students on a walk through tidal basins and coastal marshes.

In the end I wasn't hired for this position, either. The agency was financially secure and the founder continued to provide the vision so what was needed was someone with lots of hands-on experience who could lead outdoor classes and manage a retreat center. I had theoretical knowledge and good administrative skills, but this wasn't enough. The person who was chosen had directed an Outward Bound program in Pennsylvania for many years. I was disappointed to be runner-up again, but couldn't complain; people in the agency did their homework and selected someone who seemed a good fit.

Eventually I found the right opportunity for myself. You know it's the right opportunity when the needs an agency has coincide with the skills that you have to offer. Everybody wins then. The agency gets the right person at the right time and you have the chance to do what you do best and, therefore, probably what you enjoy doing most. Sometimes the pairing of the person and the job works so well that it can seem preordained.

At the time I interviewed with the crisis center, there were fifty-two other applicants. Two members of the search committee—Mike, a retired psychologist who was president of the board, and Vi, who'd been executive director of the agency ten years earlier and was coaxed out of retirement to help during the transition—took each of the final three candidates to lunch. My meal was at a Chinese restaurant (I don't know where the other two candidates ate). At the end, a waitress brought three fortune cookies. I watched Vi open her cookie, read the fortune, then smile, bemused. Mike's reaction upon reading his fortune was nearly identical, which surprised me since he and Vi weren't much alike. Then I opened my cookie. The fortune was, "You will be successful in a new venture."

That's nice, I thought, but it was hard to read much meaning into it. After all, it could apply to almost anything.

Mike and Vi shared their fortunes with each other and were astonished to learn that they were the same. Then they showed them to me. On both slips of paper was written, "The answer to your problem is very near at hand."

I showed my fortune to them and we all laughed. Two days later I was offered the job.

CHAPTER TWO

The Board: Finding the Right Jungle

The Chinese character for "crisis" means both danger and opportunity. This surprises people sometimes.

The danger part is pretty obvious. It accounts for the fear all of us feel when we confront something menacing—a physical attack, a financial setback, the breakup of a relationship, a layoff, a serious illness, an accident, a death.

The opportunity part is harder to understand. In most instances we just want to get through a crisis, to survive it and go on. Only later, from the vantage point of time, are we able to look back and see that there are ways we may have benefited.

For example, maybe the reason why we have a new job or new love is because we lost the old one. Maybe we're less afraid of being sick or poor or alone because in dealing with past crises, our coping skills have improved.

One Saturday night, as I was driving home from the video store after renting my family a movie, the engine in my car caught fire. I pulled over quickly to the side of the road and called 911. A fire truck arrived in minutes; however, by that time the car was engulfed in flames. I stared in disbelief as my trusty Volvo station wagon, with nearly 300,000 miles, became incinerated.

It was, all things considered, a small crisis. There was emotional and financial loss, and the inconvenience of having to buy another car, but no one was hurt and what was lost could be replaced. The thing that I remember most afterward is how relaxed I felt driving my new car. I never realized how much I'd worried driving my old one, how afraid I was that it'd break down.

When people call our hotlines, it's usually because they're facing a crisis and don't know what to do. They're abused, depressed, grieving, suicidal, drug addicted, alcoholic, ill, or unemployed. In the best cases, we're able to help them see that the situation presents opportunities as well as challenges, opportunities to reexamine attitudes and priorities, for example. In the worst cases, well, we just try to keep someone alive.

I'm not ready to rename my agency the Danger and Opportunity Center. It's still the Crisis Center. Yet danger and opportunity are closely related. While they rarely balance out, they remind us that good often results from bad, even when that seems unlikely.

Incidentally, the movie that I rented and hurriedly grabbed before my car burned up? It was a British comedy titled *Lucky Break*.

The challenges that I faced initially at the crisis center were different than what I expected. Moreover, I was forced to confront them before my first official day of work.

The board of directors invited me to attend the next board meeting, which was a week earlier than my start date, when I was still wrapping things up at my former agency. Several days before the meeting Mike, the board president with whom I'd shared fortune cookies, gave me a copy of the agenda. "I don't know how we're going to get through everything," he said. "The meeting is only two hours and I always promise to start and end on time."

I looked at what he'd given me. The meeting consisted of a series of reports that did, at first glance, seem substantial. The finance committee would present the first draft of next year's budget. The program committee would review progress on three new projects. A representative of the agency's thrift shop would report on recent sales, the special events committee would update board members on plans for the agency's annual auction, and the board development committee would report on its work. First, though, the search committee would make its final report and I'd be welcomed as the new executive director.

When I studied the agenda carefully, though, I realized what was missing. There were no action items. There weren't even discussion topics, just a series of briefings. Since board members weren't being asked to make any decisions, I couldn't help but wonder how much time really was required for information sharing. Couldn't each committee report be summarized in a brief handout and one or two highlights mentioned in the meeting?

I've always believed that meetings should last ninety minutes at most. Move items through. Yet here was a meeting consisting entirely of reports that was scheduled to last two hours. Moreover, the president thought two hours might not be enough time. Why?

The answer became obvious within the first five minutes. It was a social board. Board members enjoyed seeing each other and catching up on what everyone was doing. I hadn't sensed this during the hiring process even though, as the final step, I'd been interviewed by the full board in the same room where they were meeting now. The purpose then was different; all discussion was focused on determining whether I was a good fit for the position. Now the mood was relaxed. The board had done its job and board members didn't have to worry anymore about finding someone to lead the agency. Meetings became, once again, an opportunity for people to gather around the table and engage in conversations that, while starting and ending with the crisis center, meandered considerably in between.

I couldn't complain. After all, this was my first board meeting and I didn't want to make the mistake of judging all meetings based on this one. Moreover, I knew from experience that serving on a board should be fun. Board members must take their responsibilities seriously; at the same time, they could be doing other things so they have to get more out of the experience than the satisfaction of helping a worthwhile cause, important as that is.

MY OWN EXPERIENCE

A number of years ago I was asked to serve on the board of a child education center. The agency ran programs that were highly regarded, and parents throughout the area—including some who lived many miles away—vied to enroll their children in a limited number of openings. The center leased classrooms from the local school district in a beautiful, old building that was formerly an elementary school. Every classroom had tall ceilings and huge banks of windows that let in lots of natural light. All the floors were wood. The smaller rooms that weren't rented by the center were used by local artists as studios.

I joined the board in 1989, just a few months before the Loma Prieta Earthquake struck. When I started, the major topic of discussion was whether to increase enrollment fees in order to provide better salaries for staff. Many of the parents of children at the center were well-paid professionals who, like me, probably could afford an increase. At the same time, the center already was too expensive for low-income families. An additional raise would further ensure that the center's quality child development programs were available only to those with substantial means.

Throughout the discussions, which often were intense, everyone was respectful. Eventually, the board reached a compromise whereby fees were raised slightly and a scholarship fund was started to subsidize low-income children. I supported the decision; however, I didn't look forward to board meetings. There was no humor, no bantering, no sharing of personal information. It was all business.

It became even more so after the quake. A portion of the school was unusable. The rest was deemed safe by structural engineers, who recommended retrofitting that the school district couldn't afford. Partitions were set up so that multiple classes could share space while the board and the center's two co-directors began looking for a new, permanent site.

Everyone—teachers, children, and parents—proved resilient, largely because disasters tend to bring out the best in people. Several months later a former school with similar architecture unexpectedly went on the market. The price was reasonable and the location was superb. The center raised $50,000 (half from parents) for a down payment, local merchants contributed wood, paint, and other materials, and I convinced two unions to donate labor. Everyone chipped in on work crews, and within a month the center opened its doors at the new site.

Through it all, the board met continuously. We inspected buildings as they were identified, consulted with banks on a loan, submitted grant requests to prospective funders, managed a capital campaign, planned renovations, and orchestrated the move. We also dealt with staff who became increasingly frustrated the longer they had to operate in cramped, noisy quarters, and we responded to parents who at first questioned the safety of the old site and then didn't want to move to the new site. At times, the children became an afterthought.

I served four years on the board. Today, I barely remember other board members. They must have been competent, otherwise the center wouldn't have been able to buy a building; however, all of the meetings were a blur. The reason why is because even though they were productive, they weren't enjoyable. There was no social interaction; we just worked.

Now, as I observed my first meeting of the crisis center board, I was struck by the fact that everyone wanted to be there. Some people had demanding jobs, and all had families, yet each person found time to support the agency. Rarely, I was told, did anyone miss a meeting.

One thing that troubled me was that there was little diversity. Ten of the eleven board members were white, and all were between the ages of forty and sixty. None was openly gay, an immigrant, or non-Christian as far as I could tell. All lived in the central part of the county, where the agency was situated, even though many of the crisis center's clients were in the eastern and western sections of the county, which demographically were much different. More than half the board also volunteered in crisis center programs, and all had been recruited by friends who already were on the board. Given their composition, it wasn't surprising that they got along so well; they were nearly all alike.

I was still thinking about this when Hetty, who headed the board development committee, stood to make her report.

"Two months from now, Sylvie and I will be going off the board," Hetty said, motioning to Sylvie, her best friend. Hetty, Sylvie, and their husbands vacationed together every year. With their board terms ending, Hetty and Sylvie would have more time to travel, although that wasn't what Hetty was thinking about at the moment.

"If nothing is done," Hetty said, "the board will have only nine members, which isn't enough to fill the committees and do all the work that needs to be done. Given this situation, the board development committee is ready to nominate five people to the board. Each is a current crisis line volunteer. Each has been contacted by Sylvie or myself and has agreed to serve. Their names are—" She proceeded to name the five prospective members. When she finished, she said, "I move that they be elected to the board." Sylvie immediately seconded the motion.

I felt a knot in my stomach. It had happened so fast. I'd bemoaned the fact that the agenda didn't seem to include any action items and now one was presented without warning that could have a lasting, negative impact.

Hetty had a long history with the crisis center. She'd been a volunteer for nearly twenty years and had received the agency's highest honor for community service. Since joining the board six years earlier, she and Sylvie had been the driving force behind all crisis center activities, quick to make suggestions and equally quick to do the work necessary to implement them. It made sense that they thought it'd take five people to replace them. Looking around the room, I imagined that other board members thought five people weren't enough.

I knew that I wouldn't have been hired if Hetty and Sylvie had opposed it. I also knew that they were two of the crisis center's biggest donors because I'd asked about board giving while being interviewed. They bought tables at agency events, gave generously to agency appeals, and solicited donations from well-off friends. I didn't like what I had to do.

"I'm new," I said slowly. "I barely know any of you, and I haven't met any of the volunteers yet, including the ones you just mentioned, Hetty, although I look forward to doing so." I glanced in her direction; she was watching me intently.

"There are different theories about the most effective way to develop nonprofit boards," I said. "One theory is called the three W's."

I explained that the W's stood for work, wealth, and wisdom, and that work was the willingness of a board member to attend meetings, serve on one or more committees, and participate in agency events, and that wealth was the ability of a board member to make a sizable donation and also leverage financial support from others, and that wisdom was the knowledge of a board member about needs, trends, and changes in the community. I said that according to this theory of board development, every prospective board member should have not one but two Ws. It's not enough that board members be willing to work, or that they have money, or that they're wise. A strong board consists of people who contribute in multiple ways.

I paused, then added that some people refer to this theory as the three T's, which stand for time, talent, and treasure. It's the same thing. Board members invest their time, skills, and resources to help the agency succeed.

When no one said anything, I went on. "I like the idea behind the three W's; however, I believe in a different theory of board development. It's even simpler because there are only two things to remember instead of three. The first one is skills. What skills does someone bring to the agency that we don't have now? The second one is diversity. What diversity does a person add that we're currently lacking? That's what I care about in terms of new board members, skills and diversity."

I said that I didn't know anything about the people Hetty was proposing except that all were crisis line volunteers. What other skills did they have? Were any of them finance managers? Attorneys? Mental health professionals? Those were skills that I thought we needed. Had any ever been a client of the crisis center? That's a critical perspective. Did any have deep pockets? Fundraising experience? Could they open doors that were closed to us now? Most important of all, were any of them leaders? It's easier to teach a leader who knows nothing about your work to fall in love with your agency than it is to teach someone who's committed to your cause to become a leader.

Similarly, were any of the candidates ethnically or culturally diverse? Were any significantly younger or older than existing board members? Did any live in the eastern or western sections of the county, have a point of view markedly different from people currently in the room, or represent a constituency we served or wanted to serve that wasn't represented on the board now? Were any of them gay, economically disadvantaged, or disabled?

What I didn't say was that I thought the crisis center's board needed to change. I'd studied the composition, and some valuable traits were missing. Before boards change, though, they have to agree to change. This means electing new board members whose ideas, perspectives, and experiences vary from their predecessors. It also means getting rid of inactive board members, regardless of their position or status in the community. The culture of kindness that exists in many agencies prevents board members from holding each other accountable. Without this accountability, boards flounder and become filled with dead weight.

Board members are temporary stewards. The agency can and should be able to exist without specific individuals. Moreover, board members don't own a nonprofit agency, the community does. Board members act on behalf of the community to keep an agency efficient, effective, and relevant. They're the keepers of the vision, the people who tell the community what the agency stands for and why it's important. They broadly oversee staff to ensure that the vision is pursued. It's the staff, in turn, who make the dream come true.

I didn't share all of this, though. There'd be plenty of time later to work on it. My immediate concern was blocking the motion.

An awkward silence followed. Then Mike said, "John makes a good point, Hetty. What else can you tell us about these folks?"

"I can tell you that they're nice people, and that they're willing to be on the board," Hetty said. She was serious. The fact that board members probably would like them and that they agreed to serve made them qualified in her mind. It was the warm-body method of board development. We need people, here are some, let's elect them.

Mike, ever the diplomat, looked to defuse the tension. "Well that's good," he said. "They're not like Groucho Marx then, who said that he'd never join a club that would have him as a member."

Everyone but Hetty and Sylvie laughed. Mike said gently, "Is there anything else we know about them?"

Hetty said that she didn't know what any of the five did professionally. She hadn't asked them and, by her attitude, wasn't convinced that the information was important. She was pretty sure that at least two were employed, although she had no idea where. Upon further questioning, it turned out that all were white and lived near the crisis center.

The board voted to table the nominations. I was relieved, but also shaken. I appreciated that the majority of board members valued my opinion; at the same time, I was pretty sure that I'd lost Hetty and Sylvie's support permanently.

Everyone's commitment to an agency is strongest during the years when they're on the board, and peaks during the year or years when they play a leadership role, such as being president or campaign chair. They make their biggest financial gifts then, and put in the most hours of service. This is the time when they're truly invested in the agency's work, when they have the keenest interest in furthering the agency's mission. After their terms expire, though, most board members continue to be supportive. Their giving declines, and they're less likely to attend agency events or read every word of agency mailings the way they once did; still, most people are proud of their board service, remain committed to the cause, and want to continue helping whenever they can. The only ones who aren't supportive either weren't supportive to begin with (in which case the agency hasn't lost anything), moved away and adopted new causes (which the agency can't do anything about), or had a falling out with the agency.

In Hetty and Sylvie's case, once their board terms ended they stopped contributing or having anything to do with the crisis center. I talked with each of them several months later and neither said that she was angry with me, had second thoughts about my hiring, or was disappointed by the direction I was leading the agency. It was just that their terms ended and they were ready to let go.

I thanked them for their past support and left it at that. It wasn't the best resolution; however, one thing to remember about board members, just as about staff and program volunteers, is that strong agencies can survive the loss of good people because they have other good people waiting in the wings. They're never dependent on one or two individuals. I didn't know whether the crisis center had others who could be groomed to move into position, but was ready to find out.

BOARD DEVELOPMENT

Board development is much more than filling vacancies when they occur. It's about identifying, cultivating, and lining up prospective candidates who, in time, can add to the overall competency of the board through their skills, contacts, and life experiences. There are a number of steps in the process.

First and foremost, board members must understand their role and responsibilities. These need to be written and, if necessary, reviewed periodically. All boards aren't the same. Boards of arts and theatre groups, for instance, tend to focus on fundraising and leave administrative decisions to staff. They ask, "How do we get the money to stage a first-class production that I can invite my friends to?" It's not unusual for theatre boards to debate every facet of a capital campaign or the costumes, set design, and printed program for a performance while approving without discussion the administrative budget or changes to the personnel policies. This works as long as the executive director is capable and trustworthy, but it doesn't give him or her much support or guidance in managing the agency. Personally, I don't want a board that rubber stamps every recommendation I make, although I know many nonprofit executives who consider this the ideal. I'm confident of my decisions; at the same time, I want a board that challenges me to do my best thinking and adds perspectives and expertise that I can draw on and the agency can benefit from. If the board exists solely to fulfill the legal requirement that the agency must have a board, I'll look for another job.

In much the same way, boards of hospitals and health care clinics tend to focus on facility and equipment needs, motivated by a desire to have state-of-the-art technology and adequate parking for patients. The role of board members is to make sure that physicians have the latest equipment to do their jobs and that people are able to access services. Both are important, although it's equally important to specify what responsibilities go along with them. Many hospitals have fundraising auxiliaries, committees to deal with medical and ethical issues, consultants to oversee construction projects and research medical machinery, and administrators to deal with accreditation, insurance, and employee unions. What's left may be a lot or a little; either way, it should be spelled out. No one who wants to make a meaningful contribution is content joining a board of figureheads.

Boards of social service agencies tend to focus on programs. Frequently they participate or try to participate in day-to-day operation of the agency. Oftentimes they're social workers or case managers and refer clients to the agency. They know the community's needs and have good ideas about how best to meet them. At the same time, they're walking a fine line. If they're not careful, the delineation between board members and staff blurs. People become confused about where board responsibilities end and staff responsibilities begin. Moreover, one of the key duties of any board—raising money to sustain and expand services—is ignored. Staff can raise money by writing grants and securing contracts, but usually staff don't know individuals with deep pockets. Board members—the right board members—open doors that otherwise would remain closed to an agency.

The responsibilities of most boards are pretty straightforward: (1) set goals and operating policies; (2) provide broad oversight of agency finances and services; (3) raise money; (4) promote the agency in the community; and (5) hire, evaluate, and if necessary fire the executive director. Boards lead, but don't manage.

Board members fulfill their responsibilities in a number of ways. They regularly attend board meetings and read the packet of information sent to them in advance so that they're prepared to contribute to the discussions at meetings and make informed decisions if called upon to vote. They serve on one or more board committees, attend committee meetings, and perform tasks approved by the committee. They review monthly financial statements, drafts of agency budgets, and an annual audit. They make a personal contribution to the agency every year in an amount commensurate with their ability to give. They solicit donations from others to support the agency's work. They attend agency fundraising events. They provide professional expertise when needed and appropriate (for example, an attorney reviews language in agency contracts). Eventually, they also assume a leadership position (i.e., become an officer or committee chair).

Every prospective board member has two immediate concerns when considering a board position. First, what's the time commitment? It's important not to underestimate it. If it's ten hours a month, say so. The person may decline, but that's better than a subsequent resignation. If too much time is being asked of board members and you're having trouble getting people to agree to serve, consider ways to reduce it. Stick to ninety-minute meetings, always starting and ending on time.

If there are no important discussion or action items, cancel the meeting. If all business is handled in forty-five minutes, adjourn. If meetings regularly adjourn after forty-five minutes, meet every other month. Do most of the work in committees and summarize the results in writing ahead of time so that verbal presentations are brief. Use conference calls and teleconferencing whenever possible to eliminate the need for face-to-face meetings. Send everything by e-mail to expedite turnaround.

The second concern expressed by potential board members is what's the financial commitment? Again, be direct. If your agency has a specific dollar amount that every board member is expected to contribute, say so. Either it's a deal breaker or it's not; no sense avoiding it. Most agencies, mine included, don't have a set amount or even a stated range for board giving. This is because we don't want to exclude people on low incomes, especially if the agency's services are directed to the poor, and we don't want to set too low a ceiling for the people who can afford to give at higher levels.

There are numerous theories about what constitutes an appropriate board gift. One that used to be common was to "give until it hurts." This was replaced by "give until it feels good." More recently, the theory has been to give at a level that your peers would expect you to give at.

Each of these offers guidance without being specific and therefore without being limiting, which is the idea. I prefer something more concrete, though. I believe that each board member's annual donation should be the largest donation the person makes to any charity other than to his or her faith. I want board members who, during their tenures, are thinking first and foremost of the crisis center, not of another agency. It's not enough that they give their time, as valuable as that is. Their money should follow. In fact, it doesn't make sense to me when people who consider their time more important than money end up giving their time to one place and their money to another. If you serve on a board, why would you make you largest financial donation to a cause you consider less important?

One other thing about board giving: However you do it, there has to be 100 percent participation. Every board member has to contribute personally every year. Even if you don't have an overall goal for board members in terms of dollars raised, it should be clear that everyone gives—no exceptions. I've had board members who donated $10 per year and that was fine. They were disabled, lived in subsidized housing, and had no income other than Social Security. Ten dollars to them was equivalent to $10,000 for another board member. I was grateful for their support.

Every board member has to give so that each one is in this—the agency— together. Each person makes an investment and has a piece of ownership. Regardless of economic position, social standing, education, age, or other factors, board members become equal partners by giving. No one is better or worse than another, meaning no one is exempt from making a gift.

Another reason why every board member has to give is because it makes each one a stronger fundraiser. It's difficult to ask somebody to give if you haven't given yourself. People see through it. It's a lot more effective to say, "I'm proud to support the crisis center, and I hope you'll join me in donating to such a worthwhile cause."

BRAINSTORMING NAMES

Board development is the responsibility of every person in an agency. Identifying and recruiting board members shouldn't be left solely to a handful of people who serve on the board development committee, just as fundraising shouldn't be the responsibility of only those people who serve on the fund development committee. Everyone has relationships with people who can be good board members.

I consider board development one of the most important tasks of executive directors. After all, why leave the decision of who's going to be your boss in someone else's hands?

Board members and staff should constantly throw around names of potential board members. Who would be a good addition to our finance committee once Mike leaves? Who represents a diverse culture not currently represented on the board now? Who has mental health expertise, is a leader in the religious community, or is a major donor and knows other people with money?

After brainstorming names, develop a strategy for each. Is the person familiar with your agency? If not, then the first step is to invite him or her to take a tour. If the person already knows something about the agency, then he or she is approached about serving on a board committee. This is a good way for candidates to learn about the agency's inner workings and decide whether serving on the board fits their interests, while people in the agency get to assess the candidate's skills and ability to work with others.

Whenever possible, it's a good idea to bring new members on a board in twos or threes rather than individually. One reason why is because board members tend to bond most closely with those who joined the board around the same time. New board members are more likely to speak up—especially if they don't understand something—if they can turn to other new members for validation. Alone, they might remain silent. This is why board orientation is important. A buddy system pairing each new board member with a person who's been on the board awhile can speed up the learning process and make newcomers feel more comfortable. I like to see each board mentor drive his or her buddy to at least three agency meetings, during which the new person can ask questions that he or she might be reluctant to ask during the meeting itself. My present board has tended to pooh-pooh this notion, though. They prefer to get together with their buddy once, usually for lunch, and handle everything else by phone or e-mail. It's not as good as driving together to meetings, I believe, but it's their choice.

Another reason to elect board members in pairs has to do with agency change. It's difficult for a single, new board member to effect significant change, especially if the agency has been around a long time. There's too much historical precedent, too much institutional memory. One person's voice may be heard, but it's doubtful it'll carry much weight because he or she hasn't established credibility yet. Two people, though, is a different story. A pair of intelligent, strong-minded, articulate people can exert considerable influence.

Several years before I joined the crisis center, the board elected a woman named Jan who was the chief financial officer of the local phone company. She was young, smart, energetic, and full of ideas. Her second meeting on the board she proposed a whole new way of measuring the crisis center's effectiveness. She provided a detailed analysis complete with charts, graphs, and tables to support her points, which she presented expertly and with enthusiasm, confident that board members would embrace them just as the executive director, my predecessor, did. Instead, board members thanked her for doing so much work, then moved onto the next agenda item. Not easily discouraged, Jan spent several months pressing board members to consider her recommendations. When it became clear that they weren't ready for her, she gave up and resigned. She was ahead of where the board was at that time.

Conversely, a year or so into my tenure, the crisis center recruited three new board members who were elected in the same month. One had just retired as the county's mental health director. Another was a senior program manager with the county office of emergency services. The third was a private fundraising consultant. I was a little nervous about them joining the board because a lot of time was being spent at board meetings on inconsequential matters. It was partly my fault. We were doing some remodeling and I'd asked the board president, who was an interior designer, for advice on carpet purchases and paint colors. She was happy to oblige, but also wanted the board to feel included in decision-making so she brought her recommendations to the board for a vote. The last thing I wanted to do was to tie up valuable meeting time reviewing paint chips and carpet samples, but that's what happened. Once the three new members were elected, however, they made it known that they were interested in more substantive issues. Conversations about color schemes ended. Individually, each might have had minimal influence; collectively, they wielded immediate power.

THE RIGHT JUNGLE

Virtually every executive director I know who has been fed up by his or her job has pointed to the board as a source of frustration. Either board members are micro managing, inserting themselves where they shouldn't and usurping the executive director's authority, or they're not doing enough and the executive director feels overwhelmed, responsible for everything. Neither situation is healthy. Good managers leave if their position is undermined by a board that's preoccupied with day-to-day operations, or if the board is so hands-off that the director carries the entire burden.

P. Burke Keegan, a nonprofit consultant, uses the metaphor of a jungle to describe the appropriate roles for staff and board. Staff traverse the jungle floor. The executive director is in front, slashing at foliage to carve out a path for others to follow. It's slow going and there are constant challenges—dense underbrush, fallen tree trunks, poisonous snakes. Each obstacle is dealt with as it comes up. Some are met head on and dispatched, while others necessitate a detour and are avoided.

Meanwhile, board members are up in the trees, above the canopy of leaves and vegetation. From the board's high vantage point, staff look like ants, hardly moving although board members know that staff are working hard. Board members gaze into the distance. From so high up it's amazing how far a person can see. Their eyes shift back and forth from the broad horizon to the small band of people far below. Back and forth. Board members aren't trying to determine whether staff are moving in the right direction. Rather, they're trying to determine whether staff are in the right jungle.

That's what a board does, Keegan says, make sure an agency is where it needs to be. There's no reason for board members to walk the jungle floor; staff know what to do. They do it everyday. The executive director knows the general direction. The board provides perspective. No one can see above the treetops when they're on the ground. Moreover, if you're on the ground you're focused on obstacles in your immediate path, not on distant sights. It's the board that asks and answers these questions: Is the agency in the right place? Is it in the best position to make the biggest difference? Is it staying true to its mission and is that mission still valid?

There are lots of jungles. It's the board's job to see that the agency is in the right one.

CHAPTER THREE

The Staff: "I Don't Do Change"

Every fall, during football season, Cal and Stanford play another Big Game. Whenever this happens, I'm reminded of my first Big Game.

I was ten years old and my father, a Berkeley alum, got tickets for the two of us. I'd never been to an event with 60,000 people, so in my mind it was natural that this was called the Big Game, capital letters, even though I didn't know the real reason why.

The morning of the game I put on my favorite sweater, a cardigan. When my father saw me, his jaw dropped. "You can't wear that," he said.

"Why not?" I thought I looked pretty cool.

"Because it's red."

This struck me as one of those moments when parents demonstrate how weird their view of the world is.

"Yeah. So?"

"So red is Stanford's color," he explained. "We'll be sitting in the Cal rooting section. People will yell at you if you wear red."

"You can't be serious," I said. "College students aren't going to care what some kid wears."

My father tried to talk me out of it, but I was stubborn. We entered Memorial Stadium from the top and started walking down the aisle to our seats. Before I'd taken five steps someone shouted, "Take off that red sweater!" In seconds the chant seemed to thunder throughout the stadium.

My face turned as red as the fabric. I'm truly stubborn, though, and while I buried my face in my father's side, I refused to take off the sweater. People might influence my decisions, but they wouldn't make them.

That's a guiding principle at the crisis center. We inform and support people who call us, but we don't tell them what to do. They decide.

A young man phones our suicide hotline. "I'm holding a loaded gun to my head," he says. "Tell me why I shouldn't pull the trigger."

"Tell me why you want to," our counselor replies.

The caller hesitates. "It's a long story."

"That's okay," the counselor says. "I'm here."

An hour later the call ends. The man has removed the clip from his gun. It's his decision to live, just like it was his decision to call us.

At the Big Game, people stopped yelling at me after a minute or two. Play started and everyone's attention turned to the field. Near the end of the first quarter, I slipped the sweater from my shoulders. No one noticed or cared. It was my life, and my decision.

The sun seemed to shine brighter after that.

I looked around the table at the faces of my new colleagues, the staff of the crisis center—at least those staff who worked daytime hours. It was noon and the staff was holding its monthly potluck luncheon, to which I'd been invited even though, like my first board meeting, I hadn't started working at the agency yet.

The only thing I knew about the staff was that none had applied to be executive director. I asked the search committee about this and was told that staff members were trained crisis counselors who had no interest in administration or fundraising. This was a good sign because it meant that no one was disgruntled at being passed over for the job.

I also asked the search committee to give me a SWOT analysis of what I could expect. SWOT analyses are as commonplace these days in the nonprofit sector as they are in the for-profit world. The acronym stands for strengths, weaknesses, opportunities, and threats, although there's a move afoot to change "weaknesses" to "challenges" because the latter sounds less negative. In that case, the acronym becomes SCOT. Whatever you call it, the analysis is an effective way to identify what an organization does well, what it needs to improve on, what its potential is, and what might prevent it from achieving that potential.

In terms of staff, I was told that every person but one was outstanding—hardworking, knowledgeable, and committed to the crisis center's mission. I'd have to deal with the exception; however that was it. This didn't surprise me because the crisis center was highly regarded and this happens only when you have top-notch staff. Still, it was nice to hear.

Invariably, the first meeting between an executive director and his or her staff is awkward. As executive director, you're the outsider; everybody else knows each other. You have to learn how to read, relate to, and motivate a roomful of accomplished individuals who right now are strangers.

In many respects, though, the initial meeting is even more awkward for staff. Everyone has a different way of leading, and as a staff member you're never sure quite what you're getting in a new boss. If the agency has serious management problems, you want to see immediate evidence that the person hired will effect positive changes. Conversely, if the agency has been operating successfully, you want someone who won't implement sweeping reforms but rather will keep the agency going much as it has been.

During the interview process, the prospective candidate has the opportunity to ask questions of the board. In many cases, staff aren't privy to this exchange. Except at the senior level, most staff have little interaction with the board and may not have confidence that board members know the qualities needed in a chief executive right now. All of this makes the first meeting between a new executive director and his or her staff that much more uncomfortable.

Eager to get the preliminaries out of the way, I described briefly my work experience and management style. "If I had to choose one word to describe me," I said, "it'd be *accessible*. My door is always open, and unless I'm working under a tight deadline or having a private meeting, I never mind people coming in to ask a question or voice a concern. On the contrary, what upsets me is when someone withholds bad news from me. I want to be the first to know, not the last."

I said that I was thrilled to come to the crisis center, and that I knew it provided high-quality services, and that I saw my role as something of a cheerleader, encouraging and supporting employees to perform at their best. In turn, since I wasn't a mental health professional, part of the staff's role was to educate and train me so that I could do my job more effectively. Then I said that I'd like to go around the room and have each person tell me his or her name, job title, and number of years at the agency. I nodded to the woman on my left to begin.

Looking back, it would have been better to ask each person to do what I just did; that is, tell me the one word that describes him or her best. Too often when people introduce themselves, they answer mechanically, without enthusiasm or a desire to share information.

"My name is Judy," the woman said. "And I don't do change."

There was a smattering of giggles. She was in her late fifties, slender, with a caring face and keen eyes hidden behind thick glasses. She could be any child's favorite grandmother and, I learned later, was exactly that. As if to prove that she wasn't a troublemaker and would otherwise cooperate she said, "I'm the crisis line manager and I've been on staff 11 years."

Before I could ask whether she was opposed to change because she felt that nothing needed fixing or because she wasn't comfortable with the idea of a new boss, the woman sitting next to her said, "My name is Loren. I don't do change, either." She paused, waiting to see how I'd react.

I wondered what I'd walked into. No matter how well a person does something, I think it's possible to improve. Also, new ideas excite me, and the more that people challenge one another, the more stimulating I find the environment. Clearly, I had my work cut out.

THE IDEAL BOSS

There are all sorts of business books that describe the qualities most essential in a successful manager. In my early days, I wrote down key points from some of them, things like "MBWA," which was Hewlett-Packard's acronym for "Management by Walking Around." The idea was that if you circulate regularly among your employees, you catch people doing things right and can compliment them on the spot, rewarding excellence. In Hewlett-Packard's philosophy, this was far preferable to catching people doing things wrong, and resulted in higher standards of performance.

A similar practice often mentioned in business books is to expect the best from people. If you expect the best, you'll probably get it. Conversely, if you expect the worst you'll probably get that, but why would you want to?

The single best tip I've ever found is also the simplest. It came from small-business guru Paul Hawken: Be the kind of boss you want to have as a boss. It doesn't get more basic than that. Be caring, open, and honest. Listen well. Acknowledge hard work and initiative. Encourage risk-taking. Discourage blaming. Lead by example. These are qualities all of us want in a boss, and if we find them we're motivated to excel.

One of the biggest challenges for any executive director is determining the compensation of individual staff. In every nonprofit agency, some programs are bigger than others and, in all likelihood, cost more to operate. At the same time, funders have their own areas of interest. Nonprofit leaders have to balance their agency's needs with the priorities of funders. The hardest part is that funders' interests can change. Homelessness, for instance, was a hot-button topic at one time. Then domestic violence became big, spurred on, in part, by the O. J. Simpson trial. Youth violence prevention rose to the top after Columbine and was a major focus of funders until 9/11, when everyone's attention shifted to homeland security. In 2005, following the tsunami in Southeast Asia, hurricanes in Florida and the Gulf Coast, and a deadly earthquake in Pakistan, there was new interest in disaster preparedness. Today, in the wake of the tragedy at Virginia Tech, violence prevention has resurfaced. The point is, no cause, no matter how worthy, enjoys permanent popularity.

Jim, my predecessor, made the decision to tie the salaries of program staff to the program's funding. If a program was well funded, program staff had higher salaries than their counterparts in programs that were poorly funded. This isn't an unusual practice. Many executive directors tie program revenues to program expenses. For one thing, it ensures that the services funders are paying for are provided in full. No money designated by a donor for one program is used to underwrite the cost of another program. Since nonprofit agencies must be accountable to their donors— indeed, the quickest way to go out of business is to stop being accountable— establishing a direct correlation between program revenues and expenses gives everyone peace of mind. Reporting is straightforward and donors are assured that their gifts are being used as intended.

Another benefit of this approach is that if cuts have to be made, they're easy to identify. When you lose income for a program, you reduce expenses by the same amount. If staff have to be laid off, it's staff in the affected program.

Although this strategy makes sense, there are two problems with it. First, staff are rewarded or penalized for something that's largely outside their control. A person's skills, attitude, multicultural background, education, and productivity aren't taken into consideration. Second, tying salaries to funding means that funders are telling you how to value your programs. When this happens, the purpose of an agency is determined by individuals who aren't its stewards.

Early on I told crisis center staff that we're all in this together. Every employee is responsible for the agency's success and everyone benefits when things are going well, the same way that a rising tide elevates each boat in a harbor. A new grant or contract may support one program or service, but it's the funding for all crisis center programs and services that matters. If it's strong, then salaries can be raised, programs expanded, and old equipment replaced. Conversely, when things aren't going well, the impact is felt by all. The loss of a key grant or contract can mean that everyone's salary is frozen, services are reduced, and we live with outdated technology, at least until new revenues come in.

My message was simple: It makes less difference how well any individual program is doing than how well the agency is doing overall. I could say this because the crisis center's programs were integrated to the point where many expenses and revenues could be shared. Crisis line staff answered our homeless hotline after hours so a portion of their salaries could be charged to the homeless program. Grief counseling staff were called out to schools following the death of a student or teacher so a portion of their salaries could be charged to the education program. Our office manager and development director both spoke Spanish and often were summoned to our crisis line room when a Spanish-speaking person was needed, so a portion of their salaries could be charged to the crisis line program.

This integration gave me the latitude to move money where needed, yet still comply with funding requirements. Not every agency has this luxury. I had it because as the crisis center grew, its services remained consistent with its mission. Agencies that aren't so mission driven often end up with programs that operate in silos. Programs have little or nothing in common, providing different services in different ways to different population groups. When this happens, expenses and revenues must remain separate, restricting a manager's options.

THE THIRD HARDEST THING TO DO

People who've never had to fire anyone think it's the hardest thing to do. It's hard, no question, especially if the person needs the job. It's not the hardest thing to do, though. It's not even second hardest.

The hardest thing to do is to lay off staff. The difference between laying off and firing someone is that the person who's laid off may be performing at an acceptable level; you just can't afford the position anymore. Firing someone, on the other hand, is rarely a financial decision. It's more a matter of getting rid of an employee who's unproductive, divisive, or dishonest. A mistake was made in hiring the person and now the agency is cutting its losses.

The second hardest thing for a manager to do is to hire staff. The long-term success of an agency depends on employees who are talented, energetic, and committed. You don't really know about people, though, until you've worked with them for awhile. When you fire someone you know what you're losing; however, when you hire someone you're never quite sure what you're getting until months down the road. Past experience is the best indicator of future behavior, yet no two managers have the same expectations so sterling referrals from other supervisors offer no guarantees. Moreover, the way employment law is today, referrals are becoming meaningless. Employers are prevented from disclosing much negative information about an employee, leaving others in the dark. The truth is, you only find out about someone after he or she has been hired. By then it's too late.

While going through employee files I found that Jim, my predecessor, intended to fire Loren, one of the managers. He'd even written her a termination letter, although he never signed or delivered it. When it became clear that he was leaving, he left this task to me.

Loren hadn't done anything illegal or unkind; she'd just been inept. Despite a master's degree and previous experience managing a community-based agency, Loren had no planning or organizing skills, no vision, and—most importantly—no energy. She'd been at the crisis center eighteen months, yet had produced nothing of consequence—no services, no reports, no curricula of any kind. She wasn't lazy; she came to work on time everyday, answered calls, and typed away at a computer. There just wasn't anything to show for it.

Jim restructured her job responsibilities three times, lowering the expectations each time. This only delayed the inevitable. The final straw was that the agency was in the last month of a twelve-month project that Loren was responsible for and nothing had been accomplished. The funder was expecting a written report soon and there wasn't a single achievement to note. I didn't look forward to having to tell the funder that.

Loren and I talked a lot. We talked about what I expected from her and what she needed to do to prove herself to me. I reviewed with her the information in her personnel file, not mentioning Jim's termination letter but discussing his assessment of her performance. I said that she had one month to turn things around and demonstrate her value to the crisis center, otherwise she'd be let go.

Nothing that I said surprised her. She knew it, or at least suspected it; after all, she wasn't dumb. Yet she didn't challenge anything I said, either. In fact, I was a little unnerved by how calmly she accepted the warning I delivered. It was as if I was talking about a subject that had only minimal interest to her.

A month later, her employment at the crisis center ended. She didn't say good-by to anyone, just left quietly at the end of the last day. Because she'd contributed so little, it was hard to tell that she was even gone.

HIRING STAFF

The best way to avoid having to fire staff is to hire good people from the outset. This is easier said than done. Decisions tend to be made based on only a few hours of conversation with prospective candidates and a more or less pro forma check of a person's references. It helps that in recent years more and more nonprofit agencies (including mine) have become at-will employers, meaning that they can terminate an employee at any time for virtually any reason except whistle blowing or discrimination. This gives managers an out when they make a mistake in hiring; even so, there's always a negative impact when an agency has incompetent or difficult employees, no matter how temporary. Morale suffers, services are impaired, and confidence in the manager wanes.

One way to lessen the risk is to hire people already known to the agency, such as agency volunteers. They've demonstrated their commitment by giving their time, and they've probably had sufficient opportunity to show that they're caring, hard working, intelligent, and motivated. As an employer, you have a good idea how someone who's volunteering for the agency will perform in a job and fit in with others. Also, volunteers usually require less training because they're already doing a portion of the work. For some jobs at the crisis center, I prefer to hire volunteers. They know the agency culture, oftentimes can hit the ground running, and hiring them sends a good message to other volunteers that their services are valued and can lead to employment opportunities down the road (although there are no promises). The disadvantage in hiring volunteers is that you lose out on the opportunity to bring in someone new, with new ideas, different skills, and perhaps a more diverse background and perspective.

Whenever I post a job announcement, I emphasize that interested candidates should submit a cover letter as well as a resume. Cover letters often tell me more about a person than a resume. There are many services today that assist job seekers in developing resumes, so the fact that a resume is well designed, straightforward, and easy to read doesn't necessarily mean that the person has strong organizing and writing skills. A professional may have created it. Moreover, many people take liberties in their resumes to mask inexperience and hide periods of inactivity or unemployment, so the value of a resume is further diminished. In a cover letter, though, I learn how candidates present themselves, why they're interested in the job, and why they think they'd be a good fit. I also get a sense of their writing abilities as well as a glimpse into their personalities.

Many cover letters are simply form letters, generic in purpose, where only the name of the agency and the job title are changed each time they're submitted. These are easy to reject. If someone lacks the motivation to write a letter tailored to the job, why should I think he or she is really interested in it? The impression I get is of a person firing out dozens of applications haphazardly with the hope that someone—anyone—will respond. Maybe someone will; however, I want employees who are more strategic in their approach.

Oftentimes cover letters are filled with claims that sound empty without evidence. "I'm a hard worker" means nothing to me. "I'm a single mother who raised two children, then went back to school and completed my undergraduate degree while working nights to pay for it" tells me a lot about the person's work ethic. Similarly, when someone says, "I'm looking for an opportunity where I can use my professional skills in a constructive way," I'm unmoved. What does that mean? When I hired our clinical director, she said, "I'm looking for a job with a high level of satisfaction and a manageable level of stress." That I could understand. Moreover, it was a good description of the position.

An important requirement for any position is someone who's kind. I look for people who are givers rather than takers. When applicants write, "I know how important it is to listen carefully," or "It's important to me to help others," I consider them favorably.

FIRST INTERVIEWS

Usually it's possible to tell whether someone is a serious candidate in the first few minutes of the interview. It doesn't take long to assess a person's attitude, intelligence, verbal skills, and interest in the position. Readers of Malcolm Gladwell's bestseller, *Blink*, know about the accuracy of first impressions. This is important since doing first interviews with lots of candidates means that you have to be able to narrow the field quickly. If you don't, your days will be filled meeting people you'll never see again, who'll never help your agency.

I prefer a private, informal setting for first interviews, usually my office. One other staff person participates. Many questions are routine, reviewing a candidate's work history, education, skills, and accomplishments. I try to be creative, though; after all, while I'm judging the candidate, he or she is judging the agency. It's a two-way street; the candidate needs to prove to the employer that he or she has what it takes to do a good job, and the employer needs to prove to the candidate that the agency is well managed and the person who's hired will enjoy working there.

In discussing someone's employment history, I find it helpful to ask the person to describe in detail a typical day on the job. "Walk me through it hour by hour," I say, "from the moment you arrive to the time you leave at night." Afterward, I ask what parts the person liked most and least. If it's a current job, I ask what the person will miss when he or she leaves and what will be easy to forget. I like to hear that the person will miss the clients. I don't like to hear that he or she won't miss anything.

A common question employers ask candidates is to describe their strengths and weaknesses. The answer is always telling, which is why the question is asked, although most job seekers dislike it, for obvious reasons. Anyone who's trying to make a positive impression doesn't want to talk about his or her shortcomings. One of my board members, named Pete, prefers to get the same information in a different way.

"I've been a licensed therapist for ten years," he tells applicants. "Even so, ten years from now, I know I'll be better at my job than I am today. Assuming that the same thing is true for you, that you'll be a better clinician [or counselor or program manager] in ten years than you are right now, how will you be better? In what areas will you improve?"

Some people try to get out of it by saying that they'll learn to take better care of themselves and not work around the clock. Pete has heard this response so often that he can't help but roll his eyes each new time it's voiced. "Besides that," he says, "how will you improve?" He doesn't give up until the person gives a creditable response.

Another board member, named Deedee, who's a professional life skills coach, uses a different approach. She says to candidates who are applying for managerial positions, "If I asked somebody who works with you what's the only thing that keeps you from being an awesome boss, what would he or she tell me?" This question flatters the person by implying that if he or she just improved in one area, he or she would be awesome.

At some point in the initial interview I ask my own favorite question. Whichever staff person is with me invariably smiles, knowing that it's coming.

"Suppose this interview ended now," I say. "It's not going to end because I have other questions to ask and you may have questions for me, but suppose it ended now. You walk out to your car and breathe a sigh of relief, thinking, 'I'm glad he didn't ask me *that* question,' What would *that* question be?"

The first time I asked it, the woman's whole demeanor changed. Her body tensed, she pulled her legs up under her chair, and her eyes, which had been focused on mine, looked away. "I guess it would be who my husband is," she said.

I tried not to seem surprised. I had no idea who she was married to. "Who's your husband," I asked innocently.

It turned out to be an executive director I knew. She'd kept her maiden name and I wasn't aware of the connection.

"Why does my knowing who your husband is worry you?" I asked.

The woman shrugged. "I don't know. It just does."

I didn't pursue it, but the tone of the interview changed after that. The secret was out. I didn't hire her, although her husband told me later that he liked my question so much that he started using it in interviews he conducted.

Over the years I've heard a variety of responses. "Why is there a two-year gap in my resume?" "Why did I leave my last job?" "How come my college degree has nothing to do with the career path I've followed?" Naturally, I always follow it with the question that the candidate is dreading, the one that he or she hasn't been able to work out a strong answer to. Oftentimes people relax after that; the worst is over. Either they've blown it and won't get the job, or the disclosure isn't as damaging as they feared.

One woman stunned me when she gave the best answer I've ever heard. After a short pause she said, "Why, I guess it would be that question." Her ability to respond in the moment impressed me; unfortunately, in other ways she wasn't suited for the job.

A member of my board of trustees, named John, is chief financial officer of a large foundation in San Francisco. He, too, has a favorite question, directed toward people with accounting backgrounds. I haven't had to hire a finance manager at the crisis center because Walt, who manages the crisis center's finances, has been there longer than me and does an excellent job. Should Walt leave, however, one small measure of solace I'll take is being able to spring John's question on unsuspecting candidates. It's all the more clever because it sounds irrelevant.

After asking a number of questions aimed to determine someone's financial aptitude, John says, almost casually, "So, how many tires do you think there are in San Francisco?" Invariably the person looks at him in disbelief. He must be kidding, they think, so they say nothing, expecting him to ask something else. Instead, John repeats the question: "How many tires do you think there are in San Francisco?"

People shrug their shoulders and avoid looking at him. "I don't know," they say, wondering how this relates to the job they're applying for. A few candidates start trying to figure it out, though, and they're the ones who interest John.

"Well, there are about 750,000 residents of the city," they say. "If each one has a car, that's four times 750,000 or three million."

Not everyone who lives in San Francisco has a car, of course, but there are hundreds of taxis, trucks, buses, motorcycles, and bicycles to make up for people without autos, as well as new car dealerships, repair shops, and salvage yards. One or two candidates realize that most cars have spare tires so they add another 750,000 to the total. John doesn't know the correct answer and he doesn't expect people he interviews to know it; he's just wants to see how candidates go about solving a problem.

A common question asked of fundraisers is: "Who do you know?" Fundraising depends on developing relationships, so having extensive contacts is important. Who do you know who's a decision maker in a major corporation? Who do you know who could give $10,000 if asked? Who's the most famous person you know who'll return your phone call? Hiring someone primarily for his or her Rolodex is risky, though, because there's no guarantee that those names will become donors to your cause. It's better to hire someone because he or she has a good understanding of the community, good interpersonal skills, and is passionate about the organization.

One question that tends to separate novice fundraisers from experienced professionals is, "Which is more valuable, one person who gives $50,000 or fifty people who give $1,000?"

An argument can be made for one $50,000 donor; after all, it's a lot easier to ask one person for money than fifty people. Moreover, if the $50,000 donor has friends and leads you to them, you may be able to cultivate additional major gifts.

The concern with one $50,000 donor is that many donors are fickle, their fortunes change, they move out of the area, or they die. Except in instances where a deceased donor names the charity in his or her will, the agency is out of luck.

With fifty donors, an agency has more financial security than with one donor. An agency also has fifty people whose giving levels can be increased, as well as fifty times the number of family members, friends, and acquaintances of donors who become potential donors themselves. In fundraising, you don't want a donation— you want a donor.

One of the last questions I ask in an initial interview is: "What do you like to do outside of work?" I'm curious about people's interests, but more than that, I want to know whether people have interests. You spend a lot of time around coworkers, so why hire people who are dull? I don't expect prospective candidates to be standup comedians, world travelers, or daredevil enthusiasts; however, if someone's idea of fun is watching TV every night, I find it difficult to converse with the person because I don't learn anything. Oftentimes I conclude an interview by asking people to name the last book they read and last movie they saw.

SECOND INTERVIEWS

For second interviews, I purposely change the setting and the dynamics. The interview is in a different room than my office, one that's spacious rather than intimate, and there's a panel of five or six people interviewing each candidate rather than two. Panelists are handpicked by me, are ethnically diverse, and include at least one person who'll be supervised by the person hired.

The value of second interviews can't be overstated. While candidates rarely present differently, more facets of their personality surface. Usually they're more nervous, partly because the setup is more intimidating but also because they're closer to getting the job. They made it through the first round and have something to lose, whereas in the first interview the likelihood of being offered the position still seems remote.

Many employers consider nervousness a negative. They want people who are calm and composed. I do, too, especially since the crisis center works daily with people who are in life-threatening situations. Nevertheless, I generally consider nervousness a positive in interviews. I don't equate it with a person's inability to remain calm under stress; instead, I interpret it as a sign that someone really wants the job. When a person is ambivalent, it's easy for him or her to be relaxed. Whether the interview results in a job offer doesn't make much difference. If chosen, great; it's always nice to feel wanted. If not, no big deal; a better job may lie just around the corner. When a person cares, though, because something important is at stake, it's natural for some nervousness to show.

I've only had one experience where a candidate was so nervous in a second interview that he seemed like a completely different person. He was a man of about fifty who had had a distinguished career, mainly in Southern California. Although I couldn't offer anywhere near the amount of money that he was earning currently, he said that salary was less important to him than other factors, such as working for a cause that he believed in. He impressed me in the first interview, appearing thoughtful, confident, and experienced. I called him back for another interview.

He looked exactly the same the second time, even wearing the same dark brown suit. This time, though, he was literally manic. As soon as the interview started, his eyes began blinking rapidly and beads of sweat formed on his brow. He twisted and turned in his seat, unable to sit still. Whenever he was asked a question, he uttered a psychotic-sounding laugh as if responding to a sick joke.

Then he launched into a long, excited answer, barely pausing to take a breath and oftentimes not addressing the question at all.

The change was so mesmerizing that I let the second interview go on much longer than necessary just because I was fascinated. He could have been a hot-line caller who'd gone off his medication. The more he talked, the more wound up he became. John, the same board member who asks people how many tires there are in San Francisco, was on the panel and after awhile he couldn't take it anymore.

"My mother is 83 years old," he said, "and thinks that *The Sound of Music* is the best movie ever made. Is she right?"

The man's head jerked back and his eyes almost came out of his head. "No!" he said. "*Citizen Kane* is the best movie ever made, at least according to critics." As soon as he said this, he seemed to reconsider. "Wait a minute; she's your mother. Whatever movie she thinks is best must be the best, at least to her." Instantly, he changed his mind again. "Just because she thinks it's best doesn't mean it's the best movie. I don't know whether it's best or not."

He wasn't surprised by the question the way another candidate would be, nor did he hesitate to answer. Indeed, he couldn't wait. Of more interest, in just a few seconds he gave three entirely different responses. Considering that the sole purpose of the question was to test a candidate's composure (John's mother had been dead for many years and he had no idea what her favorite movie had been), the extent to which he failed was extraordinary. Afterward, I had to explain to the panel that what they had just witnessed was in sharp contrast to the man's initial demeanor.

Many managers prefer to have subordinate staff conduct first interviews, then managers participate in subsequent interviews. Certainly, this is less time-consuming for managers. Doing initial interviews with eight or nine people can take up most of a week. On the other hand, hiring competent, energetic, culturally diverse staff is one of the most important tasks for any manager. This is why, for people who report directly to me, I like to work in reverse. I review all applications when they come in, select candidates who seem qualified and/or pique my interest, and do initial interviews. In second interviews, I spend most of the time observing and listening to applicants, allowing other panelists to ask questions. Not only is this liberating—I don't have to think about questions to ask—but it also allows me to focus more intently on each person's responses. This way I'm able to see and hear things that I might have missed otherwise.

One question we always ask in second interviews has become known in-house as "the candidate killer." I don't consider it particularly challenging or threatening, which is why I'm always stunned when people provide an answer that's appalling. The question is: "Can you describe a situation where you had a negative interaction with a person from a different culture, and what you learned from it?"

One woman, a clinical psychologist, described hiring an African-American domestic and the problem she had getting the woman to prepare meals to her liking. It was clear from the way she talked that the psychologist, who was white, considered people of color to play subservient roles. What she learned, she said, is to give orders and not negotiate.

Another woman, a licensed therapist, also white, said that when she's around young people she's continually offended by their clothing, body piercings, loud music, and profane language. "I always want to ring their necks," she said. "What I've learned is to keep my mouth shut."

Many adults share this view. Crisis center counselors need to be more tolerant, though.

Most people, when asked, say that they support the notion of serving diverse cultures. Surprisingly, few, however, can define cultural competency correctly, which is another question we ask. Even an African-American clinical psychologist we interviewed defined cultural competency as treating everyone equally, which is a typical response of whites and an indication of cultural *in*competency. An agency that sees all people as being equal fails to acknowledge that different cultures have different values, perspectives, and beliefs. As a result, they use a one-size-fits-all model to deliver services, which only helps people who are most assimilated in the dominant culture, as this woman was.

TAKING CHANCES

For thirty years, until he retired, my father was a top executive at Bank of America. He had hundreds of employees working under him, most of them hired and managed by others. One day one of his managers brought him the resume of a man named Robert who was applying for an entry-level position in corporate communications. Even though my father had nothing to do with the communications department and had little interaction with people so far down in the bank's hierarchy, the manager encouraged my father to interview Robert. "I've never received a resume like his," the manager said.

My father grumbled because he had a dozen pressing items on his mind at the time; nevertheless, he read Robert's resume. The manager was right; it was the most amazing summary of work experience that my father had ever seen.

Robert was forty-two years old. He'd never worked in a financial institution. He'd never run a business, handled investments, or even taken any business-related classes until recently, when he'd enrolled in graduate school to get a MBA.

Robert was a playwright. He'd twice won the Eugene O'Neil national playwriting contest and had had his works performed Off Broadway, as well as elsewhere. For the previous ten years, to support himself, he'd been a drama teacher at the University of Southern California.

Many people work for years in a business office and dream of becoming writers. Robert was the opposite. He was a writer—a successful one—whose mid-life dream was to be a banker.

My father interviewed Robert and provided a recommendation as well, although it wasn't needed. Robert was going to be hired. He was assigned to publications where his first task was to produce the bank's upcoming annual report. It won a national award. After that, Robert never looked back. My father followed his progress and one day invited Robert to have lunch with the two of us. I'd graduated recently from college without any specific career plans and my father thought that Robert might inspire me. Instead, I looked at him, a thin, pale, average-looking man with a crew cut and black-framed glasses, wearing a dark suit, white shirt, and dark tie—the typical bank uniform at the time—and thought, "You gave up playwriting and teaching at U.S.C. for this?"

Nevertheless, Robert was happy, and so was the bank. Within five years he made vice president—a remarkable achievement for someone who'd started so low, and unheard of for a person with no previous banking experience.

Much later I learned, to my surprise, that my father had been right. Robert did inspire me. Since I've been responsible for hiring others, I've taken numerous chances on people whose experience and skills are unconventional. In virtually every instance, it has paid off. The person hired has grown into the job, been committed to the work, and added to the vitality of the workplace. I couldn't ask for more.

CHAPTER FOUR

Program Development: "Exactly How Much Blood Is Dripping?"

One of the activities that I enjoyed most when I was younger was playing volleyball. It's been many years since I played at a high level, on teams that competed for national championships. Still, it's fun today to get together with friends and hit the ball around.

There's a volleyball term that's an appropriate metaphor for our work at the crisis center. It's "improve the ball." It means that every person who contacts the ball on your side of the net needs to "improve it" in some way so that it's more playable for the next person. This can mean getting a hand on a block or dig to slow the ball down for the next touch, passing the serve to the correct spot so that the setter can run a play, or taking the spin off the ball when you set it so that it's easier to spike. When players concentrate on improving the ball, they stop making mistakes and begin playing with confidence.

Our goal at the crisis center is to improve the call—specifically, to improve the state of mind of each person who calls our crisis lines. It's unlikely that we'll be able to solve a caller's problem; after all, we can't resurrect a loved one who died, bring back a lover who left, reverse a fatal disease, change a failing grade, or rescind a layoff notice.

Improving the call means that the next person to interact with the caller, whether it's a family member, therapist, social worker, police officer, caregiver, or friend, is better able to assist the person. Improving the call can result in significant action, such as intervening in a suicide attempt, getting a battered woman to a safe place, or placing a homeless family in a shelter. More often than not, it means listening actively and discussing a person's problem in a nonjudgmental way.

A man calls our crisis lines, drunk and angry with himself. He'd been sober for five months but tonight has fallen off the wagon and wants, in his words, "to go off, to go out in the streets and start trouble." His marriage is in jeopardy, he almost hit his child, and he loathes himself for being unable to stop drinking.

"Do you have more alcohol in the house?" asks our counselor, Eric.

"Yes," the man says—"151-proof."

"Pour it out now," Eric tells him.

The man does. People want to help themselves; they just don't always know how.

The two of them discuss Alcoholics Anonymous and other options. The caller says he feels "stupid" for being in this situation.

"All of us make mistakes," Eric says. "What's important is to use this experience as a lesson the next time you think about taking a drink."

The man doesn't say anything. Eric is silent, too, letting the message sink in. Then he says, "What are you going to do the rest of the night?"

The man hesitates. "Settle down, I guess." He adds, "Thanks." Unsaid is the real message: Thanks for conveying hope rather than blame.

If we do our job—if we improve the call—that makes it easier for our teammates (other mental health professionals, doctors, the police, and people in the community) to do their jobs. The result is that everyone wins.

The depiction of crisis centers in TV shows and movies is nonstop bedlam. Phones ring continually and every caller is actively homicidal or suicidal. There's a hostage situation growing out of control, a child whose life is endangered by an abusive parent, and a volunteer who's being stalked by an agency client. Each person who comes in for counseling is an emotional wreck, so fragile that a single wrong word sends him or her over the edge. Meanwhile, budget hearings are being held to determine whether the crisis center's funding should be cut.

The reality is different. The drama that's condensed into one action-packed show is spread over weeks in real life. There are stretches when the phones are relatively quiet, clients are managing ably on their own, and funding is secure.

I didn't know what to expect when I entered the crisis center's hotline room for the first time. It was large and hexagonal-shaped. In one area there were six workstations with modular furniture, phones, computers, trays of blank call sheets, and red binders with essential information on answering each of eighteen different hotlines. In another area there was a row of black file cabinets, four drawers high, where completed call sheets were stored after data were entered into a computer. There were bookcases with phone directories, psychology texts, and pharmacology guides, a night stand with telephone relay equipment for handling calls from the hearing impaired, rolling carts with files on frequent callers, and a makeshift bed for overnight counselors. On the walls were message boards with new and urgent information left by staff, a map of the county, posters with mental health information, and emergency contact numbers for police, fire, mental health clinics, and on-call supervisors.

Twenty-four hours a day, 365 days a year, people manned hotline phones. No one other than staff and certified volunteers was allowed in the room. Even board members couldn't enter unless they were also hotline counselors.

When I walked in, three calls were in progress. Two were being handled by volunteers, who were listening to people explain their problems. Joan, the clinical director, was on the third line. The first words I heard came from her.

"So exactly how much blood is dripping?" she said.

I stopped in my tracks. She continued, "I mean, are you bleeding one drop every few seconds or is it more of a constant stream?"

I couldn't believe my ears. Her voice was even and her words were measured. "Okay. Have you put down the razor?" There was a pause. "Good. That's good."

She looked up, noticed me, and noticed the look on my face. Putting one hand over the receiver, she said, "I have a cutter. It's not too serious." Then to the caller she said, "Now here's what I'd like you to do."

It was a teenage girl who'd been slashing her wrists and arms for several months. So far no one else knew, although it was the middle of Spring and the weather was getting too warm for her to continue wearing long-sleeved shirts without her friends or parents asking questions. Each time she cut a little deeper, but today she was worried that she'd gone too far.

Joan asked if there was anyone the girl could talk to. Then they discussed counseling and Joan gave her the names and phone numbers of several local therapists. The call ended with Joan encouraging the girl to phone again whenever she felt the urge to grab a razor.

"Was that a typical call?" I asked after Joan had hung up.

"It was the first time this particular girl called," Joan said. "But it was typical of calls we get from self-mutilators. Cutting makes them feel better. The physical pain masks a deeper, psychic pain. They're numb, empty. When they cut themselves, they feel alive."

I nodded, dazed. It was clear that I'd entered another world.

THE FIRST DECISION

At that time the crisis center was nearing the end of a one-year contract with a distant county to provide twenty-four-hour phone counseling. The call volume was low; however, staff and volunteers dreaded every call. Whenever this particular line rang, people in our hotline room suddenly were busy, hoping someone else would answer.

Handling crisis calls is the heart of the crisis center's mission, and the assumption made by the previous executive director was that we could do it effectively with people who lived far away the same way we could with people who lived locally. After all, our skill was listening to a person's problem, assessing his or her situation, and providing support and resource information as appropriate. Since the distant county supplied us with a fairly current listing of services in its area, what else did we need?

As it turned out, we needed a lot. In the first place, the demographics of this particular county were far different than our own. The county was largely rural, and callers were physically as well as emotionally isolated. They had fewer occasions to receive support from others, and more chances to brood. Many of their concerns—about the weather, crop prices, the dwindling tourism industry, and rising unemployment—weren't factors in the lives of people who called our own hotlines.

Another consideration was that fewer resources were available to them. Small communities typically don't have health care clinics and social service programs. They don't have substance abuse and mental health services. Residents who need help frequently have to travel great distances to access care.

A further complication was that we didn't know anything about the few resources that did exist. We had no interaction with agencies that provided services because they were at least one hundred miles away. Our paths never crossed in meetings or community events. We also had no feedback from anyone who'd used the services, which meant that every time we gave someone a referral, we didn't know if it really helped.

Even the way the county handled 5150s was different than our own. Fifty-one fifty is the police code for emergency psychiatric hospitalization. When someone is a threat to himself or others, he or she is picked up and held in a psychiatric ward—usually in a county hospital—for up to seventy-two hours. An evaluation is done to determine whether it's safe to release the person after this time or whether further examination and possible treatment are necessary. The practice is so common in the mental health world that 5150 often is used as a verb: "He was threatening to kill himself so we 5150'd him." Locally, we'd worked closely for years with law enforcement to intervene whenever someone's life is in danger. In the distant county, though, police had no knowledge of our agency. Their protocols were different and they asked more questions before agreeing to respond.

While the distant county was satisfied with the service we were providing, we felt that we weren't helping residents there nearly as well as we were helping people in our own area. I said that instead of renewing the contract, we'd work with the distant county to set up its own twenty-four-hour hotline. We didn't receive any money to do this—and, naturally, we lost the $10,000 in annual funding to provide the service. It was a good outcome, though. Over time, people in the distant county were better served because local people were providing the service. And no one was happier than our staff and volunteers, who no longer had to answer the calls.

PROGRAM FIRST, FUNDRAISING SECOND

One of the biggest mistakes nonprofit agencies make is letting financial opportunities determine program development. It has to be the other way around—programs have to drive fundraising.

When an agency needs money, the urge to tweak an existing service to qualify for new funding is strong. What usually happens, though, if the agency isn't careful, is that it starts moving away from its mission. This is what happened to the crisis center when it expanded into a remote county. Our mission didn't include serving residents in other areas; the focus was on serving the million-plus people in our own county. In the crisis center's defense, we didn't solicit the opportunity;

the other county approached us. Still, what looked like an easy way to earn $10,000 turned out not to be easy at all.

In my second month I received a call from the president of the board of a local nonprofit. She and the executive director wanted to have a confidential meeting with me to discuss a potential merger of our two organizations. I was surprised. I'd never spoken with either woman before and knew next to nothing about their agency. More importantly, I was still learning about the crisis center; I was in no position to evaluate the merits of a possible merger. Still, it never hurts to hear what someone has to say, so I agreed to meet.

Both women were smartly dressed. After reviewing their programs and giving me literature on the agency, they moved quickly to the point of the meeting. The executive director had decided to retire and the agency was at a crossroads. One option was to conduct a search, fill the position, and continue on as before. Another option, though, was to merge with an established agency. In looking around, they thought the crisis center was a good candidate because it was highly regarded and ran programs that complemented those of their agency.

I was flattered and told them so. At the same time, I didn't think it was a good fit. Our expertise was crisis counseling while their agency provided drug and alcohol treatment services. Our work was related, yet our missions were different.

"Suppose the crisis center received a grant to assist with the merger," the president said. "Would that change your mind?"

"Who would give it?" I asked. The truth was, it wouldn't make a difference. I was just curious to know whether she had a prospect.

She named a large family foundation.

"Do you know anyone there?" I said.

Family foundations are different than community foundations. Community foundations are governed by civic leaders who tend to be process oriented. They see themselves as stewards of the community, and deliberate at length before making funding decisions. Every proposal is reviewed by multiple committees as well as staff, regardless of whether it's submitted by an agency that the foundation has supported previously or by a first-time applicant. The process is time-consuming, and knowing someone in the foundation rarely changes things. Family foundations, in contrast, reach decisions relatively quickly. Staff present a synopsis of each request to board members at regularly scheduled meetings and board members vote on it. The staff's role is important, but even more important is the disposition of the board. Since family foundations often are dominated by heirs, their actions can be emotional. Having a good contact within a family foundation is critical.

She nodded, but didn't say anything. I waited for more.

"My husband is president of the foundation," she said finally.

I might have fallen out of my chair if I hadn't been sitting with both feet on the ground. It was a good example of why it pays to be silent sometimes.

"I can't promise anything," she added, "but I think you'd have a good chance."

I was tempted to ask what role she envisioned herself playing, both after the merger and with regard to fundraising; however, it wouldn't have been fair. We weren't going to merge. I wondered, though, whether turning down the offer might jeopardize the crisis center's chances later on if we applied to her husband's foundation.

"That makes it even harder for me to say that I don't think a merger is right," I said. "At least at this time. Down the road it might make sense, but right now it doesn't. I'm sorry."

Both women were understanding and gracious. They thanked me for my time and I thanked them for their interest in the crisis center.

We never talked again. Their agency hired a new executive director, who lasted only a year, then a second director and a third. It continues to remain independent, although its services duplicate other programs that are larger and better known. Also, much of its funding has disappeared, perhaps because the president at that time has long since retired from the board. Without her connections, the agency has had a harder time raising money.

I waited a year before submitting a grant request to her husband's foundation. It was a small request by the foundation's standards, perhaps so small that it was dealt with by others and never reached his desk. To my surprise, it was funded.

KNOW THE LIMITS

These days it's fashionable in business to "think outside the box," meaning not to be constrained by past practices or conventional wisdom. In the nonprofit world this adage has a place; however, more often than not it's in marketing and fundraising, not program development. When you're actively engaged in creating and growing programs, you have to set limits. If you don't, it's easy to fall into the trap of trying to do it all.

With the exception of personnel, every decision I've made that I later regretted has concerned program development. Two things I've learned are: (1) bad decisions usually are the result of my impatience and the fact that I should have gathered more information first; and (2) every bad decision I've made has been to start or expand a service. I've never regretted saying no to an opportunity, probably because more opportunities always seem to come along.

This doesn't mean that an executive director should be averse to taking risks. It does mean, though, that he or she needs to be able to weigh those risks carefully and develop an exit strategy when necessary.

A few years ago the head of an agency that helps rape victims asked me if the crisis center would be interested in answering the agency's twenty-four-hour sexual assault hotline. Historically, the agency used an answering service, which was functional but hardly compassionate. Women who had just experienced one of the worst moments of their lives were put on hold while the answering service paged a volunteer on call and then connected the volunteer with the victim.

I was certain that we could do better, and was eager to try. The executive director assured me that volunteers responded to the page within a minute or two, so all we had to do was keep the caller on the line. She was adamant in saying that she didn't want us to do any counseling. A woman who's been raped should only have to tell her story once, the director said, and if we attempted to provide more than emotional support, it might violate client confidentiality. Also, the best testimony is the first time someone tells her story because it's the freshest. Staff at the rape agency wanted to be the ones to hear it the first time, not us.

I understood and readily agreed. The crisis center had answered a domestic violence hotline for fifteen years, so we knew the trauma of women who have been assaulted. At the same time, I didn't question what I was told about the promptness with which volunteers responded, even though at least once a month we received a call from a woman who said that she called the rape hotline and had been put on hold for ten minutes or more, waiting to talk with a counselor, before she'd given up and called our agency. Instead of addressing the issue head on, at the beginning, though, I let it go, thinking that we could work it out later.

I also didn't question the wisdom of putting callers on hold, even though it contradicted the crisis center's own policies. If all of our counselors are on the phone when a new call comes in, they communicate nonverbally to determine which one is on the least life-threatening call. That person then says into the phone, "I need to interrupt you for a minute to answer another call. Is that okay?" If the caller agrees, our counselor then lays down the receiver and goes to another console to handle the new call. He or she doesn't put the person on hold; instead, the caller can hear background sounds and in this way still feels connected. The policy on the rape hotline was the opposite, however. Callers were put on hold deliberately so that they couldn't have an extended conversation with anyone other than the rape counselor. While we waited for the counselor to return our page, we could check in periodically with the caller to make sure that she was still there, but that was all.

Given the basic difference in our two agencies' operating styles—both designed with the client's best interests in mind, yet opposed philosophically—it wasn't surprising that there were problems as soon as we began answering the line. It also wasn't surprising that the problems seemed to worsen over time.

A fair number of callers were distressed about assaults that had happened months and, in a few instances, years earlier. They needed to talk, but weren't in danger at the moment. Should a rape counselor be paged? We didn't think so; the caller could wait until a counselor was able to call her in the morning. Our partner agency disagreed.

Physicians phoned because they needed a forensic nurse for a sexual assault examination. The exam was necessary to document evidence for court, should the case go there. The agency only had a few nurses trained in this service, and they could be hard to reach. The result was that we answered repeated, angry calls from doctors wanting to know when the nurse would arrive.

By far the most difficult situations, though, were ones where a woman had just been assaulted and we couldn't reach anyone to respond. The woman would be sobbing into the phone and the only thing we could say was hold on, a counselor will be calling in any minute. The longer it took, the more agitated our volunteer became, until he or she felt as helpless as the victim. The only solace was that all of the rape counselors were phenomenal, truly remarkable people who became the victim's advocate, advisor, and friend. Once we were able to connect them, the client was well served.

After just a few weeks it was obvious that this arrangement wasn't working, at least from our point of view. Our volunteers, who were highly-trained crisis counselors, felt devalued. There was no real difference between what they were doing and the answering service used previously. I'd believed that once the other agency gained confidence in our ability to handle rape calls effectively, we'd be given more latitude to help. This didn't happen, though.

Our crisis line staff and theirs met several times and tried to work through the issues. Unfortunately, our differences were irreconcilable. They didn't want the protocols changed and we couldn't live with them as is. The fault was largely mine. These conversations should have taken place well before we started, not after the fact. If I'd owned up to our differences at the outset and discussed them openly with the other agency's executive director, the outcome would have been better. Either we would have structured the service to satisfy both agencies or we would have mutually agreed that collaborating on this project wasn't a good idea. Instead, I was so eager to start that I overlooked a critical step in planning. Bringing it up after the fact served to undermine the trust between us.

The only thing to do was admit that it'd been a mistake and walk away. I exercised the thirty-day termination clause in our agreement and the other agency went back to using an answering service. It was a disappointing end for everyone.

DOING IT RIGHT

There's one question I've learned to ask whenever a program opportunity comes up: "Would we do this anyway, even if we received no money for it?" If I can honestly answer yes, then I know it's worth pursuing. I may answer no and consider the opportunity anyway, if there are other potential benefits such as increased media exposure or access to new volunteers. I'm more wary, though, because I know that the primary reason isn't because our clients will be better served.

The crisis center's grief counseling program was born not because we received funding to start it—we didn't—but because a growing number of people called us with bereavement issues. In their grief, they were at high risk for drug and alcohol abuse, divorce, and suicide. We looked around and no other local agency offered specialized counseling to children and adults mourning the death of a loved one. Believing that we could develop the expertise, we jumped in.

Today, our grief counseling program is one of the oldest, largest, and most diverse in California. Even so, only a few funders support it directly. Despite a long and successful track record, numerous public accolades, and hundreds of testimonials from clients who completed counseling and said that it was the best thing they did for themselves and their families, the program is funded mainly by proceeds from the crisis center's thrift shop—unrestricted revenues that we allocate for this purpose. That's okay with me, it's why we raise money—to spend it on services we believe in. If we waited until outside funding was in place, the program would still be a dream.

In somewhat the same way, the crisis center began maintaining a countywide database of health and social services. In the agency's early years, all of the information was kept on index cards—hundreds of them, which volunteers meticulously updated every time a program or service changed. Today, two employees devote much of their time to managing the data electronically.

Until 2001 our agency wasn't paid to maintain the database. We did it because our hotline volunteers needed up-to-date information on local resources and no one else had a database that met our needs. This wasn't surprising since maintaining databases—especially large, comprehensive databases—is painstaking work. It also wasn't surprising that once we fully developed our database, dozens of public and private entities wanted to use it. The logical answer was to put the database on the Internet, where anyone with access to the web could view it. To do this, though, we needed an income source. The database cost us money to maintain.

My strategy was to convince three county departments to fund the database together. Each would pay one-third of the actual cost of maintenance, which was considerably less than they were paying to maintain their own in-house databases. We'd then put our database online without charge or password so that everyone, including the general public, could benefit.

Some of my peers thought I should have bargained for more, reasoning that the crisis center had a valuable commodity and could use it to leverage funding for other services. I agreed that our database was valuable and knew that if I wanted to I could have done better than break even. Still, I was content to have our out-of-pocket costs covered. In the first place, we were getting paid for something that to that point we'd done for free. Already we were coming out ahead. Second, it was important to me that the information be available to everyone, not just county employees. If the crisis center had tried to profit from the deal, county officials might have restricted access solely to those who paid for it. Instead, the county could take credit for making the database available to everyone in the community with Internet access. Third, and most importantly, I was looking down the road. In a few years' time our agency planned to be the 211 provider for the county (211, for people who don't have it yet, is a national, toll-free, three-digit phone number like 911 that people call for information about local health and social services). Our database would be the backbone of 211, and having it subsidized would enable us to develop it further.

Everything proceeded smoothly until the contract was ready to be signed. Like many government entities, Contra Costa County has long contracts filled with dense legal language that's heavily weighted to protect the county's interests. All of it except the description of deliverables (what the contractor promises to do) is nonnegotiable, I was told. This was a problem. It's standard language in all contracts for the county to own copyright of any products it funds. If we were producing a resource directory or other printed material, I'd have understood. In this instance, though, the county wasn't buying a product or a service, it was buying *access* to a product that the crisis center created, owned, and used. Unfortunately, no one with the county acknowledged the difference.

"How can the crisis center own information that's public?" county officials said.

"We don't own the information," I explained. "We own the way the information is presented, the wording, the structure and, most importantly, the way it's coded."

This is the whole value of a database. Anyone could take our print directory of 2,500 resources and put it in Access software. It'd be a lot of work, but it'd be relatively easy to do. The challenge is understanding each resource well enough that you assign the appropriate keywords and taxonomy codes so that users can find it. Frequently, this means making multiple phone calls to an agency to clarify its service.

What made my task more difficult was that the county counsel assigned to our intellectual property issue didn't use a computer. I couldn't believe it. He conducted all business by phone, Dictaphone, and handwritten notes. His staff had to make hard copies of everything for him, including his e-mail. Trying to explain the concept of an electronic database to someone who's never used one proved fruitless. The longer we negotiated, the more I worried. A lot was riding on this.

"Just go ahead and sign," county staff advised me. "We don't want to be responsible for maintaining the database, that's why we're contracting with you. The issue of who owns copyright doesn't really matter, and the sooner you sign, the sooner the crisis center gets paid." Unsaid but clearly communicated was that I could trust the county. Maybe I could; then again, the county didn't have the crisis center's interests at heart.

"The issue of who owns copyright is critical," I said. "If the county owned copyright, you could decide in the future to contract with someone else to maintain our data. You could even decide not to share the information with us, in which case we'd be prevented from accessing the very data we worked years to develop, which our agency depends on. If it doesn't matter to you, then you shouldn't object to us retaining copyright."

County officials shook their heads. "We can't do that," they said. "In the first place, we can't change language in the contract; it has to conform with state statutes. Secondly, suppose the crisis center goes out of business or decides not to let us use the database after the contract ends. We'll have to create our own database from scratch or find another one to use."

I marveled at their desire to have it all. I was offering a better product than the county had now, at a lower cost because the crisis center was merely breaking even, not profiting from the deal, and it wasn't enough.

"You don't have to change the existing contract," I said. "You just need to add an addendum, which our attorney will draft, recognizing our right of ownership and saying that it supersedes the section in the contract that gives copyright to the county. The addendum also can include language about what happens to the database if the contract is terminated."

County officials considered this. "We might agree to that," they said. "Let's talk about termination."

I said, "If it's terminated because the crisis center fails to meet conditions of the contract or because we go out of business, then we'd be willing to give or sell the database to the county. We can discuss terms. If it's terminated because the county fails to meet conditions of the contract, though, or because you choose not to fund the contract anymore, then too bad."

This wasn't acceptable to the county. At a stalemate, the director of social services called me into his office. I explained my position. "I want this to go through," I said, "but I'm not giving up our rights. They're too important to us."

"I want it to go through, too," he said. "What'll it take to make that happen?"

I said that his staff and county counsel seemed willing to add the addendum to the contract that preserved our copyright, which was the most important issue. We could spend more time trying to reach consensus on termination language, but that just meant that we continued to focus on a worse-case scenario. I'd rather think positively.

"This is a good partnership for both of us," I said. "Why dwell on a situation that we hope never happens?"

He agreed. The boilerplate language in county contracts regarding termination was deemed sufficient. It covered failure-to-perform issues without delving into transferring ownership of the database. I could live with it and, ultimately, the county could, too.

PROGRAM EVALUATION

With any program or service, it's important to know what's working and what isn't. What should be expanded, changed, or discontinued? The answers may not be obvious. People have strong emotional attachments to programs, rarely view them objectively, and can't always put them in proper perspective relative to an agency's mission.

For every program at the crisis center, we have written goals and objectives by which we measure effectiveness. The goals are what we expect the program to accomplish. The objectives are the anticipated results.

Many agencies confuse outcomes with outputs. Outputs are the measure of services provided or people served. Planned Parenthood volunteers make presentations to 500 students on avoiding teenage pregnancies. Loaves and Fishes soup kitchen serves lunch to one hundred people. Project Second Chance provides an hour of free tutoring every week to twenty-five inner-city youths. These are outputs. Outcomes are the measure of change that results when goals and objectives are reached. The teen pregnancy rate is reduced; fewer people go hungry; youths do better in school. Tracking the number of public service announcements for an anti-smoking campaign is measuring outputs. Tracking the number of people who quit smoking in response to the campaign or assessing the change in the lung cancer rate is measuring outcomes.

For objectives to be valid, they must be SMART—specific, measurable, achievable, realistic, and time-bound. Providing job training to more people is too general. Providing job training so that fifty people develop new skills and land jobs that pay enough to support an average family means something. Doing it in six months means even more.

One of the best ways to measure a program's success is through client satisfaction surveys. After all, services aim to meet the needs of clients, so client feedback is important. What do you do, though, when this isn't possible?

People who call our hotlines, for instance, don't have to identify themselves. They don't need to tell us their name to receive help. Moreover, it wouldn't make sense for us at the end of the call to ask someone who has just shared a painful experience to rate our service. We can't shift the conversation from their needs to ours and seem compassionate. We can ask permission to call back in a few days to see how they're doing, and we do ask this sometimes. Then people have to break anonymity, though, which means that the ones who say yes are a self-selecting group and not necessarily representative of everyone.

An even bigger issue for us is that sometimes when we do our best work, clients are incensed. Suicidal callers don't necessarily want to die, which is why they've called; however, they want their pain to end. When the police come because we've broken confidentiality to save a life, some people scream obscenities into the phone. We've taken away their option to kill themselves, at least for the moment. From our point of view, the call is a success. The person is still alive. We hang up relieved even though it may be hard to forget the client's closing words of anger and despair.

At least there are closing words. Sometimes a person calls us after overdosing and loses consciousness in the middle of the conversation. We don't know whether he or she is still alive until police break down the door, pick up the receiver, and inform us. We stay on the phone to keep the possibility of communication open, straining to hear any signs of life.

Once Judy, our crisis line manager, was talking with a man who said that he was holding a loaded gun to his head and wanted to pull the trigger. She tried to get him to put the gun down or to remove the bullets, but he refused. She asked him to verbally contract with her, to promise that he wouldn't harm himself or anyone else in the next twenty-four hours, and that he'd call our hotline first before initiating any potentially deadly action. The man refused again. Resigned, Judy started exploring his life with him. Then the gun went off.

Judy shouted into the phone, asking whether the man was all right. There was no response. She used a second phone to start a trace, keeping the caller's line open. Minutes ticked by. She thought she heard someone's faint breathing and kept checking with the trace operator, trying to speed up identification of the caller's phone number and address. After nearly an hour, the police arrived. The man's gun had discharged accidentally, grazing his forehead and knocking him out. He was still alive, and otherwise unhurt. Judy had stayed on the phone with him the whole time.

Experiences like this are why we use a different yardstick than client satisfaction to rate our suicide prevention program. Even though some people call back months or even years later to thank us for saving their lives, many don't. We have a lot of anecdotal evidence—heartfelt and touching letters from people who credit us with getting them through their darkest moments. That's not measurable, though.

On the face of it, a reasonable way to gauge our effectiveness would be to determine whether the suicide rate in our area has gone down. Suicide rates are based on the number of suicides in a group, divided by the group's population, multiplied by 100,000. One suicide at a school of 5,000 students, for example, produces a suicide rate at the school of 20.0 for the year. There are problems with using the suicide rate to measure success, however. First and foremost, factors outside our control, such as the economy, have a major impact on the suicide rate. No matter how well we do our job, there will be more suicides during a recession than during boom times. It's a fact. Second, suicide rates aren't accurate. If someone lives in one county and takes his or her life in another county, the death often is attributed to the second county. Third, suicides are underreported for a variety of reasons.

Because suicide is often an impulsive act, especially among young people, buying time is critical. This is why we consider a measure of our success to be whether suicidal people who phone our hotlines are still alive one month after they call. In our line of work, a month can be forever. Our grief counseling director has access to active files in the county coroner's office, so we can compare information on recent suicide victims with records of hotline callers. We may not know the names of people who call us, but we probably know their gender, age, marital status, family composition, city of residence, occupation, and other identifiable characteristics by talking with them and hearing their stories. Our objective is that 95 percent of people who call us at high risk for suicide will be alive one month later. Why not 100 percent? Because according to the SMART model, the objective has to be realistic. We strive for 100 percent but know that, realistically, we can't save everyone. Some people who are teetering between life and death choose death. It's their choice, not ours.

Several years ago we had an especially poignant moment in our hotline room. A twenty-one-year-old man, on a cell phone, said that he had a gun, ten clips of ammunition, and wanted to kill himself. Sewell, the volunteer who handled the call, tried to find out where the man was. It turned out that he was in a park, standing on a ridge top. In addition to looking down on others, he could see anyone who might approach him.

This made Sewell even more concerned. "Are you alone?" he asked.

The caller became suspicious. "Why do you want to know?"

"I just want to know if there's anyone there to help you, who you can talk with to get through this."

The man hesitated. "I'm alone," he said finally.

"Is anyone nearby?" Sewell was worried. Ten clips was way too much firepower for someone intent on suicide.

"There are a few people walking on a path below me, kind off to the side."

"Anyone else?"

The man seemed to be looking. "No," he said. "At least not right now."

Sewell listened for clues that would indicate which park the caller was in. Since the caller was using a cell phone, the call couldn't be traced.

The caller and Sewell talked for half an hour, and it seemed like Sewell was getting somewhere. The man had just started to remove the clip from his gun when Sewell heard a shout over the phone. There was a gunshot, then the line went dead.

Later the police phoned. Sewell had been able to identify the park, and police spotted the caller on the ridge at the same instant that he saw them. The man rammed the clip back into the gun, held it to his temple, and fired before anyone could stop him. Police praised Sewell for his actions, saying that he probably saved many lives considering how much ammunition the caller had. Sewell was inconsolable.

"Just a little more time," he said, his voice breaking. "Just a little more time and I might've been able to get him to put down the gun."

A few months later, Sewell was dead, too. What the caller didn't know, and would never know, was that Sewell had leukemia. While he was trying to make the most of the little time that he had left, continuing to volunteer as long as his health held up, a twenty-one-year-old with his whole life seemingly ahead of him was preparing to kill himself. Sewell didn't acknowledge the irony, and those of us who were privy to the full story kept silent. Nor was Sewell resentful. It would have been easy to tell the caller that he should be grateful for his youth, and that Sewell would trade places with him in a second. That would only make the caller feel worse, though. It wouldn't have helped.

As individuals and as agencies, it's hard sometimes to accept the fact that we can only do so much when it seems like too little. Yet society's most intractable problems—homelessness, chronic unemployment, inadequate health care, illiteracy, substance abuse, physical abuse, environmental degradation, mental illness, and more—aren't conquerable in one fell swoop. This is why we take solace in each individual success, and why we mourn each individual loss. Both are part of our world.

CHAPTER FIVE

Fundraising 101: Uncle Bob vs. Bill Gates

I had a personal and professional interest in the debate that took place regarding turning the old Orinda library into a homeless shelter. Personally, I live in Lamorinda, which is the common name for the combined communities of Lafayette, Moraga, and Orinda—all affluent, with Orinda at the top. Professionally, I direct an agency that provides services to homeless people.

I understand the concerns and fears expressed by some Orinda residents about having a homeless shelter in town. While I've never stereotyped the homeless as drug addicts or child molesters the way some opponents of the shelter did, I used to make assumptions about the homeless that were ill informed. I assumed that the homeless were predominantly single men. I assumed that they didn't work, which was why they had to beg. I assumed that if I gave them money for food, they spent it on alcohol instead.

In the past twenty years I've learned differently. I've learned that the typical homeless person isn't a single man but a parent—or two parents—with young children. I've learned that many have full-time jobs, yet their wages are so low that they can't afford housing. I've learned that those with substance abuse problems and mental illnesses need treatment, but often it's not available to them.

Even more importantly, I've learned how homeless people feel. Once you know that, everything changes.

They're sad; it's a hard life. Adults who are homeless can age ten years in a matter of months. Children can bear permanent psychological scars.

They're mad. People look past them as if they're invisible. No one seems to care.

Most of all, they're scared. The streets aren't kind.

I regret that people opposed to the shelter probably haven't had the chance to know a homeless person in any real way. If they had, I think their assumptions about the homeless would fall away, as mine did. So would their fears.

I'm concerned about my children's safety as much as any parent. I'm even more concerned, though, that my children grow up knowing that it's important to help others. If they live only for themselves, I'll feel that I've failed them as much as if they suffer from a lasting hurt that I could have prevented.

I'm sorry the shelter was turned down. I hope people will consider other ways to welcome those who are less fortunate. I'd like my community to be a model for others.
YIMBY—Yes In My Backyard.

When nonprofit agencies first form, and along their path to maturity, someone invariably suggests organizing a special event to raise money. Usually this someone is a board member, and usually the idea is greeted with enthusiasm. An auction! A golf tournament! A casino night! What fun—and we'll make money, too!

The board of the crisis center had been planning an event well before I was hired. Already, board members had solicited a number of auction prizes from local merchants. One group took responsibility for writing clever descriptions of the prizes for the event program. Another group was in charge of decorations. A third group did much of the cooking and baking to save the cost of a caterer.

Everyone was excited. The whole thing was inspiring. It was also a waste of time. Only sixty people showed up, nearly all of them agency volunteers—the same loyal, steadfast supporters who attended every event. They didn't come to bid on auction prizes; rather, they came because they were invited. In their minds, they were supporting the crisis center by being there.

Although each auction prize was worth at least $100 and was lovingly packaged by the board, most had no bids. Board members couldn't stand to see their hard work go to waste, so they started biding, hoping that would encourage others. It didn't. In the end, the crisis center cleared $8,000, mainly because board members bought the items that they had solicited.

"We should have just made a donation to the agency and saved ourselves a lot of trouble," one board member said afterward.

I had to agree. Most special events require a greater investment of time and energy than they return. Even agencies that do them well have moments when staff and volunteers question their worth.

A few years later, a woman who loved to organize events was elected to the crisis center board. She had a large circle of friends and, most importantly, was vested in the agency. Still, when she offered to coordinate a new event, I hesitated.

Patty was a former grief client of the crisis center. Her husband had been clinically depressed for years; even so, she wasn't prepared to find him dead one day, the victim of a self-inflicted gunshot wound. The thought of it today, more than fifteen years later, still produces tears.

"If you've ever lost someone you love," she says, "you know how empty you feel. Nothing matters. Even the simplest thing, like opening a can of soup or reading a newspaper, is overwhelming."

She never imagined that she would feel helpless. She had a wonderful husband, two young daughters, a nice home, and a fulfilling, professional career.

"It's amazing how quickly your life can change," she says. "One moment you have everything, the future looks bright. Then, in the blink of an eye, it's gone.

You don't know how you're going to get through the next five minutes, much less the day. A week seems like 100 years."

The crisis center's grief counseling director called Patty and asked her to be part of a support group she was starting for survivors after suicide.

"I said okay without any idea what I was committing to," Patty says. "I'm so glad I did. I learned through the group that I wasn't alone. I learned that others shared the same feelings, thoughts, and pains as me. I learned that I could talk about the shame, the guilt, and the hard times, and receive back understanding and support."

There was no way that I could say no to Patty when she asked to organize a gala on our behalf, especially when she said that her volunteer committee would do most of the work—solicit auction prizes, book the facility, order food and wine, coordinate the design and mailing of save-the-date cards, invitations, and the event program, and hire the entertainment. Staff had one main task: to solicit corporate sponsorships. Other board members also had one task: to invite well-to-do friends and acquaintances to attend.

Today, the gala grosses about $100,000 and nets $65,000 annually. We could do it for less; however, we splurge on a sit-down dinner, hosted bar, gaming tables, and live entertainment to make sure people have a good time. This is important because we want our guests to come back the following year. All things considered, it's a good profit. If I calculated how much time and energy is put into the event, though, the return probably wouldn't equal minimum wage. It's always a fun night and we'll continue doing it; however, it's important to remember that there are other ways to raise money.

DEVELOPING A PLAN

When I started at the crisis center, the agency received little grant funding and few individual donations. This was because most of the agency's operating costs were borne by government contracts. Staff and board members assumed that this funding would continue, so no one felt a strong need to fundraise. Consequently, there wasn't a fundraising plan.

The problem with this is that government support is unreliable. An agency that banks on it always being there can go under if it suddenly goes away.

In putting together a plan, it's important to understand the difference between single-issue agencies like a food bank, homeless shelter, or domestic violence program and multi-issue agencies like a crisis center. In the first place, the purpose of single-issue agencies is easy to understand—you're feeding people who are hungry, housing people who are homeless, or protecting people who are threatened. Donors don't need to know much more than that in order to decide whether to give. What's the purpose of a crisis center, though? Why do people call? How do you help them? The benefit isn't immediately clear.

As a fundraiser for a multi-issue agency, you have to educate potential donors about the problems the agency is addressing and the ways you're doing it before you can ask for money. This takes time. Studies show that most people give emotionally and only later, if asked, justify their giving intellectually. With only a few words or a single photograph of a despondent child, the Children's Defense Fund can motivate donors to write a check. The American Civil Liberties Union, though, which has a broader mission, needs to tell its story before someone will donate. Many people don't give it the chance.

Single-issue agencies have another thing going for them—their donors usually are committed. Not everyone cares about helping people with AIDS, but those who do tend to be passionate about it. They give often and generously because the cause is dear to them.

In contrast, donors to multi-issue agencies, like the agencies themselves, often have diverse interests. Instead of concentrating their giving in one area, they support a large number of causes that they consider important. Multi-issue agencies can attract more donors than single-issue agencies because their services touch more segments of the general population; however, donations tend to be smaller since donors are less invested in the work.

This isn't to say that one kind of agency is easier or harder to raise money for than another kind. Rather, some fundraising strategies are more likely to succeed for certain kinds of agencies and it's important to know this.

There are three factors to consider in a fundraising plan. The first is the purpose of the funding. Will it provide seed money for a new program, operating costs for continuing services, one-time capital for a building (frequently referred to as bricks and mortar), or long-term security such as an endowment that assures the agency's financial independence?

The second thing to consider is the source of funding. For most nonprofits, there are four main sources: individuals, corporations, foundations, and government. A few nonprofits derive substantial income from other sources such as religious groups and service clubs (Lions Blind Centers, for instance). Some nonprofit agencies—mine included—have developed for-profit subsidiaries that generate revenue for their work. Still, for most agencies the primary revenue sources are individual donations, corporate gifts, foundations grants, and government funding.

The third thing to consider is the stimulus. How will funds be solicited—face-to-face, by phone, by mail, or in a grant request? Each has a place.

RULE NUMBER ONE

Here's a test. Who's most likely to become a donor to your agency: (1) your Uncle Bob who lives 3,000 miles away; (2) Mr. and Mrs. Smith, who live locally and give generously to several charities, though not yours; or (3) Bill and Melinda Gates?

If you answered Uncle Bob, you're right. The first rule in fundraising is that people give to people. Specifically, people give to people with whom they have a relationship, not people they don't know. This applies across the board, regardless of the funding source. When a foundation grants money to an agency, it's often because of the relationship between a program officer of the foundation and the executive director or development director of the nonprofit. Trust has been established. The foundation is confident that the agency's need is real and accurately presented, that the agency will spend grant funds as intended and deliver the services it has promised, that the agency will publicize the grant in a manner that reflects positively on the funder, and that the agency will submit grant reports in a timely fashion.

Foundation staff also know that if any major problems arise during the course of the grant period, the agency will discuss them as they come up, not wait to disclose them until the grant expires, when it's too late to do anything. Funders are partners and want to be informed in advance of bad news as well as good news.

Uncle Bob, being so far away, probably doesn't benefit from your agency's services. This doesn't matter, though. What's important is that he knows you. He knows you wouldn't ask him to donate unless it was needed, that his money will be spent wisely, and that it'll support a worthy cause. Uncle Bob is an ideal prospect.

Mr. and Mrs. Smith may be good prospects, too, but it's less certain. They have the capacity and inclination to give, which are essential. In addition, they support several local agencies and could be willing to donate to yours. Without knowing the specific reasons why they give, though, it's hard to assess their potential. They may contribute to the Leukemia Society because their son died from the disease, but this doesn't mean that they'll give to the American Cancer Society, much less to an unrelated cause, such as a literacy program.

The bigger issue is that the Smiths don't have a connection to your agency. If they don't know anyone in it, or anyone served by it, or anyone who donates to it, they have little incentive to give.

The same is true, but even more so, for billionaire philanthropists like Bill Gates and his wife. Just because someone has an unimaginable amount of money and donates a lot of it to various causes doesn't make him or her a good prospect. Yet many charities send appeal letters to the wealthiest people in their community, or to the wealthiest people in the country. It's usually a waste of time, paper, and postage. You need to develop a relationship first.

RULE NUMBER TWO

When people solicit someone they don't know, such as Bill Gates, they're ignoring the first rule in fundraising. On the other hand, they're following the second rule of fundraising, which is that you have to ask. If you don't ask, you won't receive.

Donors who are surveyed about their giving habits cite numerous reasons why they haven't given to a particular agency. They don't know anything about it. They're not interested in the cause. They don't know whether the need is real. They're not sure if the agency will handle their money responsibly. They're strapped at the moment and can't afford to give. One reason high on almost every donor's list is because no one asked. No one asked, so the donor never had to decide whether to give. This is why our mailboxes are filled everyday with solicitations from various charities. Each is gambling the cost of the mailing that at least a few people will give if asked. Sometimes it's a small gamble that's worth the price, especially if an agency can afford to be patient. You don't measure the success of any mailing solely on the immediate return. It's possible—even probable—that an acquisition mailing (a mail appeal to people who have never donated to your agency) will fail to cover costs. If it produces enough new donors, though, who give more frequently and more generously over time, it's worth it.

In asking people to give, it's important to remember what you're doing and what you're not doing. You're not going to donors, hat in hand, asking them please, pretty please, be so kind as to favor your poor agency with a gift—any amount will be appreciated. You're not asking them for spare change. Fundraising isn't begging.

Instead, what you're doing is presenting donors with an investment opportunity. By giving to your agency, they're making something good happen in their community. People who are unemployed will get job training. New mothers will receive "Welcome Home, Baby" information. Troubled teens will be mentored, lonely seniors will be entertained, stray animals will be adopted.

Words like "gift," "giving," "donation," and "contribution" make fundraising sound one way, from donor to agency. It's really a partnership. The agency gives the donor a chance to improve his or her community in some way, and receives funding to make that happen. The donor, in turn, provides needed support, receives appreciation for it, and knows that he or she is helping to make a difference. It's value for value. Fundraising isn't something to be embarrassed about. It's a necessary part of running a nonprofit agency. With money, an agency can fulfill its mission. Without it, the agency's services will disappear.

CRISIS FUNDRAISING

Imagine that you're a new executive director and your first day on the job, your very first day, the major benefactor to the agency dies. This actually happened to a colleague of mine. A woman who gave the agency more than $200,000 annually died suddenly and the new executive director started her job with a huge hole in the agency's budget. The hole grew quickly because the donor had encouraged many of her socialite friends to contribute and suddenly their support began evaporating, too.

The natural inclination whenever an agency befalls misfortune is to sound alarm bells. The agency is in a crisis and needs donations fast. The problem is that most people don't want to support a sinking ship. They want to contribute to a successful cause.

It's tempting, especially in times of trouble, to focus on the agency's needs. Yet most people—especially major donors—give because of needs they have, not needs that the agency has. This is the third rule of fundraising.

Some people give because it makes them feel good. They consider themselves fortunate to be in the position they're in and want to help others. What they get for their money is the knowledge that lives are being saved, human dignity is being restored, important causes are being furthered.

Public recognition is a compelling incentive for many donors. Being listed in a program or newsletter with others in the community—particularly others you admire—can elevate your status, or at least put you in good company. For businesses, being recognized as a generous contributor to local causes boosts your public image and frequently leads to increased sales. Major donors give to endowments and capital campaigns to have a lasting effect, to play a key role in an agency's future. If the donor's name ends up on a building or wall as a result, well, it's a nice legacy.

Many people give because they get something tangible in return. It may be a small premium, such as an article of clothing, tote bag, or magazine subscription, or it may be something more valuable, such as preferred seating at a symphony performance or the chance to meet someone famous. Even donors who say that they give for nobler reasons often are swayed by incentives, even in mail appeals. They read the solicitation letter in the privacy of their homes and don't have to admit to anyone—including themselves—that they're attracted by a free gift.

The biggest benefit of all for some donors is one that costs the agency nothing at all—a tax break. Donors who itemize their charitable contributions can support causes they consider worthy and deduct it from their income.

Whatever the donor's motivations—and frequently they're numerous, such as a desire to do good, the need to be recognized, and the chance to benefit personally— you can't forget them if you're a fundraiser. This is easier said than done. When you work at a nonprofit agency, it's natural to think that people should give because the agency deserves it. You see the value of the agency's work everyday, in a way that no donor can. What we're doing is important; people ought to support it. Unfortunately, donations aren't a right that every agency is entitled to merely because it's providing a needed service. Successful fundraising focuses on the donor's point of view.

PERSONAL IS BETTER

In England, charities take out ads in newspapers when they need money. I don't know how successful that is, but I know it wouldn't work in this country. Here, the more personal the ask, the more likely people are to give. That's the fourth rule of fundraising. A newspaper ad can be ignored easily, which makes it the least effective way to solicit donations.

The most personal way to raise money, and therefore the most effective, is face-to-face. Meeting with a prospective donor, telling him or her about the agency's work, hearing the donor's concerns, answering questions, and requesting a gift— usually a substantial one—is the most successful method of fundraising. It hinges on having the right person ask for the right amount at the right time. By this I mean someone who's close to the donor, who asks for a donation that's neither beyond the donor's means nor beneath them, at a time when the donor is in a position to give.

A lot of research goes into determining these three components. Information is collected about the donor's interests, hobbies, education, professional life, family, friends, clubs, political beliefs, and religious affiliation. To gauge the donor's giving potential, the agency gathers data about his or her income, real estate, stock holdings, and other assets, as well as about the assets of family members, plus information about gifts the donor has made to other charities. From this, the agency decides how much to ask for. The amount shouldn't be so high that the donor recoils in horror, or so low that he or she breaths a sigh of relief.

Two people then meet with the donor (any more can be intimidating). One is usually a friend of the donor who has given to the agency already, preferably at a level as high or higher than the donor will be asked. The other is the president or executive director of the agency who can talk knowledgeably about its services. They decide in advance the amount they're going to ask for, the purpose, and who's going to do the ask.

Less personal than a face-to-face ask is a solicitation by phone from someone close to the donor. Depending on the caller's relationship with the donor, there can be enormous pressure for the donor to say yes to the request, at which point the only question is how much the donor will give. If the caller is skilled, he or she tries to get the donor to agree to a specific amount—usually more than the donor's typical gift. The donor may be able to negotiate it lower—"I don't know, Jerry. It sounds like a good cause but having two kids in college is really killing us financially"—although it's understood that he or she will donate something.

Less effective than a phone call from someone the donor knows is a call from a board member or volunteer at the agency. The caller is donating his or her time to perform a fairly distasteful task—calling strangers and asking them for money—because the agency's work is important. Saying no is harder than saying no to a telemarketer who's been hired by an agency. It's also harder than ignoring a mail solicitation.

Lower down in terms of effectiveness is a personal letter sent by someone close to the donor like a family member or friend. The donor is sure to read it, and unless he or she is willing to reject the friend's request—something most of us aren't comfortable doing—the donor will write a check. It'll be for a small amount, though, if the donor isn't interested in the cause or the agency.

Last in effectiveness is a form letter that's customized as much as possible to appear personal. Sometimes it starts out "Dear Friend," although with the advent of high-speed laser printers many have personal salutations now. It's probably signed by someone the donor doesn't know—the president of the board, the executive director, a volunteer, a client, or, if the agency is well connected, a local celebrity. The person may not have written the letter; in fact, as a general rule, the larger the agency the less likely it is that the person who signed the letter had anything to do with crafting it. He or she simply agreed to provide a signature. The letter tries to sound personal, though, and with modern technology the donor's name can be inserted in several places to foster that impression.

The response rate for mail appeals is low—on average, under 1 percent for new donors and 5 to 10 percent for repeat doors. The average gift also tends to be low—around $25 for new donors and $75 to $100 for repeat donors. Agencies use mail appeals to build their base of donors, then over time work to increase the size and frequency of each donor's gifts. The goal is to move impulse donors to become habitual donors, giving regularly, and eventually upgrading them to thoughtful donors who make giving to the agency a high priority.

FUNDRAISING SOFTWARE

How quickly can you put together a list of donors who gave $100 to your agency last year? $500? $1,000? Which donors gave Last Year But Unfortunately Not This year? (In fundraising jargon, these are LYBUNT donors.) Which Gave Some Year But Unfortunately Not This year? (SYBUNT donors.) How many haven't given at all in the past three years? (Lapsed donors.) When were your donor records last purged, meaning the names of lapsed donors were removed?

When board members provide names of friends to be solicited, is it easy to generate reports every month on the results? Can you add personal notes to a donor's record in order to develop profiles of them? Can you track memorial gifts? Maintain pledge information and send reminder notices?

Which zip codes have produced the largest gifts? Which have the highest average gift? Both are good to know when it comes to buying prospect lists.

It's one thing to enter information on donors and donations in a database; it's another thing to do something with it. That's why there's no substitute for fundraising software. With it you have a powerful fundraising tool. Without it you just have a mailing list.

Donor information, like client information, should be treated confidentially. Some people in an agency need to be able to see it but not edit it, while others need to be able to see contact information (address, phone number, e-mail address, etc.) but not someone's donation history. Select individuals need to be able to add information, including written notes on a donor's assets, values, and priorities that result from research, as well as a log of personal contacts between the agency and the donor. Good fundraising software has multilevel security codes to control exactly how much data any individual user can view.

Depending on the software, you also can perform special, sophisticated functions such as: (1) archive data so that when donors die or move out of the area, their giving histories are retained in a separate file that's linked with relatives and friends who are still active donors, but are omitted from reports; (2) track noncash donations such as stock, vehicles, auction prizes, and volunteer hours; and (3) maintain addresses of vacation homes so that if a donor spends winters in Florida, for example, the agency's holiday appeal is sent to the Florida address rather than to the person's primary residence. Most programs also allow users to create their own codes and customized reports, import and export data in a variety of formats, and integrate seamlessly with word processing, spreadsheet, and accounting software.

Whenever I hear that an agency won't buy fundraising software because it's too expensive, or that the agency relies on a database created by a volunteer, I cringe. It's so shortsighted. Next to an agency's reputation, a fundraising database is its most important asset. Over time, it can be worth hundreds of thousands or even millions of dollars. It makes sense to spend a relatively small money to manage an asset this valuable.

There are dozens of fundraising programs. To find the best one for an agency, get references from sales reps, call other users, and ask questions. Nonprofit Genie, a web site with information on lots of subjects, lists some good questions to ask.

THE FINAL RULE

Thank you, thank you, thank you. You can't say it too often.

The process of soliciting a new gift starts with acknowledging the last one. The best way to encourage donors to give is to express, often and sincerely, gratitude for their support.

Just as the most effective solicitation is personal, so is the most effective way to say thank you personal. A letter is good, a phone call is better, and a face-to-face, heartfelt expression of appreciation—perhaps during an event, when the donor receives public recognition as well—is better yet. Best of all, do all three.

At the crisis center, I start many mornings by affixing my signature to new thank-you letters. Whenever I begin to tire of it, I think how much harder it'd be if the agency didn't have these and other donors supporting our work. I also remember how I feel when I donate to another agency and receive a note of thanks. It makes me want to give again.

I always use blue ink when signing letters, and I instruct my staff to do the same. Black ink looks photocopied, and other colors look unprofessional to me. If I'm going to go to the trouble to sign, I want it to look personal.

One can't forget to thank foundations. Frequently, when I talk with foundation staff, I'm told that many agencies never thank them. This amazes me. Agencies seem to think that because foundations are in the business of giving away money, they don't require the same care and nurturing as individuals. Nothing could be further from the truth. Foundations are made up of people, just like agencies. Thanking them is part of the process. An agency that treats any funder as an account that's closed once a donation is received may be in for a shock when funding runs out and the agency goes back to ask for a new grant.

Imagine being in a job where 90 percent of all the phone calls, e-mail, and paper correspondence you receive consists of people asking for money. This is what it's like to work at a foundation. Then imagine that you open a letter from the executive director of an agency who says, "You made my day! Because of your grant, we're going to be able to provide free mammograms and other breast cancer services to 500 Spanish-speaking women who don't have health insurance. Thank you so much!"

Three sentences, just thirty-five words. It took only a few minutes to write. Still, wouldn't you feel good to receive it? And later, if several of the women sent you personal notes as well, in broken English, meaning that they labored over it, telling you that the service saved their lives, wouldn't that make you look forward to the agency's next grant request? You can't say thank you enough.

CHAPTER SIX

Volunteers: "I'm John and I'm Nude Here"

Some milestones we look forward to: being able to drive, to vote, to drink legally. Others we're not sure about: the first day of school, of a new job, of retirement. Still others we dread: turning thirty, forty, fifty, sixty.

At the crisis center, we pay a lot of attention to milestones. We know that people suffer from holiday depression ("How am I going to survive another Christmas?") and postgraduation blues ("Now what?"). We know that some children can't wait until their eighteenth birthday in order to be emancipated, yet when that day comes they feel lost, unsure what to do next. The same is true of parents after their last child leaves the nest.

Our crisis line counselors pay particular attention to anniversaries because we know that people often think of suicide on the anniversary of a loved ones' death. The attraction can seem magnetic.

"My mom killed herself a year ago," says a teenage girl a week before the anniversary of her mother's death. "I have pills and in seven days I'm going to do what she did."

You want to scream "No!" Instead you say, "I'm so glad you called."

"I don't think I can make it," she says.

"Is there anyone you can talk to? Maybe your dad?"

"He checked out a long time ago. I live with my aunt, but she hardly speaks to me."

Your heart goes out to the caller. You take a deep breath. "How can I help?"

The two of you develop a plan. She'll divide difficult days into hours and try to get through them one by one. When she has trouble, she'll ask for help just like she's doing now. She'll also consider joining one of our support groups for teens who are grieving. Sometimes just talking with others who share similar feelings can make a big difference.

Before I turned fifty, the idea seemed foreboding. Afterward, I forgot about it. It was a thing of the past, like Y2K.

That's the nature of milestones. The good ones pass so quickly that often-times there's a letdown afterward, yet the hard ones pass, too. They may take longer but somehow, with support, we survive them until they no longer seem like millstones.

The atmosphere inside the van was electric. "Is this great or what!" said Peter, a volunteer from Atlanta.

Thousands of people lined the street on both sides. Helicopters circled overhead. Despite Friday evening rush hour, police cordoned off every lane of traffic in both directions.

That's when all of us in the van, fifteen people chosen to carry the Olympic torch through San Francisco and four escort runners, realized that the event was bigger than we ever imagined. Two of the fifteen were former Olympians who had won medals (a silver in women's basketball and a bronze in men's rowing); however, they were as awed the rest of us.

The van pulled out onto 19th Avenue, a major thoroughfare, in front of a procession of motorcycle police, support vehicles, and a Caltrans truck with the marquis flashing "1996 Olympic Torch Relay." Directly in front of us was another van filled with reporters and photographers. The back door was open and TV cameramen were preparing to film live footage for the six o'clock news.

Everywhere people were hanging out of windows and standing on the tops of cars. When we passed the San Francisco Conservatory of Music, a band out front struck up the Olympic theme song. A moment later we stopped briefly so that Peter could relay a message to the vehicle behind us. A girl no older than eight or nine unabashedly mounted the steps of our van, stuck her head inside, and said, "I just want to let you know how much I appreciate what you're doing. We've been studying the Olympics in school, so I know what it means."

Each of us was prepared for the moment when we'd carry the torch. Now, though, it started to seem like a dream.

"Here's what the torch feels like," Peter said. We passed it around wordlessly, focusing less on the gold-plated bands with the names of previous host cities, on the Georgia pecan-wood handle, and on the twenty-two aluminum reeds representing the former Summer Games when the torch was run, than on the height (thirty-two inches), weight (three-and-a-half pounds), and balance. It was taller and heavier than I thought it would be. "You-all want to hold it away from your body," Peter said, "because the flame gets awfully hot."

Each of us had his or her own torch. The flame was lit by the sun in Greece and would be passed from torch to torch until it reached Atlanta, the host city.

Ironically, the only time I was in Atlanta was 1992, right after the last Summer Olympics. At that time I was flown in to manage a large food distribution center that was set up to help victims of Hurricane Andrew. I didn't have much time for sightseeing.

As the van slowed to let each of us off at our starting point, Peter gave us our torches. A few minutes later, torch in hand, I descended into a crowd of 200 people, including family members and friends. Everyone wanted to touch the torch.

"They can touch it," Peter said, "but don't let anyone hold it. Don't let it out of your hands."

I posed for photographs with babies in strollers and answered questions about why I was chosen to carry it.

"My wife nominated me," I said. It was true. At a press conference in San Francisco several weeks earlier, Mayor Willie Brown and three retired professional athletes greeted the fifty-two so-called "community heroes" from the Bay Area who were chosen by United Way from a thousand nominees to carry the torch. I was the only one who was nominated by his spouse. Since Suzan had served the community selflessly for many years and also directed a nonprofit agency, we could have traded places.

Ten other torchbearers in the van were chosen for their community work. Gary spent his "off" hours consoling people with terminal illnesses. Letha directed a mental health clinic. For fifty-nine years Dorothy, a victim of cerebral palsy, was confined in institutional homes until she found a social worker who listened to her story, knew that she had the ability to take care of herself, and moved her into independent living. The final two people were employees of Olympic sponsors who were selected by company lotteries.

"There it is!" someone shouted.

I turned. Keith, a young man who mobilized volunteers to restore an abandoned cross-country racecourse and started a multi-city program of youth soccer leagues, was running toward me. His body was backlit by the sun and his face glowed from the light of the torch.

We met in the middle of the street. He lit my torch with the flame, then I took off, surrounded by six motorcycle cops who led me past Golden Gate Park.

Peter's advice was simple: "It doesn't matter how fast you-all go, whether you walk or run. This is a once-in-a-lifetime opportunity for each of you. The main thing is to have fun."

People waved, car horns sounded triumphantly, TV cameras blazed. On one side of me and a few steps behind was an escort runner, in case I tired or fell and was unable to go on. That wasn't likely to happen since each of us carried the torch only half a mile or so; still, the event organizers were prepared.

Leading up to the event I thought, or assumed, that carrying the torch would be among the most lucid moments of my life. Instead, it passed in a blur. Before I knew it I saw Nancy. Eight years earlier she'd received a heart-lung transplant from a teenager who'd died in a car accident. In turn, she donated her good heart to an elderly man (at the time, medical science couldn't separate the heart from the lungs so Nancy received both when her lungs failed). Now she traveled the country promoting organ donations. I passed the flame to her, then watched as she started running. Her feet hardly seemed to touch the ground.

Immediately, another van appeared. Inside were the torchbearers who had completed their segments before me. We exchanged high-fives and exalted in our unique experience. Then we picked up each of the remaining torchbearers in turn. John, the Olympic rower, was now a high school algebra teacher in San Francisco.

We followed in the van as dozens of his students ran alongside him while he carried the torch through Haight Ashbury. Dorothy was the last one. A special holder had been fitted to her motorized wheelchair so that she could carry the torch across Market Street. After she finished, her wheelchair was lifted onto the van and all of us began talking at once.

Hours later, with family and friends at Justin Herman Plaza for another Olympic celebration, one that included former gold medalists and true local heroes Kristi Yamaguchi and Chris Mullin, I still couldn't stop talking. It'd been an incredible day. Meanwhile, the torch was retired for the night, to be carried across the Golden Gate Bridge early the next morning by another group of people who'd have their own moment of glory.

The Olympic Torch Relay was an important moment in my life, and not just because it proved to be an unforgettable experience. I learned something valuable from it: when you honor people, they're motivated to do even more.

Like many individuals who work at a nonprofit agency, I've never sought personal honors. The work is reward enough, I always say, and I mean it. Bringing a smile to the face of someone in need or hearing a client's heartfelt thank you means infinitely more than a plaque or award or lofty words of praise. Something magical happens, though, when you single people out for recognition. More often than not, they're embarrassed. If they agree to be honored, it's only because the agency will benefit from increased media exposure. What they think is that they're undeserving, that they haven't done anything special. They vow to work even harder to prove themselves worthy of the attention they've received.

Following the Olympic Torch Relay, I made the same vow. I also vowed that volunteers at my agency would receive greater recognition. They deserved it, but that was only half the reason. The other half was selfish: Recognizing volunteers is a good way to keep them volunteering, just like recognizing donors is a good way to keep them donating.

COMPARING VOLUNTEERS WITH DONORS

In many respects, volunteers are like donors. They need to be found and nurtured, they need to believe that helping others is important, and they need to value the agency and its cause. In addition, they need to feel that their support is making a difference and that it's recognized. If not, then volunteers, like donors, stop contributing.

In other respects, though, volunteers and donors are different. Volunteering is a lot more complicated than writing a check and, generally speaking, requires more commitment. You have to decide to make time in your life to volunteer and determine how you're going to do it. Are you going to volunteer on a one-time basis or become an ongoing volunteer? What specific tasks do you want to do? Some accountants may want to lend their financial expertise to an agency, while others may decide that they work all day with numbers and want to do something entirely different. Do you want to be indoors answering phones or outdoors cleaning up a beach? Do you want to help people in need directly or work more anonymously, behind the scenes?

From an agency's point of view, the differences between volunteers and donors are significant. First, to accept volunteers, agencies must think through the roles that volunteers play. They need an application process, training program, and some sort of ongoing supervision. In contrast, to accept money, agencies just need an accounting system.

Second, volunteers must have skills, agreeable personalities, and a schedule that fits the agency's needs. It doesn't do any good, for example, if someone works during the day and wants to volunteer nights or weekends when the agency isn't open then. Donors, by comparison, need only money and the willingness to part with it.

Third, nonprofit agencies have to continually sustain a volunteer's interest and enthusiasm while donors need only think about the agency periodically. Conversely, it takes time for any volunteer, even a board member, to make a large impact, yet donors can contribute once and, if their donation is big enough, the effect is immediate and lasting.

Fourth, agencies accept money from almost any source while volunteers have to apply, be screened, and sometimes are turned down. Some individuals who want to volunteer at the crisis center lack the emotional stability to answer crisis calls. Others are unable to put their own problems on hold and focus on another person's need. A few are too judgmental, motivated by a desire to save the world or tell others how to right their lives, which is inappropriate in our line of work.

A major difference between volunteering and donating is that volunteering generates a ripple effect of goodwill in the community while money usually is spent and is gone. For donors, it's forgotten about, largely because giving money is a passive act. How many times have you heard people talk over a dinner table or at a cocktail party about charitable donations they've made? Practically never. Yet how often does someone who volunteers regularly talk about the experience? All the time.

People give to live. Consider this Chinese proverb: "If you want happiness for an hour, take a nap. If you want happiness for a day, go fishing. If you want happiness for a year, inherit a fortune. If you want happiness for a lifetime, help someone else."

THE VALUE OF VOLUNTEERS

There are many reasons why agencies prefer money to volunteers. The main one is because cash is simpler to handle. Recruiting, training, managing, mentoring, scheduling, and recognizing volunteers is demanding.

Agencies that don't use volunteers, though, or who use them only sparingly, are missing out on an enormous asset. For one thing, volunteers can save an agency thousands of dollars in personnel costs. At the crisis center, people volunteer more than 28,000 hours per year providing crisis counseling, grief counseling, and other direct services. Those 28,000 hours equal 13.5 full-time employees.

Funders love agencies that are cost effective, and the best way to be cost effective is to utilize a large number of volunteers. When donors tour my agency, look through glass windows into our crisis line room, and ask how many people in the room are volunteers, I say, as if it's the most natural thing in the world, "Why, all of them." Then I tell donors that each volunteer completed eight to ten weeks of training, that each is taught to answer all eighteen hotlines, not just one, and that each works one or more four-hour shifts every week. I add, almost as an afterthought (though, of course, it's planned), "Many of our volunteers have been doing this ten years or more." Who wouldn't be impressed?

A third reason why volunteers are so important is because studies show that people who volunteer tend to give more money to charity than people who don't volunteer. It makes sense that individuals who give their time because they see firsthand the good that results from it are also more likely to give their money. Not only that, they may leverage donations from family members, friends, and coworkers, as well as from employers that have matching-gifts programs. Whereas annual donors can lose interest in an agency over time, volunteering keeps people's interests alive, sustaining and deepening their commitment.

VOLUNTEER SECRETS

Ever notice how the most selfish people usually are the first ones voted off the island? It's not coincidental. People who care about others tend to be well-liked. So how does an agency find, recruit, and retain these individuals?

Finding them is easy, mainly because they're everywhere. Every community has them. The trick is helping them find you. The best way is through word of mouth—a current volunteer tells friends about the agency and they decide to try it. Advertising in newspapers, on school campuses, and through your agency's web site all work. Emphasizing the need for volunteers in news articles and when making presentations in the community is effective, too.

Many people feel that once they find themselves they can help others. They come to an agency after handling a variety of challenges, and the richness of their experiences enhances the quality of the work. It's equally true, however, that in helping others we can find ourselves. No one has a magic wand that makes people's problems disappear. We can listen, though, and discuss options. In doing so we empower people to help themselves, and our own lives develop added meaning as a result.

"Everybody can be great," said Dr. Martin Luther King, Jr., "because everybody can serve. You don't have to have a college degree to serve. You don't have to make your subject and verb agree to serve. You don't have to know Einstein's theory of relativity to serve. You only need a heart full of grace, a soul generated by love."

Just as it's important to be the kind of boss you want to have as a boss, so is it essential for an executive director to create the kind of agency that he or she would want to volunteer at. For me this means an agency that's welcoming and inclusive, that respects and values differences, that provides essential services in a thoughtful, compassionate, and cost-effective manner, that conducts every aspect of its work with utmost integrity, that stands by its clients, and that operates by the measure of what's right rather than what's most expedient, politically advantageous, or financially beneficial.

One way I do this is by making sure that volunteers feel informed about what the agency is doing and have ample opportunity to provide feedback and voice concerns. Throughout the week I circulate among different shifts, asking volunteers how things are going and giving them verbal updates on agency activities. I also write a monthly newsletter that's distributed by e-mail to current and former volunteers, as well as to donors and friends. This newsletter is less formal and more chatty than the agency's "official" newsletter, which is published quarterly and geared for people in the community. At least once a year I also hold a state-of-the-agency meeting in which all volunteers are invited to a town hall-type gathering to hear about and discuss a variety of topics related to the crisis center's work.

Giving volunteers a voice in the running of the agency helps make them feel valued. It's not a substitute for the encouragement and support they need to receive from other staff, or for the need to recognize their contributions publicly, but it's part of developing their commitment to the agency and its mission.

A LESSON LEARNED

At one time I decided that it'd be a good idea for the crisis center to start doing criminal background checks on all staff and volunteers. We'd never had an incident; still, it's better to be safe than sorry, I reasoned. Moreover, when I talked with executive directors of other counseling services in our area, they were aghast that we weren't doing background checks already. Convinced that the crisis center needed to meet the standard of care that existed in our community, I discussed the issue with staff. The primary objection raised was that background checks seemed unnecessary. We already had outside psychologists and therapists who did free, one-hour mental health screenings of all prospective volunteers. In addition, clinical staff worked side by side with new volunteers, constantly assessing their performance. If anything was wrong, they'd find out much faster and with far greater certainty than any kind of background check would tell us.

A secondary concern was that background checks would be inconvenient to administer. We'd have to buy fingerprinting equipment, schedule times to have volunteers printed, send the prints to the state Department of Justice, and set up a system to receive the results in a way that respected confidentiality. Staff thought that some volunteers would be upset, not because they might fail the check, which was for criminal wrongdoing, not financial failings, but because they'd consider it an invasion of their privacy.

When I presented the subject to board members, they had the same concerns. I said that staff could handle the administrative part, and several of our volunteers were retired police officers who could do the finger printing at no charge. I didn't think many volunteers would have misgivings, especially after they learned that one of the reasons for doing background checks was to protect volunteers so that if a client falsely accused them of some deed, the person's spotless record would provide contradictory evidence—a kind of indemnity insurance, in a way.

In the end, the board supported my recommendation and we implemented the checks. Several volunteers grumbled, but only one person refused to be printed. Okay, I thought when it was over, that wasn't too bad. A few weeks later I attended a meeting with executive directors of other crisis centers. I mentioned that my agency had implemented criminal background checks and asked whether theirs did them, too. I expected to be praised for being proactive; instead, two of the directors thought I'd lost my mind.

"What makes you the morality police?" one director said. "If someone's been convicted of a crime, accepted the punishment, and served his or her time, who are you or I or anyone to say that that's not enough, that the person can't volunteer?"

"Many of our best volunteers are the ones who have had the most life experiences," the other one said. "They made bad choices at one time and suffered the consequences. They know firsthand what some of our callers are facing, which makes them better suited to help someone than a volunteer who's never been there."

I was stunned. Why hadn't I consulted them before proceeding? The kicker was a story that one woman told. The previous year she'd been at a conference in Oakland where the director of the state's prison counseling program spoke.

"I'm not going to ask how many of you have ever been convicted of a crime," he told the audience. "Some of you may be here with bosses or coworkers and I don't want to embarrass anyone. Instead, I'm going to ask those of you to stand if anyone in your immediate family—your spouse or children—has ever been convicted of a crime."

Fifteen to twenty people in the audience, which numbered about 300, stood. The man said, "I want you to join them in standing if you've ever had a parent, or brother or sister, stepbrother or stepsister, grandparent or in-law convicted of a crime."

More people got to their feet. "If you've ever had a cousin, uncle, aunt, nephew, niece, or close friend convicted of a crime," he said, "please stand."

By now nearly half the people in attendance were standing. The speaker paused. His eyes surveyed the room. "Look around you," he instructed. "What do you see?"

People literally gasped. Every single person of color in the room was standing. Almost every single white person was sitting.

"Justice isn't carried out equally in this country," the speaker said. "Remember that when you go back to your agencies."

I went back to my board, admitted my mistake, and recommended that the crisis center's policy be changed. I still thought there were compelling reasons why staff and volunteers who conducted counseling in schools and clients' homes should have background checks—also the finance manager position—but other volunteers, especially those who answered hotlines, should be exempt. The board could decide, I said, whether a background check was required of the executive director. It was a better policy, and the board approved it unanimously. I just wished that I'd been enlightened enough to suggest it in the first place.

EXPECTING THE UNEXPECTED

The crisis center holds trainings for new hotline volunteers twice a year. Most of the people who sign up have never done this kind of work before and they're nervous. They want to succeed, but they have doubts. They have to learn protocols and procedures on a variety of complex issues—suicide, depression, child abuse, rape, domestic violence, substance abuse, elder abuse, homelessness, unemployment, bullying, and mental illness. Not only can this information be overwhelming, but it can seem impossible to remember at a moment when someone's life is in your hands.

The second day of class I greet new volunteers and tell them my story. It helps put things in perspective and lets them know that our expectations, while high, are achievable.

"Like many of you," I say, "I'm not a mental health professional. Some members of our staff are, and some of our volunteers are, but I'm not. When I first went through the training, I didn't know what to expect. I didn't know if I could remember the appropriate protocols for each of our hotlines. I didn't know if I could respond in the moment to someone with urgent needs. I didn't know if I could help a person who threatened to kill himself or whether that person would die on me. In short, I didn't know if I'd measure up, something many of you may be worrying about—and something that's really embarrassing if you don't and you've just been hired to be the new executive director."

Invariably, people laugh. Really, though, I didn't know whether I could continue working at the crisis center if I wasn't fit to do what volunteers do.

"Fortunately," I say, "there are a lot of people here to teach you, just as there were people to teach me. No one is a born crisis counselor. With training, though, and a caring heart, almost anyone can do it."

Everyone's worst fear is picking up the phone the first time and hearing a caller who's acutely suicidal. This doesn't happen often since only a small percentage of our callers are in immediate, life-threatening situations, even on our suicide hotline. In the few instances when it has happened, the volunteer has handled it perfectly, with the help of an experienced volunteer. Afterward we just had to convince the new volunteer that this wasn't a typical first call.

"My own first call," I tell the class, "wasn't nearly so nerve-wracking. In fact, it was rather humorous."

Some callers are what we call "regulars," which is, people with persistent and severe mental illnesses who call often during the week seeking assurance that they're okay. Many have private therapists; however, they need to touch base with someone in between sessions. There's not a lot we can do for them, other than listen and try to be supportive.

"Sheryl is one of our regulars," I say. "She's not dangerous and sometimes is even charming, although that depends on her mood."

I didn't know that she was a regular when I answered the phone the first time, nor anything about her state of mind. "Hello," I said. "May I help you?"

There was a pause, then she snapped, "This is Sheryl. Who's this?" She called often enough to know that my voice was unfamiliar.

Taken aback, I managed to say that my name is John. I added, not to erase any doubts she might have but to lower her expectations about what assistance I might be able to provide, "I'm new here."

Now there was an even longer pause. I thought I heard a sharp intake of breath.

"What!" she said finally. "What did you say?"

I was completely lost. All I'd done was answer the phone and tell the caller my name.

"I said my name is John," I repeated, "and I'm new here."

Sheryl started laughing hysterically. I thought to myself, "Even with the training, I don't know the first thing about mental illness. She's completely bonkers and I don't have a clue what to do."

Finally, she stopped laughing long enough to share the joke with me. "I thought you said my name is John," she said, "and I'm nude here."

It was my turn to laugh. I also breathed a sign of relief—there was hope for me yet. We proceeded to have a brief, pleasant conversation about nothing of note. It was one of Sheryl's good days and she just wanted the agency to know it. I thanked her for calling and she thanked me for adding humor to her life.

When I hung up, I realized that I'd learned a valuable lesson: hotline volunteers need to be ready for anything. The next call, I was.

CHAPTER SEVEN

Marketing: Cooking without Looking

I didn't know Mike well. No one did. He was the kind of person you saw once or twice a year, were reminded how intense and intellectually curious he was, told yourself that you should see him more often, but somehow never got around to it.

Women fell in love with him on sight. He had jet-black hair and movie-star looks, but that was only half of it. There was a hint of danger in him, of someone who trusts his instincts completely, without thought that they could be wrong.

Men envied his knowledge of machines. Mike was a longtime mechanic at a major airline. He could take apart any kind of engine and put it together again. He also could build anything from scrap. Need a compressor to paint your house? "Here," he'd say. "Let me pull the motor off this old lawnmower, weld a stand for it, and mount some wheels. It'll just take a minute."

Despite having seniority, Mike worked weekends and holidays at the airline because it didn't matter to him, he didn't have a family. He rarely traveled, even though he could fly free to anywhere in the world, because there was no place he wanted to see. He never bought a house, although he could easily afford one. He did buy a junkyard, though, a real junkyard so that he had plenty of material for his building projects.

About ten years into his career at the airlines, Mike fell from the wing of a 747. He hit the tarmac and shattered both legs. Doctors inserted pins to hold his bones together, but said that he'd probably never walk again. Mike didn't hear them. He built a customized wheelchair to propel himself around his shop, then invented a series of walkers and pushed himself maniacally to become more mobile. In eight months he was fully recovered; years later doctors still wrote about him in medical journals with awe.

Long after his accident, Mike learned that I used to teach tennis. He challenged me to a match even though he couldn't remember the last time he'd played.

He was dressed in his customary black T-shirt, black jeans, and black, nonathletic tennis shoes—the only clothes I ever saw him in, except when it was cold and he added a black leather jacket. The racket he played with he'd retrieved from a dumpster.

After we rallied for a few minutes, Mike insisted that we play a set. As soon as we started, he tried to hit a winner on nearly every shot. Usually he failed, although a few times—almost by force of will—he surprised me.

"Relax, Mike," I said at one point. "Have some fun. We don't need to keep score."

"It's only fun if you do something you don't think you can do," he said.

A lifelong smoker, Mike developed lung cancer in his forties. He didn't tell anyone or seek any treatment. Early one morning, before his health began to deteriorate, he drove his pickup truck to a park, strapped a rifle to the doorframe, and shot himself in the head while sitting in the driver's seat. There was no suicide note. Only later, when going through his effects and finding x-rays, did friends learn about his illness. Meanwhile, police marveled at the gun's construction. In typical fashion, Mike made it himself.

All of this happened years ago. His death still haunts me, though. If only, I think. If only he had told someone. If only we had known.

Mike died the way he lived, alone with his thoughts. He never called or wanted help. I respect that. I wish it had been different, though.

I attended a media relations workshop once where the initial session featured a panel discussion with representatives from two major newspapers, a TV station, a radio station, and a national wire service. A woman from the *San Francisco Chronicle* arrived late, after other panel members had been introduced. She was carrying a large, wire box that was filled with pages of loose paper. With great showmanship and no small amount of relief, she dropped the box on the table in front of the panel. It landed with a thud. The whole room became silent.

"Sorry I'm late," she said. Then, without further apology and no explanation, she introduced herself and said, "These are all of the press releases and public service announcements that I received . . . " she paused for effect, "yesterday."

Before any of us in attendance—representatives from fifty nonprofit agencies—even began to comprehend her statement, she added, "I received roughly the same number of press releases the day before and the day before that. In fact, this is how many I receive on any typical work day."

I stared at the wire-rim box. There were 1,000 pages or more. Not all were from nonprofit agencies, she said; many companies had sent announcements, too. Each was competing for a small amount of space and a few seconds of a reader's attention.

The focus of her presentation was how to improve an agency's chances of getting its news releases printed when the shear number of releases issued every day is overwhelming. She displayed some rather unusual attempts by agencies and companies to stand out from the crowd, sending press releases in solid black envelopes, on paper that was cut into unusual shapes (circles and ovals and asymmetrical patterns), using colors and fonts that were different and eye-catching. It only took a few samples, though, for the novelty to wear off and these releases, like the hundred of others that were more conventional in appearance, to blend into the rest. And that was her point. There are no tricks or gimmicks to getting media attention. It often comes down to one thing: the relationship you have with individual reporters. In this way it's no different than fundraising, where who you know and how well you know them tends to supersede everything else.

If you've worked with a reporter before, you can pitch your story more effectively and with greater likelihood that it'll receive coverage than you can when you send a news release cold, to a person you've never met or spoken to before. In the latter instance you're hoping that the story is picked up, whereas in the former you're making it happen.

To pitch a story, you have to have something to pitch. As obvious as that sounds, many people don't follow it. Just because something is new doesn't make it newsworthy. A new logo, new agency name, new executive director, new board president, or new building may be important to staff and volunteers, but to people outside the agency they're not that interesting. Something is newsworthy if it's public (public hearings, court cases, etc.), timely, affects a large number of people, is local but relates to a regional or national story, or involves a newsworthy person such as a celebrity or politician.

When you have something that is of interest—a new service, special event, notable award—your media contacts will be likely to listen, unless they're not working on deadline. It's always a good idea when calling a reporter to start by asking if he or she is on deadline. If so, find out when would be a good time to call back.

When you're able to have a conversation, be prepared. Develop a list of reasons why you think your story merits coverage. If you're pitching a TV reporter, make sure you have compelling visual elements. Radio, in contrast, is quick, immediate, and needs sound. Newspaper stories are more in-depth. After that, follow up. Call the reporter, verify that he or she received the press release you sent, and ask if you can provide additional information.

Whether your story ends up aired or printed is out of your hands. Oftentimes, it's out of the hands of your media contact, too; people higher up make the final decision. One thing I emphasize in working with reporters is that the public is always clamoring for good news. While there's truth to the adage that blood sells, people also grow tired of bad news and look forward to something positive, if only for the reassurance it provides that the world isn't doomed. Nonprofit agencies, by the nature of our work, offer good news. Every day we help people who are hungry, abused, sick, disabled, poor, and otherwise disadvantaged.

Even bad news can have a positive news bent. For instance, suppose the top-of-the-fold story on page one is about a local woman who's beaten to death by her husband while her two young children watch in terror. The story is tragic, gruesome, and unnerving. Invariably, the focus is on who, what, how, when, where, and why. Neighbors and friends report past arguments between the husband and wife, or express shock because they saw no indication of something like this happening. The husband is arrested and booked on charges of murder. The children are placed temporarily with relatives or in the custody of child welfare workers. Funeral services for the deceased will be held in a few days. That's the story as it's covered by the media. The lingering image is a shrine of flowers around a photo of the mother, with heartfelt, penned messages to her and her children. There's a lot that's missing, though. In the first place, the children are going to need extensive counseling. Who provides it? In many communities, it's nonprofit agencies. If no relatives are fit or willing to be guardians, the children will be placed in foster care or a group home. Often these are operated by charities. Victim assistance programs will start a fund to raise money for the children and, if necessary, for their caregivers. All of this happens within days, weeks, or even months after the initial act. As such, it gets little or no attention.

Even in the moment, media miss an opportunity to report good news. Many communities have shelters for battered women and their children. Naturally, the addresses are secret to protect women from their batterers, yet staff are available to answer a reporter's questions. The day of the murder, how many women were in local shelters, safe from harm? For every woman who's killed, dozens of others live because of the nonprofit agencies that operate shelters and the people who support them. That's worth knowing. Also worth knowing is the phone number of the domestic violence hotline that women can call for help. Both the phone number and the information on what to do if you're being battered can be included in a sidebar article, to prevent future instances of violence.

Another topic for a related article is why women stay in abusive relationships. From an outsider's perspective, it's easy to say that you'd flee the first time it happened. In reality, though, it's much harder. All sorts of psychological, social, religious, cultural, and economic conditions influence the decision.

There's always more to a story than the basic journalistic elements. In developing relationships with reporters, I continually stress that.

News stations and publications balance a lot of factors when determining what gets covered and what doesn't. Oftentimes, I pitch stories that go nowhere. This doesn't mean they're bad stories. Maybe they're just not immediate enough for radio. Maybe they lack depth and aren't detailed enough for newspapers. Maybe they lack good visuals for TV. Alternatively, maybe the station or publication covered another, similar story recently and is looking for something different. I can't do anything about those situations except be aware of them and bend my story, if possible, to fit.

TV IS KING

One thing I've learned is that most people today get their news from TV. I've written, been featured in, and been quoted in dozens of newspaper stories, most of which have escaped the attention of people I know. Yet anytime I've been interviewed on TV, even on a local cable segment that aired at six o'clock on a Sunday morning, people tell me later that they saw me on the tube.

In being interviewed, here are a few things to keep in mind:

- Remember that while you're speaking to a reporter, you're addressing the public.
- Have two or three message points and keep coming back to them. This way any brief clip that's aired is likely to include them.
- Keep your answers short. When you've conveyed your message, stop talking.
- Control the interview. If a reporter asks a question that you don't want to answer, steer the conversation back to your message. Say, "I can't address that issue right now, but I can tell you that ... " or "That's an interesting point, but I think the real issue is ... " Get back to your message points no matter what's asked.
- Stand up for phone interviews; your voice projects better. Face a wall to avoid distractions.
- Avoid jargon or organizational language; it's not familiar to most people.
- Wear appropriate clothing for TV interviews. Flashy jewelry, bright colors, and intricate patterns are distracting.
- Don't fill awkward silences; they're only awkward to you. Some reporters deliberately say nothing after someone stops talking to get a person to say something he or she might not have said otherwise. Just wait for the next question, or ask the reporter a question.
- Don't say "no comment." If you can't comment on something, emphasize what you can say and return to your message points.
- Don't be afraid to say, "I don't know," adding, "But I'll try to get the answer."
- Don't say anything is "off the record." The best way to keep something from being printed or broadcast is not to say it at all.

If you're being interviewed in a TV station, as opposed to being filmed at your office or another site, you often have the opportunity to wear makeup. Take advantage of it. TV uses bright lights and people look paler than normal, so makeup compensates. Also, because TV lights are hot, people sweat more and powder keeps your face dry. My experience with cosmeticians at TV stations, though limited, is that they're masters at making you look as good as possible.

BRANDING

Branding is the practice of putting your identity on something, the same way ranchers put their brands on cattle to let people know whom each cow belongs to. One of the best-known brands is Nike's swoosh. It's so successful that the company doesn't even have to use its name anymore, the swoosh is enough. Nonprofit agencies, with the possible exception of the Red Cross, don't have this kind of recognition, largely because nonprofits don't have marketing budgets the size of Nike's. Nevertheless, there are things that agencies can do to improve the chances of becoming better known.

First and foremost is to develop consistency in all marketing materials. This way, over time, people associate the message with the agency. The place to start is with the logo. There are two parts to most logos, the mark and the signature.

The mark is what most people think of as the logo. It's the graphic image that represents an agency or company. Nike's swoosh is a mark. The image of an apple with a bite taken out of it is the mark of Apple Computers. The signature is the name of the agency or company, often in distinctive type. Together, the mark and signature comprise the logo. Unless an agency is exceptionally well known, the mark always should appear with the signature, in the same position. Don't place the mark to the left of the signature one time and above it, below it, or to the right of it other times. Be consistent in the treatment of the logo.

Contrary to popular belief, the agency name and mark aren't the most important things on a page. The message is. The first thing people notice in any written piece is the headline, especially if it speaks to needs they have. The name and mark just brand the message, connecting it to an agency. For this reason, they don't need to be big and they shouldn't be prominent. Just put them off to the side or at the bottom, someplace where they're visible but don't detract from the message.

In terms of design, there are many books and classes that teach basic principles. I'm a stickler for things lining up. They don't have to be symmetrical and, in fact, too much symmetry is as annoying as too little. Nevertheless, the human mind appreciates order while the human eye is quick to notice disorder—things that don't line up—and this creates tension.

I'm also a stickler for white space, as much as possible. Text is easier to read if it's framed by large margins and empty space. You don't need to blow up letters to fill a page, or cram in artwork. There's a visual relief in nothingness, the mind relaxes.

Too many different fonts, varying point sizes, and multiple typefaces are distracting. I try not to be dictatorial about most things; however, I insist that my staff use the same, designated fonts in all materials distributed to the public (in-house, they can use whatever they want). When everyone uses the same fonts, materials start to look like they came from the same agency.

MARKETING VERSUS PUBLIC RELATIONS

The conventional wisdom is that your agency's name has to appear in print at least seven times before people remember it. Even then, there are no guarantees. So why do all of us in the nonprofit sector try so hard to get our agencies in the news if the competition is so fierce and the payoff is so small? It's because we confuse public relations with marketing.

Public relations is promotion. It's about making something popular or at least better known. Marketing is different. It's about producing behavioral change. When you market, you get people to donate, volunteer, use agency services, come to an event, etc. Increasing awareness isn't marketing. Marketing is influencing the way people act.

To be successful, you have to think: Who is my market? What do they need? How can I meet it? The most effective marketing messages usually are about feelings. What does the market (customer, client, patient) feel? Need? Want?

Suppose you're with an agency that provides services to low-income, home-bound elderly people. Currently the services are being underutilized, and you'd like to increase their use. One way to do it is to market the services to social workers so that they'll refer more clients to you. What do social workers feel? Often they feel overworked, tired from long hours in the field. What do they need? They need services that are free or low cost and tailored to the needs of their clients. What do they want? They want to know that when they refer clients to a service, the clients are helped. With this information, it's possible to develop a marketing strategy that achieves the desired goal.

Once I listened in awe as a marketing whiz named Gerald Bartlett created off the top of his head a plan to get blind people to sign up for self-sufficiency classes. A woman in the audience asked him how her agency, Lions Blind Centers, could create interest in the classes, which currently were under-enrolled.

"Tell me a little about them," Bartlett said. "What do people learn?"

"They learn all sorts of things," the woman said, "how to keep house, cook, balance a checkbook, sew, plant a garden, do basic home repairs."

Bartlett thought for a moment. "Cooking," he said. "Let's focus on that. There are lots of advantages in knowing how to cook. You can feed yourself, of course, which obviously is important. Beyond that, though, if you know how to cook you can prepare meals for other people. You can invite guests into your home. Suddenly you're able to entertain rather than always having to go out or eat by yourself. Imagine what a boost that must be to someone's self esteem."

The woman was thrilled. A whole new world opened up to her. "Blind people definitely would be more likely to come to a cooking class if it was marketed to them like that," she said.

Bartlett nodded. "Now you need a catchy name for the class," he said. "How about this: Cooking Without Looking."

The woman clasped her hands in rapture. Perfect! She couldn't thank him enough.

One of my glimpses into the marketing mind came several years ago when I invited twenty sales, marketing, advertising, and public relations people to lunch. For the most part they weren't people I knew; I just looked up their names in the phone book and called them cold. Twelve individuals showed up—a good turnout, I thought. Only a few were familiar with the crisis center, which was fine. In return for a free meal, they agreed to spend an hour using their expertise to help us come up with the start of a marketing plan.

I began by giving a quick, five-minute overview of our services. When I finished, a person who owned a small marketing firm said immediately, "I get it. You guys are like the General Motors of crisis intervention."

I looked at him in amazement. That was exactly the image I wanted to convey. We weren't anywhere near the colossus of G.M., but we were pretty big in our community.

After that, the group developed a slew of marketing ideas for us. Some were off the mark, but many were good and a few were excellent. Considering that the meal cost the crisis center under $200, it was one of the best investments I've ever made.

PUBLIC SPEAKING

When people are asked to name their greatest fear, dying is number seven. Higher on the list are going blind and being alone. Number one is public speaking. According to research, people would rather do anything—even die—than speak publicly.

A friend of my wife and mine is a stage manager in Hollywood. He does all the big shows—Academy Awards, Grammy's, Emmy's—as well as many TV specials. He's on a first-name basis with many actors, actresses, and musicians. A surprising number, he says, experience stage fright, even though they're professionals who've been performing for years. The idea of getting up before an audience can be terrifying, no matter who you are or how often you do it.

Executive directors of nonprofit agencies do a lot of public speaking. Presentations to service clubs and religious groups, to city councils and county supervisors, to foundation boards, business leaders, and community groups are part of the job.

The first public presentation I made, long ago, could've been a disaster. I was invited to a local college to address graduate students who were interested in working in the nonprofit sector. I spent several weeks preparing remarks, which I transferred to a series of index cards. When I was introduced, I stepped to the podium and laid the cards in front of me, next to the microphone, out of view of the audience but within my sight.

"Thank you for inviting me," I began, then involuntarily my hand jerked and knocked all the cards off the podium and across the stage. I froze. It would take several minutes to collect them, and several more minutes to put them in the right order. The audience seemed to freeze too, waiting to see what I would do.

I had no choice but to go on without them. Much to my surprise, I remembered most of what I'd written and the presentation went well.

When you're doing public speaking, decide in advance how you're going to present information, either chronologically (past-present-future), by degree (most important-less important-least important), by balance (advantages-disadvantages-conclusion), or by inquiry (who? what? how? when? where? why?). Write the introduction and conclusion, and think about transitions (how you get from one section to the next). If you use Power Point, don't rely on it too much; equipment can fail, as mine has from time to time. Create slides that are visual, and keep text to a minimum.

Every presentation has three objectives: to inform, to persuade, and to move people to action. Think about what you want the audience to take home from your talk. Whether it's something to remember or feel, make sure it's the focus of your presentation.

When it comes time to speak, I tell people what I'm going to tell them, then I tell them, then in the end I tell them what I told them. This way everyone in the audience knows what to expect, hears it, and leaves satisfied. I stand tall, take deep breaths from time to time so that I don't rush my words, and maintain eye contact throughout. Most importantly, I smile. People respond more to visual cues than verbal ones. While the content and delivery of a speech obviously matter, the way a person looks when he or she talks is what members of the audience remember most. Just by smiling a person is likable and so, by extension, is his or her agency.

CRISIS COMMUNICATION

One of the biggest impacts of the Internet and all-news stations like *CNN* is that news is conveyed immediately now to every corner of the world. It wasn't so long ago that heads of state had several hours after a bombing, airplane crash, or another person's spoken comments to formulate a response. Today, there's no time. Seconds after a tragedy, TV cameras are thrust in front of world leaders and they're expected to articulate heartfelt words to the victims' families as well as a plan of action to assure people that the situation is under control.

Similarly, nonprofit leaders are expected to respond immediately and publicly to crises involving their agencies. As with public speaking, preparation is key. Too often, nonprofit executives don't plan for the worst. Even when disaster looms, they're in denial, thinking one of four things: (1) it won't really happen; (2) it'll happen, but not to me; (3) it'll happen to me, but it won't be too bad; or (4) it'll happen to me and be so bad that there's nothing I can do.

The purpose of crisis communication isn't to allay people's fear. It's to help people manage their fear and not become hopeless. The initial message must be short, relevant, positive, and repeated. In a crisis, first messages carry the most weight. The role of the spokesperson is to reduce fear for the audience and build trust and credibility for his or her agency. The rules are simple:

- Tell the truth.
- Stay within your scope of responsibility.
- Express sympathy.
- Emphasize that there is a process in place to deal with the crisis.
- Express wishes rather than regrets ("I wish we had the answer today; we're working on it," not "I'm sorry I don't have the answer for you").
- Give people things to do.
- Don't over-reassure (people accept uncertainty if they're told the next steps).

Although the crisis center has operated since 1963 and never been the subject of a negative news story, I don't rest easy. One of the questions I posed to my staff was, "What keeps you awake at night?" No one can respond effectively in a critical moment if he or she hasn't prepared for it. We brainstormed some worse-case scenarios:

- A distressed person calls our hotlines, isn't helped, dies by suicide, and the family holds us responsible.
- A volunteer overreacts to a caller's story, sends police to intervene when it isn't necessary, and the caller sues us.
- A student calls our school violence tipline and says that another student is threatening a rampage. Instead of reporting it right away, the counselor handling the call waits for our education coordinator to come in the following day to deal with it. In the meantime, the attack is carried out and people are killed.
- A prominent representative of the crisis center, such as a member of the board or a high-level staff person, dies by suicide.

For each scenario, we're now developing three message points. My greatest hope is that none of these events occur. At the same time, all of us will sleep easier knowing that if one does, we're ready.

WHAT'S IN A NAME?

The crisis center has been in business over forty years. During this time we've gone through four name changes, or an average of one every ten years. The last one I instigated.

When I started, the agency was called Crisis and Suicide Intervention of Contra Costa County—a mouthful. Board members and staff referred to it as C.S.I., which was more manageable but didn't mean anything to people outside the agency (this was before the TV series *C.S.I.*, which would have really confused things).

A bigger problem was that "suicide" is such a powerful word, it's oftentimes the only word anyone hears. People would call our crisis line and say, "I'm not suicidal, but . . . " They'd pause, then say that there were just battered, raped, or otherwise victimized. It was as if they were apologizing in case we thought their situation wasn't serious enough to merit a call for help. In addition, individuals and families came to our grief counseling program and felt uncomfortable because the person they were mourning didn't die by suicide. The final straw was that we started two new twenty-four-hour hotlines, one for homeless people and the other for runaway youth, neither of which had anything to do with suicide. I thought the agency's name needed to be changed, and I set out to do it.

The process of change can be hard, especially for people who have been associated with an agency for a long time. I've found that throwing open an idea for discussion without formulating options first often frustrates everyone. Thus, before even broaching the subject, I thought about a name that I felt was appropriate. In recent years, a growing number of agencies across the country that provided similar services were calling themselves crisis centers. I liked this; it was simple, descriptive, and broad enough to cover a variety of programs.

Since our service area was Contra Costa County, California, I thought this needed to be reflected in our name as well. There were four options: (1) Contra Costa Crisis Center; (2) Contra Costa County Crisis Center; (3) Crisis Center of Contra Costa County; and (4) Crisis Center of Contra Costa. I eliminated the second option immediately because I didn't want people to think that the agency was part of county government. The third and fourth options I discarded in short order because the editor in me sought the most concise name possible. That left Contra Costa Crisis Center.

I began approaching staff to get their reaction to the name. Everyone liked it. Then I talked with officers on the board. They liked it, too. I shared the idea with several volunteers and donors, who also were supportive. A few weeks later the board of trustees met and voted unanimously to change the agency's name. The whole process, start to finish, took two months. The only costs were the filing fee to register the new name with the Internal Revenue Service and the State Franchise Tax Board, and the printing of new marketing materials. It couldn't have been easier, which speaks to one of the advantages of being a nonprofit agency. Change can happen fast because nonprofits tend to have maximum flexibility and minimum bureaucracy.

At exactly the same time, my brother-in-law, Mark, was considering a name change for the high-tech Silicon Valley company he founded. The way he went about it, though, was much different. First he hired a marketing firm, which spent several weeks coming up with a list of 100 potential names. Next, the company bought as many Internet addresses as possible, connected to the names. If a web address wasn't available, the name was dropped from consideration. This reduced the list to about fifty. After that there was a yearlong winnowing process as the merits of each name were debated. Finally, the marketing people recommended one name, Artisan Components, which was approved. I asked Mark what he thought of it.

He shrugged. "It's all right. It wasn't my first choice."

This surprised me. Since he was chief executive officer, I knew it was largely his decision. I asked him why he went with the marketing firm's recommendation.

"Because they're the experts," he said. He added, "If the company continues to grow, we may change the name again in a few years anyway." In other words, he didn't consider it a permanent decision.

I thought about this. It made sense. Why hire people with expertise if you're not going to follow their advice? One definition of an expert is someone who knows when to call in other experts, who knows the limits of his or her talents and brings in the right people at the critical moment. Mark did that.

I didn't regret being unable to do the same thing. The crisis center couldn't afford it, so it wasn't an option. Moreover, I was pleased with the new name and remain so today, ten years later. At the same time, I wonder sometimes whether marketing consultants would have validated the name I chose or recommended a different one. If it was the former, the crisis center saved time and money. If it was the latter, the agency lost an opportunity to have its identity reassessed.

One thing worth keeping in mind when you're considering a name change is what staff and volunteers will say when they answer the phone. Whatever the name, invariably it's shortened when someone calls. At the Contra Costa Crisis Center, people say, "Crisis center, may I help you?" Our web address is www.crisis-center.org. I discourage everyone from using the initials CCCC, despite the convenience and alliteration. Unless you know what the letters stand for, they provide no indication what the agency does.

Several years ago, one of the best-known nonprofit agencies in my area, working with marketing consultants, changed its name from Battered Women's Alternatives to STAND! Against Domestic Violence. There were a variety of reasons for the change: (1) the agency provided services to children and also to batterers, and agency leaders wanted a name that was more encompassing, (2) the agency's mission included advocating for policies of zero tolerance for domestic violence, and the old name didn't reflect this, and (3) the word "battered" doesn't translate easily into other languages.

All of these were good reasons to consider a change. At the same time, I questioned the new name. For one thing, people in the agency insist that STAND be written in capital letters even though it's not an acronym. Also, the exclamation point is part of the official name, which looks odd, especially when the possessive is used (STAND!'s programs).

Another problem became apparent when staff and volunteers started answering the phone. "STAND! Against Domestic Violence" is a mouthful. It was shortened to "STAND! Against D.V.," but that didn't last long. It's still a lot to say, and few people know what D.V. is, even when they're victims of it. Pretty soon everyone just picked up the phone and said, "Stand, may I help you?"

Callers were confused. "Stan? I'm not trying to call anyone named Stan."

After a lengthy period of adjustment, the community has accepted the new name. If it hadn't, well, a name can always be changed again.

That's what happened with Mark's company. The new name lasted only a few years. The company grew, despite economic downturns elsewhere in Silicon Valley, and in December 2004 he sold it, making millions on the deal. One of the first things the new owners did was change the name. Their marketing experts suggested it.

I was happy for Mark. He worked hard and accomplished his dream—to start, build, and sell a successful business. He had a right to be proud. There was only one thing I wished: that somewhere along the way, someone was willing to pay a large sum of money to buy a successful nonprofit agency. That was my dream.

CHAPTER EIGHT

Strategic Planning: Big Hairy Dreams

In 1969, the Apollo space program was in full swing and astronaut Neil Armstrong took the first historic steps on the moon. Today, many people around the country, starting with the president, want to invest in a long-term effort that one day will put men on Mars. The rationale most often cited for this quest is that it'll unify America much the same way that John F. Kennedy's lunar program did.

There's no question that America needs unifying. Recent elections have divided families, separated friends, and created deep fissures between the two major political parties that won't be easily traversed. There's also no question that space exploration is a great cause. The masterminds of science who tackle technological challenges far beyond my comprehension, and the courageous astronauts who risk everything dear to them in order to expand our knowledge of the universe, have my utmost respect.

At the same time, I can't help but think that there are even greater causes here on earth. Conquering them would do more to bring America and the world together than trips to every planet in the solar system.

One problem, of course, is that for every great cause there are myriad opinions about how to address it. What to do in Iraq, how best to reduce the national debt, and the answers to improving education and funding Social Security depend largely on your point of view. Space travel, in contrast, we leave to scientists to figure out.

The bigger problem, though, is that some of the greatest causes don't concern us directly. More than 500 million people in the world today have experienced war, imprisonment, torture, or starvation—but not me. More than one billion people in the world live in fear of harassment, arrest, or death if they attend church, temple, or another form of religious meeting—but not me. Two billion people in the world are illiterate, unable to read—but not me.

I don't suffer from malnutrition, as 50 percent of the world's population does. I don't live in substandard housing, as 80 percent of the world does. I have money in the bank and spare change in my car's ashtray—unlike 90 percent of people in the world.

I also have transportation, health care, a college education, employment, and privileges that come from being male and white in a culture where members of my gender and race still make the rules. All of these things are easy to take for granted, and I do sometimes—until the next hotline caller, grief client, or homeless person contacts our agency and I'm reminded again how fortunate I am.

It's exciting to stretch the boundaries of our imagination, to set our eyes on a distant star or planet and wonder what it'd take to actually get there. Ironically, though, it's tackling hard, ugly, everyday realities that requires true vision. May we have the fortitude and commitment—as individuals and as a country—to do it.

A few months into my tenure at the crisis center, the agency held a one-day retreat to begin developing a new agency strategic plan. Mike, the board president, used a novel approach. Rather than reviewing the previous long-range plan or starting with an overview of current services, both of which quickly lead people to focus on details, Mike said, "Let's start by doing some blue-sky thinking. Let's assume, for the moment, that money is no object. We can hire as many staff as we need, buy as big a building as we want—or multiple buildings, if we choose—and create programs that truly make a difference to people in our community. Now, what are our goals?"

Everyone began throwing out ideas. As one might expect, some suggestions were grandiose, befitting an agency ten times the size and influence of the crisis center. A few were fanciful, amusing to consider but not particularly realistic. Most of them, though, made a lot of sense. Moreover, they weren't so far-reaching as to be unattainable.

Roland was the agency's treasurer, a kind-hearted man and a worrywart—desirable characteristics in a treasurer. He could be counted on to consider the human cost of any decision; at the same time, he obsessed over numbers in our financial statements, performing much-needed due diligence and providing peace of mind to other board members who really only wanted to know whether we were continuing to operate in the black.

"I think one goal should be that every board decision is unanimous," Roland said. "That way we'll know it's the right decision and everyone will be behind it."

Mike had instructed all of us, at the beginning, not to comment on another person's suggestion. He didn't want to limit the flow of ideas, so I didn't say anything. Later, though, during a break, I went up to Roland.

"I have to let you know that I disagree with your suggestion about wanting all board decisions to be unanimous," I said. "I think it's important to build consensus; however, I also think differences of opinion are healthy. If every decision we make is unanimous, I'm going to worry that we're missing important points of view."

Roland was one of my strongest supporters on the board. He seemed hurt that I criticized his suggestion.

"I didn't mean to imply that we should start out agreeing on everything," he said. "I just think that after we've discussed something, we should be able to reach a decision that all of us support. I don't want to serve on a board where people are fighting all of the time."

"No argument there," I said. "Fighting isn't constructive. At the same time, if people have deeply-held views, I wouldn't expect them to change based on a conversation in a board meeting. None of us is that persuasive."

"And yet," Roland said, "board members need to be open minded. If we refuse to hear and possibly support what someone else says, that's not helping the agency."

I saw where he was going. If everyone isn't on the same page, the cause suffers. We're not moving forward in unity.

"My point is just that unanimity shouldn't be the goal," I said. "The goal is to make good decisions. Some of the best decisions of the United States Supreme Court have been ones where the vote was five to four."

Roland was quick to speak. "But don't you think some of those decisions would have been accepted more readily if the vote had been nine to nothing? They'd have been less likely to be reversed later on."

"Perhaps," I conceded. "Then again, without dissent, people get lazy justifying their opinions."

Roland laughed. "So what you really want, then, is for the board not to become lazy. That's why we hired you, to keep us on our toes."

It was my turn to laugh. "Right. And the job of every board member is to keep me on my toes so that I don't become lazy, either."

Several years later, board members faced a defining moment, deliberating over whether to purchase 4,000 square feet of office space that suddenly became available next door. We owned our own space, which was about the same size, yet it was now too small to accommodate a growing number of services. If we didn't act quickly, we'd be stuck with our current space or have to move, neither of which was a desirable option.

After much discussion, an informal poll was taken. Eleven board members were in favor of the purchase. There was one dissenting vote—Roland's.

"I agree that it looks like a good opportunity," he said. "We could merge the two units and have the space we need. But what if we can't raise the money? This would be more ambitious than anything we've done before. I don't think we can afford to take that risk."

"I don't think we can afford *not* to take the risk," other board members said. "We need additional space and this is the first time in years that the property has gone on the market."

Roland pointed to our most recent financial statement. "We don't have much cushion," he said. "If something goes wrong, the whole agency could be in jeopardy."

It was a sobering point. Board members turned to me.

"Some decisions, when you get down to it, require a leap of faith," I said. "I know that's not how the business world thinks, but it's how nonprofits operate."

I said that twelve years earlier, board members debated a similar purchase: whether to buy our current offices. At that time the crisis center had a smaller budget and less developed fundraising program. Even so, everyone had voted to go ahead.

"Looking back," I said, "that was one of the smartest decisions the board ever made."

Board members approved the purchase. People felt good about it, in part because Roland had challenged the group in a way that made everyone aware of the risk and committed to the goal.

Today, the crisis center has a state-of-the-art facility and space for all of its programs. Our counseling rooms are soundproof, and all offices have natural light. Board meetings are conducted in a new room specifically designed for that purpose.

The first thing anyone sees walking in our front door is a beautiful oak receptionist's desk and credenza, where our office manager sits. Both were donated by Roland—part of his gift to a successful campaign.

OPERATING IN FUTURE MODE

One of the biggest challenges for any nonprofit board is operating in future mode. Typically, board meetings focus on the past and the present. They're filled with information about what happened last month—minutes of the previous meeting, a review of the agency's latest financial statement, recent program statistics—as well as reports by the executive director and various committees about work in progress, which often concerns fires that staff and perhaps the board are in the process of putting out. Rarely, it seems, do board members spend time examining the future.

This may be one of the biggest differences between nonprofit agencies and for-profit companies. Companies devote significant resources—time, money, and expertise—to research and development, knowing that they're only as good as their next product or service innovation. If they rest too long on their laurels, they'll disappear from the marketplace. To be successful, businesses must continually evaluate where their products and services are relative to consumer demands and competitors' offerings, then develop strategies to increase their edge, if they're ahead, or close the gap, if they're behind.

Nonprofit agencies, in contrast, almost never invest in research and development. When we engage in long-term thinking, more often than not we approach it as a constructive exercise rather than an essential business practice. We spend a year or more formulating a new strategic plan, then file it away in a drawer where it sits untouched for months.

Anytime we do begin to plan, the first step, invariably, is to review the agency's mission statement. Why does the agency exist? What do we want to accomplish? Long-time board members and staff groan at this exercise. Reaching consensus on a clear, concise mission statement is time-consuming and tedious. It becomes especially challenging when an agency has developed new services that don't fall under the current mission statement.

Rather than think in terms of mission, some nonprofit agencies ask, "What's the dream?" I prefer this, although my agency still has a mission statement. One reason why I like it is because dreams don't have boundaries. They're not confined by money, time, or reality. Another reason why I like it is because you don't have to explain what a dream is. Everyone has them. People don't walk around with mission statements in their head, though, and someone who's unfamiliar with the term may be slow to grasp its meaning. The third reason why I like it is because dreams change. The dreams you had as a child undoubtedly are different from the dreams you have as an adult. Periodically asking, "What's the dream?" is a good way to keep everyone focused on the future.

Hand in hand with this is developing an ends policy. An ends policy is a statement that says what the agency is working toward. When the crisis center was founded, it had one purpose: to end suicide. Over the years, the agency's services expanded, as did the purpose.

An ends policy for my wife's food bank would be to end hunger. An ends policy for an agency that provides emergency shelter would be to end homelessness. An ends policy for an agency that helps battered women would be to end domestic violence.

Unstated and often unrecognized in an ends policy is that if the agency is truly successful, it'll put itself out of business. If suicide is eliminated, suicide prevention becomes unnecessary. If hunger is eliminated, there's no need for soup kitchens or food pantries. If homelessness is eliminated, homeless shelters will disappear. In the nonprofit sector, going out of business because your services no longer are needed is the greatest end. It's also the rarest. Much more common is going out of business because your funding has dried up.

Whether an agency has an ends policy, vision statement, or mission statement, it should be posted prominently. Ours is hard to miss—it's printed and framed in our lobby, in individual staff offices, and in our boardroom. It's also printed at the top of every agenda for board meetings. When discussion wanders, board members are conditioned to point to the mission statement and say, "This doesn't really relate to our mission. Do we want to continue talking about it?" Sometimes the answer is yes, which is fine; at least they think about it. Having it available and referring to it often helps keep everyone on track.

GETTING STARTED

Every consultant has interactive exercises designed to get people in a group comfortable with each other. When the crisis center held its last board and staff retreat, the facilitators started both morning and afternoon sessions with icebreakers. Each was effective.

In the morning session, the facilitators divided us into groups with each group consisting of one to two board members and three to four staff. Each group had two tasks: to find something that every member of the group had in common, and to find something that was unique about each group member. The groups then shared the results with everyone. Since the primary goal of our planning was to better serve people of diverse cultures, determining similarities and differences between people was particularly appropriate.

In the afternoon session, each person was given a piece of paper and asked to write on it something about himself or herself that no one else in the room knew. Then the slips of paper were folded and collected in a jar, after which everyone chose a piece of paper and had to find the person who'd written it. Like before, the results were then shared.

There's so much about people that we don't know. One of my favorite icebreakers is when people talk about their name (first and last). Do they like or dislike it? Does it have meaning? Does it reflect their culture? Were they named after anyone? Did they or their ancestors ever change their name? If so, why? Is their name ever mispronounced? How do they feel when that happens? What do they do about it (correct the person or let it go)?

One icebreaker that works with a group of ten to fifteen people is called two truths and a lie. Each person is given five minutes to think of two things they've done that seem improbable but are actually true, and one thing that they've never done. Then you go around the room, and after each person describes his or her three experiences, the group decides which two are true and which one is a lie. Invariably, people are hard-pressed at first to come up with two unlikely truths, although anyone older than twenty (and many people who are younger) has had at least a few unusual experiences. The gifted participants—and the ones who earn everyone's admiration—are those who can think of a clever lie as well, and tell it convincingly.

One thing to keep in mind about icebreakers is why you do them—to help establish cohesiveness in a group. A potential downfall is that everyone's energy goes into the icebreaker and not into what comes afterward. Icebreakers can and should be amusing; however, if they don't lead to substantive conversations, their value is lost.

BUILDING TO LAST

Many nonprofit agencies come and go. They spring up, usually inspired by an idea, a strong personality, and a funding opportunity, operate for awhile, then fade into oblivion. To stand the test of time, agencies need more. One of the better management books is *Built to Last: Successful Habits of Visionary Companies*. In it the authors, James Collins and Jerry Porras, describe five attributes that they consider critical to sustaining and growing a business.

First, and most important, is having a strong, core ideology. This is the mission or vision that drives the agency's work. It should be clear, relevant, and unique (at least unique in the community; it may be duplicated elsewhere). All programs should be aligned with the mission, as should the internal culture. It's the primary management tool.

Second is developing "big, hairy, audacious goals." Mediocre organizations think small; great organizations think big. No one is inspired when an agency sets its sights low. Being successful when you measure success with a tiny yardstick means little. On the other hand, when you aim for something far beyond your reach, people are moved. You may come up short, despite everyone's best efforts the goal may be unattainable; however, you'll probably get a lot closer than if you start out content to achieve less.

The third key attribute of lasting organizations is a strong internal culture. The crisis center had been in business more than thirty years when I arrived, so the internal culture was well established. Some things, such as a high regard for volunteers, the clinical competency of staff, and a strong sense of teamwork, were essential to the agency's success and I made sure that they continued. Other facets I changed, though. One had to do with money. Throughout its history, the crisis center had operated on a shoestring budget. Purchases over $10 were agonized over, and people literally saved paperclips. Donors, if they knew, probably appreciated such tight fiscal responsibility. At the same time, it was inefficient. Instead of paying $200 to fix the copier, staff made numerous trips to Kinko's to get things printed.

It's important for agencies to be cost effective, but they must be effective, too. "Nonprofit" is a tax status, not a strategic plan. With good equipment, we now have faster access to information, are able to serve clients better, and can give funders a more timely and complete accounting of our work.

A bigger and more difficult change is one that I've been working on from my first day at the crisis center: developing an internal culture that embraces diversity. People are different. They're different physically, culturally, emotionally, and psychologically. To deny differences and pretend that everyone is the same doesn't make sense. Instead, differences should be celebrated. They're what make life varied and interesting.

Recognizing, understanding, and appreciating differences isn't easy, though. It requires a fundamental shift in the way individuals think and the way agencies operate. This shift is challenging, especially to people who have been affiliated with an agency for a long time, are comfortable with the status quo, and are part of the dominant culture.

The crisis center's current strategic plan includes a number of objectives and tactics designed to promote diversity and increase the agency's cultural competency. If we're successful, more people of diverse cultures in the community will report that our services are valuable to them. Usage in communities of color will increase. Minority clients who come to our offices will find the environment warm and welcoming.

The fourth key attribute of agencies that are built to last is being able to stimulate progress while preserving the core. Organizations, to be successful, have to grow and change. They have to continually assess new opportunities in light of what the agency does well, its mission, and the potential for generating revenues. Then they have to make smart decisions. Personally, this is one of the things that I enjoy doing most. It's fun to consider new possibilities and determine whether they're a good fit for the crisis center. It's harder to do, naturally, during tough economic times when it's tempting to secure funding from any source, even it means straying from the mission. A better approach under these circumstances is to make sure that the core is identified, then cut costs that aren't related to preserving it. This may mean reducing or even eliminating services that the agency holds dear; however, it can't be helped. The core has to be maintained. It's analogous to a flower; you can cut back to the bulb and the plant will regrow, but if the bulb is damaged there will never be new blossoms.

A common exercise of agencies doing strategic planning is determining what to keep and what to change. Typically, the staff, board members, volunteers, and sometimes donors are asked to name three things about the agency that they never want to see changed and three things that they think need to be improved, ranked from most to least important. When the two lists are shared with everyone, usually there's widespread agreement on the "never change" items and considerable differences of opinion on the "needs improvement" issues. A team within the agency then winnows down the "needs improvement" list to the five most pressing issues, and these are the ones that everyone focuses on.

The last key attribute is striving for excellence. An agency that settles for less than the best becomes complacent and, soon, irrelevant. Of course, striving for excellence and achieving it are two different things. It's possible to aim high and still be mediocre. At the same time, if you're content to accept less than the best, it's almost certain that that's what you'll get. It's hard for anyone—staff, board, volunteers, or donors—to feel good about that.

HUNKERING DOWN

Dealing with financial setbacks is one of the biggest challenges for executive directors. No one has ever founded, fostered, grown, or led a nonprofit agency in order to lay off staff, dismantle programs, and eliminate services. Nevertheless, when times are tight, coping with cutbacks is a reality. Sometimes an agency has no choice but to hunker down, absorb painful cuts, and ride out the storm.

Reducing payroll costs is the obvious first step since salaries and employee benefits constitute a large portion of any nonprofit's expenses. There are a variety of ways to do this. The easiest ways are to implement a hiring freeze, delay salary increases, offer unpaid leave, and terminate employees who are underperforming. Beyond these, the choices are tougher. You can reduce hours or the work week, reduce benefits, implement job sharing, implement across-the-board salary reductions, and lay off staff, replacing them with volunteers and graduate interns if they're available to you. Personally, I dislike any action that's administered across-the-board such as a 10 percent salary cut for all staff or mandatory reduction of the work week from forty to thirty-five hours. While I understand the rationale—everyone is treated equally; we're all in this together—I don't agree with it. Everyone isn't equal. Some employees are more productive than others, some have special skills that can't be easily replaced, and some provide cultural expertise that the agency must have. Penalizing your most valuable employees the same as everyone else doesn't make sense to me. These are the people you count on to carry even more of the workload when staffing is reduced. Because they're high performers, they're also the employees with the most options, the ones who have the best chance of finding jobs elsewhere. I don't want them looking, which is why I make sure that they're unaffected by staffing cuts. During good times I can ill afford to lose them, and during bad times I absolutely need them.

Another way to cope with cutbacks is to control costs. Analyze purchases to see if they're necessary; seek competitive bids and new suppliers; consolidate or restructure debt; delay maintenance; share space; eliminate or consolidate publications.

It's also possible to manage money differently to improve cash flow. Invoice receivables promptly, submit grant requests before the deadline, invest cash reserves in ways that produce maximum return, borrow money at subsidized rates, and sell all unneeded assets.

Another option is to generate new income. Find new donors, seek new grant opportunities, add a special event, build an endowment. You can sell staff time and expertise to other entities, create an income-generating service or product that fulfills the agency's mission, rent out office space, charge a fee to serve as a fiscal agency for others, or sell valuable information that others need, such as data on local human services.

You may have no choice but to start charging fees to provide various services, or to increase existing fees if they're not covering the costs, although here you have to be careful. When I came to the crisis center, the agency charged a modest fee for its grief counseling services. Individuals paid $45 per year and couples $60 per year for an unlimited number of counseling sessions. Because many clients were middle income and a few were upper income, it was reasonable to think that they could afford it (low-income people could request a waiver, which was always granted). The problem was that with the fee, many people felt that they had paid for the service so they didn't donate to the agency. Mail appeals and other solicitations went unanswered. Even though the service was worth far more than the actual fee, which was merely an attempt to recoup some of the operating costs, people didn't think of it that way.

I convinced the board to eliminate the fee, which had multiple benefits. First and foremost, grief clients ended up contributing more money. Those with moderate to substantial means gave a lot more than when they paid the fee. Even some low-income clients donated whereas before they accepted the waiver. Second, the crisis center could publicize that all of its services were free to clients. Grief counseling was the only service in which a fee was charged, and the exception created problems when we promoted the agency as a whole. Getting rid of the fee simplified things; now we could say that all services were free. Third, the fee was frustrating to administer. We had to track who paid and who didn't, who had requested a waiver, and bill people who were delinquent. The small amount of money raised wasn't worth the paperwork required to collect it. Lastly, eliminating the fee meant that poor people didn't have to request a waiver. They could receive service without the embarrassment of disclosing their financial state or seeking charity, the same as people with greater means. Grief counseling became more attractive to them.

In truly dire circumstances, when an agency's existence is threatened, there are additional options. This is a time when eliminating services that aren't aligned with the mission isn't enough. All possible cuts have been implemented and the agency is still hemorrhaging. More needs to be done. You can spin off struggling programs to other agencies that have a better chance of keeping them going, co-locate with one or more agencies and share office expenses, merge with an allied agency, or change the mission to take advantage of new programmatic and funding opportunities. You also can sell all remaining agency assets and schedule a final retreat of the board and staff in Tahiti, although it's not recommended.

WORKING OUT

In many respects, a strategic plan is like a workout video. Both offer a method of achieving a desired result—building a strong agency and developing a physically fit body. Both require dedication, hard work, and long-term commitment. Both have personal trainers (consultants in the case of agencies developing new strategic plans) who lead, cajole, and otherwise motivate their clients to get into better shape.

I like thinking of a strategic plan as a workout video for another reason: you have to use it to see results. If the video stays on a shelf it's worthless, the same way that a strategic plan, filed away, does nothing. You can't get trimmer and healthier by wishing it. Similarly, an agency can't grow stronger if once its strategic plan is completed, everyone goes back to focusing on day-to-day concerns.

At the crisis center, we treat our strategic plan as a living document. Agendas for board meetings are structured to include discussions and updates on the plan, and committees review their portion of the plan regularly. Periodic staff meetings are devoted to the plan as well. The result is a constantly evolving blueprint for the crisis center's future, anchored by core values and ambitious goals as articulated in a document that everyone helped create.

It'd be difficult to continually review and revise the plan if it was a large document. Some agencies have strategic plans that are hundreds of pages. The heft may seem impressive to everyone who participated in the planning process, and make the agency feel like it got its money worth from the consultants who helped. The reality, though, is that once the plan is finished, no one reads it. People rely on the executive summary to understand the gist—unless the executive summary is more than two pages, in which case it tends to be ignored, too.

I edited our plan so tightly that it contains only essentials. I eliminated every unnecessary word and clarified every loosely phrased thought so that the writing is as clear and concise as possible. I didn't get the crisis center's strategic plan down to one page. It's nineteen pages including attachments, with one-inch margins and eleven-point type. This isn't bad, especially since more than seventy people actively participated in the planning process, which took twelve months. Included in this were ongoing focus groups of African-Americans and Latinos who served as cultural informants for our cross-cultural goal. They provided a lot of good feedback, which I wanted to incorporate in the final draft.

For the executive summary, I did fit the three goals, nine objectives, and seventeen measurable outcomes into a single-page table. It's what we use in working groups, and what we give to funders.

After the plan was approved by the board, we threw a party. Everyone deserved to celebrate. The plan was a milestone for the crisis center, the first to be guided by professional consultants, the first to include a number of participants outside the agency, and the first to articulate a specific multicultural goal, which was agency-wide. In addition, unlike previous plans, this one covered a three-year rather than a five-year period in recognition of the fact that needs and funding had become more volatile. Five years is too far out to make projections with any confidence. The condensed timeframe added urgency to the work ahead.

As of this writing, we're in the middle of year three. Some elements have changed, which is okay. If all of our assumptions still seemed accurate thirty months later, and all of the tasks laid out in the plan were being completed on time, I'd worry that we weren't paying close enough attention. As it is, we're ahead in some areas, behind in others, and have let one or two things go. What's important is that the plan continues to guide our work—at least until the next plan, which we're starting to draft.

CHAPTER NINE

Fundraising 102: Crossing the Divide

Like everyone else, I was awed by the destruction and saddened by the misfortune caused by Hurricane Katrina. At the same time, I knew there was more to the story.

In the aftermath of Hurricane Andrew, which hit Florida in 1992, I was flown by America's Second Harvest to Atlanta to manage a large, temporary, emergency distribution center. Donations of food, water, blankets, cots, and other items poured in from across the country. Hundreds of volunteers sorted them into boxes, then loaded the boxes onto trucks so that they could be transported to the hardest-hit areas.

The fourth week, a dozen volunteers from Florida arrived. They'd lost everything—homes, pets, nearly all of their personal possessions. Still, they felt fortunate to have escaped serious injury and wanted to help. One man had photos that he'd taken with an Instamatic camera. *CNN* aerial views of widespread destruction seemed sanitized compared with these hand-held snapshots. A large, steel light standard was bent by the wind, its top touching the ground. People stood on a table in a living room, water up to their knees. There was a photo of a dead body, close up.

The man with the photos said that his Volkswagen car had been lifted by the storm. He found it accidentally a week later—five miles away.

Among the many disturbing elements of Katrina—the lack of preparation, the looting that followed, the slow Federal response—was this: the people most affected were the ones most vulnerable to begin with. Those who could afford to leave and who had transportation evacuated immediately. It was the poor who were left behind.

Because many of the victims were Hispanic, the National Suicide Prevention Lifeline set up a special hotline for Spanish-speaking people. We answer all local calls to the Lifeline, and our Spanish-speaking staff began answering some of the national calls from hurricane victims. The calls, like the cleanup, continue.

Despite Katrina's fury and devastation, most people are recovering from it, just like they recovered from Hurricane Andrew. Their lives may never be the same, though. Natural disasters remind us of our place in the world and that efforts to control nature rather than live in concert with it are unwise.

As I think back to my time in Atlanta, I remember that the days passed in a blur. There was so much to do. It's ironic that for victims of a disaster, unlike for relief workers, time stands still. There's no job to go to, no home to maintain, no recreational or social activities to enjoy. Everything is frozen in images of the past.

Hope is frozen, too. It takes awhile to rebuild. We do, though. Eventually, we do.

In 1976, three volunteers of the crisis center went on a ski trip together. One night in the lodge, relaxing after a day on the slopes, they talked about ways to raise money to support the crisis center's work. After considering and ruling out a number of options, they hit upon an idea that they thought was promising—start a thrift shop. None of the three had ever run a business before, but that didn't deter them. They scoured the community for a suitable site, one that was small enough to be affordable and not so far off the beaten track that no one would find it. With backing from the crisis center (another one of those leaps of faith that nonprofits make sometimes), the three signed a one-year lease and went to work.

They solicited donations of clothing, jewelry, scarves, and handbags. They recruited friends and neighbors to volunteer in the shop and set up schedules. They bought an old cash register, tags to price each item, and racks to display the merchandise. Then they posted flyers around town and hung a hand-painted sign above the door.

Nine months after that ski trip, Leftovers Thrift Shop opened for business. It was called Leftovers because that's what it sold, other people's unwanted yet still usable things. The first year, after expenses, the shop made $128. Another lease was signed. The second year, profits were $1,000 and Leftovers moved into a building that was a little bigger.

In 2004, Leftovers raised its one-millionth dollar for the crisis center. Thirty years after its founding, it continues to operate entirely with volunteers. An auxiliary of women does everything from collecting, sorting, pricing, displaying, and selling all merchandise to handling the finances, coordinating advertising, and negotiating the shop's lease.

On the face of it, operating a year-round business seems like a lot more work than organizing an annual event. In many respects it is; however, there are mitigating factors. First, the thrift shop is self-propelling. It has developed its own base of customers who go there not because they want to support the crisis center but because they're looking for a good deal. We can count on their patronage regardless of the weather, the time of year, or the condition of the economy—all factors that influence the success of a special event.

Second, by working at the thrift shop, volunteers are first in line to buy new merchandise that comes in. For people living on fixed incomes, as many thrift shop volunteers are, this is important.

Third, Leftovers volunteers have the opportunity to feel useful. As you get older, and once you retire, life presents fewer chances to be productive. Although some Leftovers volunteers are quite elderly, the hours they give every week make many of the crisis center's services possible. We couldn't do what we do without them.

A final consideration is the social value. By working at Leftovers, people get out of the house regularly, interact with others, and make new friends. Sadly, because nearly all Leftovers volunteers are seniors, there are frequent funerals. Every time I attend one, I marvel at the turnout. Usually, the older someone is, the fewer friends he or she has. In the last stages of life, there's no one left to mourn. Leftovers is just the opposite. The longer people volunteer at the shop, the wider their circle of friends. We should all be so fortunate.

Leftovers is unusual, but it isn't unique. Many nonprofit agencies now operate for-profit businesses to raise money to support their mission. Restaurants, bakeries, cleaning services, and print shops are just a few of these enterprises. They go head to head with private companies and often hold their own. Sometimes they do more than hold their own because they're able to operate with lower profit margins. It's not all gravy, though. For-profit businesses run by charities have to pay tax on unrelated business income, which is not so different from the tax that private companies pay. And customers, whether they buy from a nonprofit thrift shop or a for-profit department store, still have to pay sales tax.

In general, the most successful businesses operated by nonprofit agencies are closely aligned with the agency's mission. Goodwill Industries and St. Vincent de Paul have thrift stores around the country, which produce considerable income. Just as importantly, though, the stores offer valuable job training that enables the agency to help its clients become self-sufficient workers.

GETTING GRANTS

By far the most common way that nonprofit agencies raise money is by seeking foundation grants. It used to be that any agency doing good work could count on foundations for support. Today that's no longer the case. Funding is limited, competition is keen, and foundations often have to choose between hundreds of proposals, all of them worthy.

There's no magic formula for obtaining a grant. There are, however, several basic principles to follow:

- *Know what you want.* Know what you want to do, how much money you want to do it, and what the community benefit will be as a result. Know who potential collaborative partners are, whether there are similar or competing services in the same geographic area, and how to document the need for your proposed project.
- *Do the research.* Find out if your project matches the funder's interests, if the amount you're asking for is consistent with the funder's giving range, and if the funder has made any recent grants for similar projects, in which case the foundation may feel that it's done enough in that area, at least for the time being.

• *Adhere to a funder's guidelines.* Don't submit a full proposal if a letter of intent is expected first, don't request funding for services outside the foundation's interest areas, don't submit incomplete information, and don't be late—meet all deadlines.

The first thing I do when crafting a grant proposal is develop the budget. I know fundraisers who do this near the end, which amazes me. I find that working out all of the budget details—staffing, occupancy, equipment, supplies, printing, and other costs—helps me shape the project clearly in my mind. If I did it the other way around, I'd have to do a lot of rewriting.

The best budgets have four columns and fit on one page. The first column lists revenues and expenses for the project. The second column breaks down how funding from the particular foundation will be allocated by line item. The third column details funding from matching sources. The last column is the agency's total budget. Displayed this way, a funder can see at a glance where his or her money will go, how other funding will be used, the total needed to complete the project, and how the project fits in with other work the agency does.

Every foundation is different, and everyone in a foundation scrutinizes different parts of a grant request. Money people study the budget, a recent financial statement if it's enclosed, and the agency's annual audit. Program people analyze the service, whether it's needed, whether the agency is capable of providing it, and whether it's partnering with other agencies. Staff make sure that all required attachments are included and that if the agency received funding previously, it submitted complete reports in a timely fashion.

Some funders—particularly community foundations—assess the composition of an agency's board, staff, and volunteers, as well as the composition of people being served. Is the board comprised of leaders? Do staff have the necessary skills and training to manage the project effectively? Are volunteers utilized? Are clients satisfied? Do all—board, staff, volunteers, and clients—reflect the diversity of the community?

For corporate foundations, a major consideration is the opportunity for positive press. Unlike family and community foundations, which exist to grant money, corporate foundations exist to support the company's work. Foundation revenues are tied to corporate sales, and the primary purpose of corporate grantmaking is to boost the company's image. Few grants are made to controversial projects or to agencies without proven track records.

Staff in corporate foundations tend to differ from staff in family and community foundations in two important ways. First, they have more influence in decision-making. Without a board to oversee their grantmaking, they have considerable latitude. Second, they often have little philanthropic experience. Many times, staff at corporate foundations are promoted from other departments, such as marketing. They may have never read a grant proposal before, and are inclined to fund agencies that the company has supported previously. To have a chance, a new agency has to show that funding will provide positive marketing opportunities for the company, not just social benefits for the community.

Before writing a proposal, I always contact the foundation. I want verbal feedback on our project prior to submitting anything in writing. This helps me structure the request in a way that foundation staff and board members are likely to support. More importantly, it lets me know what the chances are for funding. No one can afford to spend time tailoring proposals that are rejected because the funder isn't interested. When I submit a grant request, I want some assurance that it's going to be approved.

It's never a good idea to submit a laundry list of needs to a funder. Most agencies have multiple needs and it's tempting to mention them all with the hope that one will resonate strongly. The problem is that funders have limited money and want to grant it to projects that have high impact. A laundry list just tells the funder that you don't know which need is most important, so you're going to let the funder decide. This doesn't inspire confidence in the agency. It's better to do your research, determine the funder's primary interests, and submit a proposal that fits.

When I prepare attachments for grants, I make sure that they have the same layout, type treatment, and look as the body of the proposal. It's important to me that everything appears consistent and professional. Budget information, the list of board members, profiles of key staff, agency fact sheet, and other addenda convey an image of the agency that inspires confidence if presented well. Conversely, information that's thrown together haphazardly, that shares no common design elements, that's poorly copied and slipshod in appearance, calls into question the agency's competencies, as unfair as that might seem. It doesn't take much time to redo a program manager's resume so that it matches other elements of a proposal. Moreover, once you do it, it's done. It's a little thing, perhaps, but little things add up.

Whenever a proposal is funded, I have two reactions simultaneously. The first is to pump my fist in celebration—we got the money! Now we can deliver the service; people are going to be helped. The second is to ask, "What are we going to do next year when the money has run out?" Most foundations want to see some sort of plan for sustainability after their grant expires. They don't want to be permanent funders of a project. This means that you have to find other sources of support. You can't hold things together with grants alone.

MAIL APPEALS

One of those other sources is mail appeals. To people outside the nonprofit sector they're "junk mail," but to those of us who rely on individual donations they're part of our life-support system. Many agencies couldn't survive without them.

I love to receive mail appeals from other organizations because each one is a source of ideas. Did the agency use a tag line on the outer envelope? One of the biggest challenges in any mail solicitation is getting people to open the envelope. A clever tag line or compelling photo often accomplishes this. Some agencies not only don't put a tag line on the outside, they don't put a return name or address, figuring that people will open it to find out who it's from. The disadvantage with this approach is that once they know, people may resent being misled. With the house list, which consists of current donors, you always use the name.

When I open an appeal, I look first at the salutation. If it's addressed to me, the letter and inserts were laser printed, which is more expensive than traditional offset printing. If the mailing isn't addressed to me, the salutation is generic, usually "Dear Friend." There are variations—"Dear Neighbor," "Dear Caring Person," "Dear Friend of the Crisis Center." None is an improvement on "Dear Friend," although every time I open a new appeal I wonder whether someone has found a better greeting.

Next I look at who signed the letter. Was it the president of the board, the executive director, someone well-known, a volunteer, or a client? Odds are that whoever it was, he or she didn't write the letter, especially if it's a larger agency. The name offers clues, though, about the strategy behind the solicitation.

After seeing who signed the letter, I read the postscript. It's one of the most important elements in the letter. The reason why is because most people who open an appeal letter do this: they read the first sentence or two, glance at highlighted text, skip to the end and read the last sentence, then read the P.S. At that time they decide whether to go back and read the whole thing or throw it all away. The P.S. has to capture the essence of the appeal in such a way that people want to read more. If a letter doesn't have a P.S., it's a mistake.

Other elements I note in passing. Was a live stamp or postage indicia used on the mail envelope? What inserts were included and why? Were there giveaway items or other inducements? Was return postage paid? Does the reply card work as a stand-alone piece? (Frequently, people who decide to give save the reply card and return envelope and put them with bills that'll be paid at the end of the month. When that time comes, however, they may forget why they wanted to donate. If they don't have the solicitation letter anymore, the reply card has to serve as a reminder. If it doesn't, the donation is lost.)

In crafting an appeal, here are a few things I've learned:

- Use "I" and "you" but mostly "you" in the letter. You're not writing to the masses, just to one person (even couples read a letter individually, which is why you use a singular salutation—"Dear Friend"—rather than "Dear Friends"). To establish a personal relationship with someone, appeal to him or her directly, thus "you."
- Use words and stories with emotional impact. People give because they're moved; only later, if asked, do they justify their giving intellectually.
- Inform and educate, but don't moralize. The purpose of an appeal letter is to motivate people to write a check, not change the way they think or believe. Facts and statistics presented objectively can add credibility, although their use should be limited. Write from your heart—not your head.
- Create a sense of urgency so that people give now. Sometimes there's a genuine reason why donations are needed immediately. Even if there's not, there can be consequences if a fundraising goal isn't met: "Without your help, someone like Tracy will continue to be ignored."

Many people labor endlessly over the appeal letter, as if it'll be preserved for posterity. It won't. A successful letter elicits a donation while an unsuccessful one doesn't, but either way the letter is thrown away afterward. No one saves it. Moreover, the letter isn't the most important element of a mail appeal. This fact was brought home to me a number of years ago when I wrote an appeal letter that I intended to be laser printed with a personal salutation. At the last minute I changed my mind, deciding that I couldn't afford the extra days it'd take to run the appeal through laser printers and hand match the letter with the mailing envelope. I forgot to alter the salutation on the original document, though. When I received my appeal in the mail, I was horrified to see that it began, "Dear [Salutation]." The agency had spent thousands of dollars on the mailing; even more importantly, it was banking on a strong return. Anyone who opened it would see something far more off-putting than "Dear Friend"—they'd see "Dear [Salutation]." To my surprise, and with great relief, I found that people responded generously anyway. It wasn't the letter that sold them; there were other factors at work.

The single most important aspect of any direct mail campaign is the list of people it's sent to. The same package sent to one list can raise ten times more money than sending it to a different list. In the case of my mistaken salutation, the appeal was mailed to the house list, which consists of people who had donated previously to the agency. They opened it because they saw who it was from, and were more forgiving than if the agency was unfamiliar to them.

In doing prospecting (mailing to people who probably don't know about your agency), fundraisers ascribe to a variety of theories regarding lists. One is buying the names of known givers to other causes. These are people who are used to giving, whether it's to Catholic Charities, Children's Defense Fund, Mothers Against Drunk Driving, the soup kitchen down the street, or Greenpeace. If your cause aligns with one they support, then they'll probably give to you. Many national charities sell their mailing lists as an additional way to raise money. I don't advise agencies to sell or trade their own mailing lists—I feel it's important to be able to tell our donors that we value and protect their privacy. I'm always willing to buy someone else's list, though, if I think it'll be a good source of donors for the crisis center.

Another theory is to use real estate records to target people in selected neigh-borhoods, whose homes are valued above a certain amount, meaning they're well off financially and may have disposable income, and who have resided there for at least three years, meaning they probably have ties to the community. If you analyze your current donors and find commonalities with these demographic indicators, so much the better.

A third theory is to find donors to political causes and tailor you message accordingly. For Republicans, emphasize your agency's cost-effectiveness and use of volunteers. For Democrats, talk about the people you help. Political donations have to be declared and are public information. A number of web sites track them. Two of my favorites are Fundrace.org and Opensecrets.org. Fundrace.org has a "Neighbor Search" page where you can type in your address and see everyone in your neighborhood who has donated, complete with each person's address, how much the person donated, and to which candidates or political action committees. Opensecrets.org allows you to search by name (finding out how much and to whom Hollywood director Steven Spielberg donated, for instance) or by cause (finding out who donated to Senator John McCain, for instance, or to the National Rifle Association). You also can get breakdowns of the total amount of money donated during the past year by residents of a particular city, as well as a list of the biggest donations and top recipients by zip code. While it may be alarming to learn how much personal information is available on the Internet, good fundraisers take advantage of it.

The second most important thing in direct mail fundraising is segmentation. You don't want to send an appeal seeking $50 donations to people who you know are capable of giving $500. In segmenting a mailing, you put together different packages for different groups of people. A general rule of thumb is that the higher the giving potential, the more personal the mailing is. Most personal of all is a handwritten or one-of-a-kind letter with a hand-addressed envelope, first-class stamp, personal greeting, reference to past giving, personal signature, and personal postscript. Needless to say, it's the most expensive.

Third in importance is the time of year you mail. Everyone mails in November and December because people generally are more charitable then; however, the competition is greatest, too. Mailing in October gives you a head start; in addition, you can send a followup mailing a month later to everyone who didn't respond to the initial solicitation. Spring is another popular time, in part because it's opposite winter but also because kids are still in school so people are home, they haven't gone on vacation yet. Another reason why spring is good is because many people who do their taxes chide themselves afterward for not having given more to charity. If your appeal hits then, they may feel guilty and decide to donate.

Fourth in importance is the offer made in the mailing. There are different kinds of offers—membership acquisitions (join us), membership renewals (join us again), program appeals (make this service possible), capital appeals (help build this building or buy this piece of equipment), and matching gifts (someone else will give $1 for every $1 you give). How much you ask for, how you say the money will be used, and what, if anything, you promise in return for a donation make the offer distinctive.

Fifth—far down the list—is the letter itself. Some agencies design their appeals to lead donors through the life of the agency. In the spring appeal, a homeless family is admitted to the agency's emergency shelter. In the fall appeal, the same family uses the agency's revolving loan program to pay first and last month's rent on an apartment. In the winter appeal, the breadwinner has a new job thanks to career counseling provided by the agency.

Whatever strategy is used, it's important to have only one call to action per piece. Don't ask people to give to a specific program, volunteer at the agency, and write their congressman regarding an issue. Multiple messages confuse donors and often end up producing no action at all. Instead, focus on the goal—raising money.

This raises the question of how often a charity should solicit its donors. One response is, "As often as you need the money." Personally, I think four times per year is appropriate; however, I understand why charities solicit more than that. Contrary to popular belief, donors don't mind being asked frequently. If they did, we wouldn't have houses of worship; after all, religious groups ask people to give every week and few people complain. They've come to expect it. What people don't like, though, is being asked to give before their previous gift has been acknowledged. This is why Kim Klein, a premier fundraising consultant and editor of the *Grassroots Fundraising Journal* (an excellent publication for fundraisers at all skill levels) says, "Thank before you bank," that is, call or write the donor even before you deposit the donation. Practically speaking, this may not be possible; however, it's a strong reminder that prompt acknowledgement is essential.

GOVERNMENT FUNDING

One of the ironies of nonprofit work is that agencies with government funding depend on it and agencies without it don't want it. Even agencies that provide similar services often disagree on the value of government funding.

For agencies that receive one-third or more of their funding from government sources—local, state, or federal—it's critical. Government funding provides core support that's enhanced by grants and individual donations. Although some government programs, such as Medicaid, have extensive reporting requirements, many programs—especially those at the local level—don't. This reduces the administrative burden on agencies and actually ends up making government funding more efficient than private sector support. Also, unlike grants, which usually are short-term—twelve to twenty-four months—government funding can last for years, giving agencies the time needed to develop sufficient infrastructure to address long-term community problems.

The downfall, as agencies that don't receive government funding are quick to point out, is that there are no guarantees and being dependent on any single funding source is risky. Administrations change, political winds shift. Moreover, accepting government funding often means that agency representatives have to spend time befriending elected officials in order to protect revenue sources.

Another challenge for agencies that accept government funding is that you have to deal with large bureaucracies. Whereas most nonprofit agencies are small and facile, able to make decisions and initiate them quickly, government departments tend to be big and slow, with many layers of administration. A contract may move across the desks of ten or more government employees before it gets mailed to the contractor. This can take months.

Once I was contacted by the deputy director of a county department who wanted to grant the crisis center $20,000 in special, one-time funding so that we could provide additional emergency motel vouchers to homeless people. He called me in April and said that the money had to be spent by December 31st. That didn't seem like a problem. The crisis center has arrangements with a number of local motel managers to provide rooms to homeless individuals and families based on a phone call from us.

"Great," I said. "Get me a contract and we'll start housing people."

Spring ended. So did summer. Every few weeks I called Bart, the deputy director, to find out the status of our contract.

"It's in the works," Bart said. "We've had a lot of people out recently, but everyone's back now and you should have it in another week or two."

Since the money was for emergency lodging, which homeless people need most in fall and winter, I didn't worry. Then September passed, and October. Now my calls to Bart were more frequent and more strained. At one point, I snapped.

"Damn it, Bart. How much longer are we going to have to wait?"

"Not much longer," he said. "November 15th at the latest."

It'd be tight, but we could do it. Once the contract was signed, we could put up the money knowing that we'd be reimbursed. While it'd be frustrating to front money to a big county department, at least we were able to. I wasn't about to dip into savings, though, without a contract.

"If it's after November 15th," I cautioned, "we'll have to turn it down. We won't be able to spend it responsibly by the deadline."

"You'll have it by November 15th," Bart said. "You have my word on it."

Needless to say, I didn't receive the contract by November 15th. I didn't receive it by December 15th or even December 30th. His secretary hand delivered it to me at noon December 31st, literally the last day of the year.

"What am I supposed to do with this?" I said to Bart, holding the contract like a dirty rag, as if he could see it over the phone. "We can't spend $20,000 in twelve hours."

"I know," he said. "Here's the thing, just call the motels you work with and tell them you want to prepay several thousand dollars each. Cut the checks today so that the money is encumbered by the deadline, then draw on it in January and February, like a line of credit."

"Is that allowed?" I asked. It didn't sound right.

"Sure," Bart said. "We do it all the time. Don't sweat it."

I didn't know of any government funding that could be spent that way. At the same time, I rationalized that it was the department's money. As long as the crisis center was paid back, I didn't care. Moreover, the idea of being able to help homeless people in January and February, when they really needed it, was appealing.

"Okay," I said. "But first I want you to fax me signed authorization to do what you just described." I'd learned by now not to trust Bart's verbal promises.

He faxed it to me and I went ahead with his plan. As it turned out, it wasn't allowed and Bart got into a lot of trouble for it. Fortunately, because of his signed authorization, the department had to honor the contract and the crisis center was reimbursed.

SHOOTING THE PUPPY

In recent years across the United States, and especially in California, there has been an ongoing funding crisis. Some of it's due to skyrocketing costs of employee pensions, health care, and workers comp insurance. Some of it's the result of economic downturns, which have diminished assets and provided lower rates of return on investments than budget planners anticipated. Some of it's attributable to state government siphoning off more and more tax revenues from counties. Whatever the cause, and frequently there are many, creating what local officials find solace in calling "a perfect storm" of worst-case scenarios playing out simultaneously, county funding for health and social services—including many provided by nonprofit agencies—becomes threatened.

A strategy that's employed sometimes is for county departments to target high-profile, high-impact services for cuts, primarily as a way of demonstrating to the public how dire the county's fiscal situation is. Invariably, there's an uproar. Agency leaders describe the potential devastation of critical programs. Newspapers print editorials decrying the situation. Clients storm the chambers of the county board of supervisors. No one is happy, least of all elected officials who don't want their names associated with the elimination of a vital service. Somehow they find the money to keep it going, which is what the people who put the agency's contract on the chopping block in the first place are counting on. They don't want to lose the service, just have the money come from somewhere else.

The practice has become so commonplace that nonprofit agencies have a name for it: shooting the puppy. Local charities take turns being the puppy that people in the community fall in love with, who's then pushed before angry budget cutters and is the target of abuse.

On several occasions, the crisis center has been the "puppy" that a department head attempted to shoot. Each time I've fought hard to preserve our funding. So far I've been successful; however, it's taken a toll. By the end of budget hearings, I'm emotionally exhausted, and so are many other executive directors. This is why I continually strive to reduce our reliance on government support. When I started, 70 percent of the crisis center's budget was borne by government. Today that's down to 30 percent. A part of me hopes that one day we won't need government funding at all, although another part of me believes that my agency represents one of the best uses of taxpayer dollars.

HOW FUNDERS CAN HELP

When government at all levels reduces funding for important services, the philanthropic community can't make up the shortfall. The gap is too big and their resources aren't adequate. At the same time, there are two things that grantmakers can do to help nonprofits.

The first is to provide general operating support. During difficult economic periods, nonprofit agencies have one primary goal: to survive. If the only money available to them is to start or expand programs, that's what they'll do. Consequently, funders who concentrate their giving on program support oftentimes encourage ill-advised growth that diminishes rather than increases the capacity of grant recipients. Agencies become over extended and start to lose focus. General operating support enables agencies to spend money in ways that they think are best, providing flexibility and enabling agencies to preserve core systems and infrastructure, which are most critical. Granting money for operating costs requires funders to place more trust in agencies to make the right decisions in setting priorities, and means that more due diligence is needed by funders in selecting grant recipients. The payoff is increased sustainability for nonprofits and, oftentimes, more creative use of grant dollars.

The second way that funders can help nonprofits is by committing to long-term support. Like grants for general operations, this strategy runs contrary to the giving practices of most foundations, whose executives worry that agencies will become dependent on their funding. The thing is, with long-term support, agencies can focus on services and have greater impact on problems in their communities. Just as it's easier for foundation staff to administer one three-year grant rather than three one-year grants, so is it easier for nonprofits to manage one multi-year grant rather than several single-year grants. Moreover, with longer-term funding commitments, agencies can take the time necessary to develop well-conceived strategies that have a greater chance of success.

No one is served when a foundation provides seed funding for a service that's discontinued several years later, or when a grant is made to an agency that subsequently goes out of business. Successful agencies are committed to the long haul, and funders should be, too. This means that foundations have to turn down even more grant requests, something they're loathe to do. Some foundations avoid saying no by making many small grants to a large number of agencies. If they thought about it, though, they'd realize that this doesn't make sense. No single grant has much impact, and the foundation ends up wasting its resources. Making fewer, larger, longer-term grants is the best way for a foundation to maximize the benefits of its philanthropy and increase the capacity of the nonprofit sector.

The model that foundations should follow is that of individual donors. This may seem surprising since foundations tend to be staffed by thoughtful professionals while individual donors, in general, are considered unsophisticated, giving emotionally rather than strategically. In practice, though, the results are the opposite. Foundation giving often ends up being capricious while individual giving is deliberate and meaningful.

Many foundations provide short-term grants for new projects that may or may not last and make a difference. By contrast, individuals donate money year after year to the same select agencies, thereby providing stability. Foundation funding usually is restricted to meet the needs of the funder. Individual donations, on the other hand, usually are unrestricted, meaning that the charity has discretion in how they're used and can apply them to meet the agency's most critical needs. Foundations try to spread their money to as many qualified organizations as possible, giving preference to agencies they haven't funded before. Individuals, conversely, focus their support on a few specific agencies that they're really committed to, saying no easily and regularly to other charities. Foundations place many requirements on their funding, before and after a grant is made. Individuals tend to give unconditionally, confident that their contributions are being used wisely without needing significant proof of it.

The result of these differences is that charities that rely on foundation support spend a lot of time writing reports and doing evaluations of services that may not last. Charities that rely on individual donations, in contrast, tend to start programs that matter and are sustained.

CROSSING THE DIGITAL DIVIDE

A few foundations have recognized the negative effects of their philanthropic practices and implemented programs that offer charities greater flexibility in how they spend grant funds. One of these was an initiative started several years ago by the San Francisco Foundation called "The Digital Divide." Through it, grants were made to selected agencies that the foundation had funded in the past to upgrade their equipment and thereby strengthen their infrastructure. There was no application process; in fact, many local charities didn't even know about the initiative until they received an award letter from the foundation.

This was the case with the crisis center. We received $25,000 for technology. We could replace our phone system, upgrade our computer equipment, buy specialized software, a new copier, a backup emergency generator—whatever we deemed most important.

Technology is evolving quickly and many nonprofits can't keep up. They make the best of outdated equipment, but it hampers their ability to serve clients efficiently. The result is a "digital divide" between the for-profit sector, which invests in new technology, and the nonprofit sector, which is stuck with old, slow, expensive-to-maintain equipment.

I've received many grants over the years, some for considerably more than $25,000. I've never been as surprised or as delighted by a grant as this one, though. Asking a funder to give money for equipment is a difficult sell. Almost every nonprofit agency needs new equipment, so funders can't distinguish between the benefits of competing proposals. In addition, foundations prefer to fund direct services rather than infrastructure development. Added to this is the fact that most charities are reluctant to spend unrestricted money on equipment. We know it's important; however, program needs have priority. To receive a grant that's unsolicited, has few strings attached, and is for the specific purpose of enhancing an agency's technological needs is unique.

In typical nonprofit fashion, we leveraged it to the hilt. First, we researched the cost and performance of workstations and a new file server. Then we selected a vendor and negotiated a bulk discount. After that we went to individual software vendors and requested donated, licensed copies of the latest versions of all the programs we needed. In a few instances where we couldn't get software donated, we bought it from a wholesaler. With hardware and software in hand, our next step was to approach the largest employer in our area, Chevron Corporation, and ask members of the information technology department to donate their time to set up everything for us. They were happy to help.

We had to give up the dream of a new flat-screen monitor for every workstation; our budget wouldn't allow it. With faster computers, though, we did opt for faster Internet access.

We used every dime of the foundation's $25,000 grant. The effect on staff morale was immediate. No longer did we have a patchwork system comprised of donated computers from a variety of sources. Everyone had new, matching equipment with the latest software and high-speed Internet access. Tasks that used to take agonizing minutes to perform now were completed in seconds.

Other than the purchase and remodeling of our facility, no other change at the crisis center has been so transformative. Thanks to the wisdom and vision of foundation staff, and to the generosity of companies that donated in-kind products and services, a relatively small amount of money, granted with maximum latitude and trust, produced a huge return. Every time I turn on my computer at work, I'm grateful.

I only wish that the initiative had continued. Sadly, it ended after a year. The benefits couldn't be measured to the satisfaction of foundation trustees.

CHAPTER TEN

Cultural Competency: The Platinum Rule

Whenever Grandma Helen reached another milestone, someone in our family would ask her what it's like to be seventy, seventy-five, eighty years old. Invariably, she'd say how much she enjoyed being able to tend her roses and watch her grandchildren grow. Her words reassured us, giving us reason to think that aging wasn't bad at all.

On her ninety-second birthday, Grandma Helen was still living on her own. She'd had knee replacement surgery, needed a walker, and seemed increasingly forgetful. She didn't complain, though, so it was easy for the rest of us to overlook these changes.

During the family celebration of her birthday, when we were alone, I said, "Grandma, how does it feel to be ninety-two?"

I expected the same warm-hearted response as always. Instead, she lowered her voice and said, "It's awful. Be thankful you're still young."

I was stunned. In that moment, my attitude about aging changed forever.

Grandma Helen isn't alive today. Neither is my father; he succumbed to prostate cancer that caused incontinence and required him, a retired executive, to wear diapers the last five years of his life. The days of leisure he looked forward to when younger ended up filled with trips to the bathroom and constant dressing changes.

It's still possible to age gracefully, but it's difficult to be grateful. Growing old is hard. It means declining health and mobility. It means increased loneliness and fear of being a burden to others. Many older Americans face serious financial problems as well.

Other cultures revere elders. Ours, unfortunately, places higher value on what people own and how they look than on what they think and how they feel. No wonder senior citizens—especially senior men—have the highest suicide rate of any age group in America. Unless you've accumulated lots of money, being old doesn't count for much.

As I creep closer to old age, I'd like to think that attitudes will change and society will embrace senior citizens for what they offer all of us: a chance to relive history, a distinctive perspective, and an abundance of knowledge and skills hard earned and still valuable. I see an elderly man or woman and think: What languages do they know that I wish I could speak? What talents do they have for woodworking, finance, botany, or art that I envy? What places have they been to that I'd like to visit?

The elderly can teach us a lot, if we let them. Now is a good time to start.

"I have a question for you," says Terry, a consultant I hired to do multicultural training at the crisis center. "What does being white mean to you?"

I shrug. "It doesn't mean anything."

She nods. "You take it for granted."

I consider for a minute. The subject never came up at our dinner table. I never discussed it with friends. I never thought about it. "Yes, I guess that's true," I say.

At different times in my life, I've thought about what it means to be black. I went to school at Berkeley in the seventies when the student body was especially diverse and Black Power had meaning. I read James Baldwin, Langston Hughes, Ralph Ellison, *Black Like Me*. Professor Harry Edwards' class on racism was a rite of passage for sociology majors, myself included. Terry's question catches me off guard. What does it mean to be *white*?

When Minerva, our homeless services manager, is asked to describe herself, the first thing she says is, "I'm a black woman." Her ethnicity and gender are essential to who she is. They're directly and indirectly responsible for the majority of her life experiences.

Until the training, I never described myself as "a white man." It didn't seem necessary. Terry was right; I took my race and gender for granted. Then I started learning that being white in a society dominated by white culture means having privileges and powers I didn't know I had—benefits that others lacked.

Peggy McIntosh, a white woman, published a groundbreaking essay on white privilege a number of years ago. In it she said, "I was taught to see racism only in individual acts of meanness and violence, not in invisible systems conferring dominance on my group." The latter, she maintained, were even more destructive because they were hidden and, thus, never addressed.

McIntosh identified forty-six ways in which she experienced unearned advantage on a daily basis. The following are a few of the ways that she, I, and other whites benefit because of the color of our skin.

- I can walk into any store and clerks don't follow me with their eyes, worried that I'm going to steal something.
- I can criticize my government without people telling me to go back to the country I came from.
- I can go to a movie, watch TV, or read a magazine or newspaper and see people of my race widely represented in a positive manner.

- I can go into a supermarket and find foods I grew up with or into a barbershop and find someone who can deal with my hair.
- If a cop stops me, I know I haven't been singled out because of my race.
- If I'm unable to rent an apartment or buy a house, it's not because of my race.
- I can take a job without coworkers thinking I got it or am able to keep it because of my race.
- I can discuss issues of race without being seen as self-interested or self-serving.
- I can ignore without consequence the opinions of people who are not my race.

WHITE CULTURE

Being white, I never thought about having a culture or what it meant. Culture was something that people of other countries and ethnicities had. If asked, as Terry did, what my culture was, I said I was "American."

"America is a place, not a culture," Terry said. She pointed out that African-Americans, Native Americans, Koreans, Hispanics, Chinese, Laotians, Pacific Islanders, and everyone else who's a citizen of the United States is American, too. It's not their culture, though, just as it's not mine.

Now I make a point of saying that I'm a white man. And I have a culture, or more precisely, two. They're the European cultures of my parents.

My father was born in England. My mother grew up in a Norwegian community in North Dakota after her father (my grandfather) emigrated from Norway on his own at age twelve.

I was raised in a small, northern California town named Terra Linda, across the Golden Gate Bridge from San Francisco. Friends and I slid on pieces of cardboard down rolling hills and caught tadpoles and frogs in surrounding ponds. In what could have been an ominous sign, the biggest and best pond was filled in soon after we arrived and became the site of the new elementary school.

When I was young, I only knew of one black family. Their four-year-old son got out of the house one night, toddled over to some construction equipment parked nearby, somehow set in motion a big bulldozer, and was run over. Hundreds of people showed up for the funeral. The only people of color present were relatives.

Over the next ten years, the community grew, yet nearly everyone who moved in was white. When I was a senior in high school, I had 2,500 classmates, yet I knew only two blacks and three Hispanics, and the only reason I knew them was because we played sports together.

My experience, I think, wasn't much different from many other whites in suburbia. Virtually everyone was like me. It was a community of privilege, although I didn't recognize it as such. There was no crime, few serious problems, and little hardship. I was never a target of prejudice or oppression because of my race. Moreover, the system was designed for me to succeed. The rules were made by people like me; the tests were developed by people like me; the jobs were offered by people like me. As I excelled in school and later in professional life, I benefited from untold advantages I wasn't even aware of. So did other whites. It was a shocking thing to learn.

WHERE I LIVE

One of my concerns at the crisis center was that agency services were being used significantly less by African-Americans, Asians, and Latinos than whites. These groups constituted 40 percent of the population of our service area yet represented only 20 percent of our clientele. Moreover, their numbers were growing. If the crisis center didn't change—and change quickly—it would be irrelevant for many people in the community.

Contra Costa County is the thirty-eighth largest county in the United States, with a population of more than one million people. Directly east from San Francisco, across San Francisco Bay, it's divided by rolling hills into four distinct geographic areas, each with its own character.

West county consists primarily of blue-collar cities that are home to major oil refineries. Huge tankers fill up at private docks owned by Chevron Corporation, which is headquartered in Contra Costa and is the area's largest employer. A lot of barrack-style housing still exists, remnants from World War II when local shipyards needed a large workforce to support the war effort. School test scores are low, crime and gang violence are high, and whites are a minority.

Central county is made up of bedroom communities that all run together like a mini Los Angeles. They're populated by a growing mix of people who commute to jobs elsewhere, mainly San Francisco and Oakland. When they drive through West county, they stay on the freeway.

East county remains devoted mostly to agriculture, and many Latinos are employed in the harvest. Farmland is disappearing fast, though, because it's become too valuable for crops. Several years ago I asked the largest farmer in the county what he was growing. "Two-by-fours," he said, happy about it. Every new acre that he sold for housing added to his wealth—and didn't require plowing. One day the whole area probably will be subdivisions and shopping centers, much to my regret.

South county is more affluent—and more white—than any other area of Contra Costa with the possible exception of Lamorinda in Central county, which also is affluent and predominantly white. South county and Lamorinda are the major reasons why Contra Costa has one of the highest per capita incomes of any county in California. Tear-down homes cost $1 million, and $5 million may buy only the second or third-best house on a street.

Two places in Contra Costa have gained national reputations, for different reasons. Blackhawk was one of the first "turn-key" communities in the United States. Built by Ken Behring, who at one time owned the Seattle Seahawks football team, Blackhawk is home to numerous professional athletes and corporate CEOs. When the original houses were first sold, they came fully furnished, not just with sofas, beds, tables, and chairs but with towels, linens, food, and fine wine so that buyers could literally turn the key, open the front door, and move in. The idea was that people left everything they owned previously behind them. Not only was this convenient but they didn't have to rely on their own questionable tastes; everything was chosen and styled to match.

A few miles north of Blackhawk but a world away is Port Chicago. It was the scene of the deadliest home-front disaster of World War II and one of the biggest miscarriages of justice in U.S. history. Port Chicago was a weapons depot, the largest on the West Coast. Sailors worked around the clock loading bombs, torpedoes, and depth charges onto naval ships that fought in the Pacific. It was dangerous work, made more dangerous by bets between officers as to which ship would be loaded first. Because the U.S. Navy was segregated, only black sailors did the loading. White officers supervised.

July 17, 1944, two munitions ships exploded at the dock, killing 320 men and injuring 390 others. Two-thirds of the victims were black. A Navy inquiry ruled out sabotage, as well as absolved white officers of any responsibility. Instead, black sailors were blamed for "rough handling" of the explosives. While white officers were granted thirty-day leaves after the tragedy, black sailors were told to collect the remains of fellow sailors, then immediately ordered back to work. Most refused, afraid of another explosion. They were threatened with charges of mutiny, an offense punishable by death from a firing squad. Fifty black sailors didn't care; they'd seen enough.

In the largest mass-mutiny trail in U.S. Naval history, thirty-two days of court hearings ended after only eighty minutes of deliberation. All fifty sailors were found guilty and sentenced to fifteen years in prison. A half-century later, in 1994, the Navy reviewed the cases and upheld the original convictions. Today, the town of Port Chicago doesn't exist and the only remnants of what happened decades ago are pilings from the pier. The Concord Naval Weapons Station now encompasses the site, as well as much of the surrounding countryside, although the base has closed and may be turned into a commercial development in the future. Local congressman George Miller continues to fight to clear the sailor's names, so far without success. The few who are still alive, as well as all who perished, await justice.

DIVERSITY MATTERS

According to the U.S. Census Bureau, the number of Hispanics and Asians in this country will triple by the year 2050. The Hispanic population is projected to grow from 35.6 million in 2000 (12.6 percent of the total population) to 102.6 million in 2050 (24.4 percent). The Asian population is expected to jump from 10.7 million in 2000 (3.8 percent of the total) to 33.4 million in 2050 (8 percent of the total). The number of African-Americans is projected to rise by 71 percent, from 12.7 to 14.6 percent of the total. By 2050, half the population of the United States will identify as people of color, up from 31.6 percent in 2000.

Coincidentally, the projected composition for the country at that time will mirror the current composition of California, my state. Already, nearly half of California's population consists of people of color, and the number is growing. Agencies like mine that don't make a concerted effort to become culturally competent will find their services ignored and devalued.

There are several definitions of cultural competency. A common one is "a set of congruent behaviors, attitudes, and policies that enable an agency to work effectively cross culturally." Another is "a set of skills, knowledge, and attitudes encompassing awareness, acceptance, and appreciation of difference." A third is "the ability to think, feel, and act in ways that acknowledge, respect, and build upon ethnic, cultural, and linguistic diversity."

These all sound good; however, people at the crisis center had a hard time understanding what they mean. If we treat everyone equally, they said, isn't that being culturally competent? No, it's not. Before I explain why, let me share my personal definition of cultural competency. It's not precise or scientific. It's more like the old Supreme Court decision on pornography in which the justices said that they couldn't define pornography, but they knew it when they saw it. Cultural competency is equally hard to pin down.

I do a lot of public speaking, and whenever I walk into a workplace I can tell almost immediately whether a business has institutionalized multicultural practices. Sometimes it's reflected in the colors of people's faces and the way they dress. Sometimes it's evident by the way space is configured or the artwork and promotional materials that are displayed. Mostly, though, it's in the air. The workplace just feels different—alive. As a newcomer, you get the feeling that everyone who enters these offices—regardless of his or her ethnicity or culture— is valued.

And that's part of my definition of cultural competency: When anyone of any race or culture walks in our front door, he or she feels immediately welcome, not by people saying it but by subtle cues all around. The other part is that when people seek services from my agency, they feel understood, respected, and valued whatever their ethnicity or culture.

Not everyone at the crisis center accepts this definition. They understand it, though. This made it easier when we adopted three goals: (1) our services are valued by everyone in the community; (2) our services are used by everyone in the community; and (3) our agency looks like the people we serve.

Before we could start working on these goals, we needed information. How many African-Americans, Asians, Hispanics, or Pacific Islanders were we serving? We didn't know; we never collected this data. How many people who spoke little or no English called our hotlines? Again, we didn't know. We subscribed to a teleinterpretation service, accessing third-party language translation, but didn't track how often it was used or whether the results were positive for callers. Our first challenge, then, was getting everyone to ask clients a simple yet highly charged question: "What ethnic or cultural group do you identify with?"

No one wanted to ask. White people didn't want to ask and people of color didn't want to ask. The feeling was that when someone is in crisis and calling for help, it adds to his or her stress level to ask questions that don't seem related to the problem. At the same time, volunteers didn't hesitate to ask people what city they lived in or a caller's age. Volunteers understood that we needed this information because our agency receives funding from numerous cities and we have to report the number of residents served. We ask people their age because it helps us understand their situation and enables us to provide better referrals.

In our grief counseling program, we provide free individual and group counseling to youths and adults mourning a death. If someone is interested, we determine the person's age, gender, residence, relationship to the deceased, age of the deceased, when the death occurred, and method of death (accident, illness, homicide, or suicide).

The consultants asked why we collect all this information. "So that we can provide the best possible match between the client and our pool of grief counselors," staff replied.

"Why don't you ask a client his or her ethnicity?" said the consultants.

Staff recoiled in horror. "We could never do that," they said. "When someone is mourning the death of a loved one, we don't want to trouble the person any more than is absolutely necessary."

The consultants considered this. Then they said, "Don't you think that a person of color might prefer to be counseled by someone from the same culture or race, the same way he or she might prefer to be counseled by someone who's roughly the same age, has had similar life experiences, and lives in the same community?"

They turned to the people of color on staff, who confirmed that this was true.

"Asking someone's ethnicity or culture is another way of ensuring that the agency's services meet the client's needs," the consultants said.

Once everyone understood this, people started asking the question. Many still are comfortable; however, they make the effort. The more often they ask, the easier it becomes.

One of the first questions our consultants asked me was, "What percentage of staff and volunteers are multilingual/multicultural?" I didn't know offhand, but few enough that it was easy to figure out. They asked, "Does your salary structure reward multilingual/multicultural employees?" Ah, no. "Is cultural competency a goal in your agency's strategic plan? Is it mentioned in the mission statement? In job descriptions and employee reviews?" I looked at them blankly. Say what?

WHERE WE ARE TODAY

When I started, there was one person of color on staff, and she was part-time. Nearly all of the crisis center's 250 volunteers were white. Program materials were in English only.

Today, half the employees are people of color, including two of four program managers. We have Spanish-speaking staff on our hotlines every day from 8 A.M. to midnight. All job descriptions and employee evaluations stress cultural competency.

We're also recruiting and retaining a more diverse pool of volunteers. By creating a more inclusive environment, we're able to keep them.

Many of our outreach materials are printed in Spanish now. Our countywide resource database can be viewed in twelve languages. We started a monthly diversity film series, showing popular and lesser-known movies that focus on ethnic and cultural differences, and afterward host a facilitated conversation. Perhaps most importantly, we collect ethnic and linguistic information on all of our clients. We've also begun to measure our effectiveness serving people of diverse cultures, including those who don't speak English.

It's a good start—and it hasn't been easy. Institutionalizing multicultural practices requires a fundamental shift in the way an agency operates and delivers services. This shift is challenging to staff, volunteers, and clients, especially those who have been affiliated with the agency for a long time, are comfortable with the status quo, and are part of the dominant culture. The next steps, though, are even harder.

In 2004 we completed a new strategic plan at the crisis center. For the first time, people outside the agency participated in the process. They asked questions that we never considered. For instance: Is our goal to increase the number of people of color who call our hotlines, or is it to see that more people of color who are in crisis get help? If it's the latter, then maybe we should use our expertise to train more community-based agencies to provide crisis intervention and suicide prevention services because that's where people of color are likely to go. They won't be served directly by us, but their needs will be met. In fact, a positive outcome, according to our cultural informants, might be that *fewer* people of color call our hotlines because they're helped upfront, before they need our services.

We've always believed that we could serve a large geographic area from a single location because most of our counseling is phone-based. One central office is more cost-effective than multiple sites. Yet how well can we serve any community if we don't have a physical presence there? Put another way, will people be more likely to use our services if they're provided by individuals who know local needs and speak the community's language? We can't afford offices in every community; however, we're exploring the possibility of staffing one or more satellite offices and routing calls from those communities to the satellite office rather than to our centralized location.

Our clinical model has been that whoever answers a hotline call stays with the caller. We make exceptions, of course; someone who speaks Spanish is transferred to a Spanish-speaking counselor, or a woman who's been sexually assaulted can speak with a woman if a male volunteer picks up the phone. Now we're wondering, though, whether a caller who identifies as African-American should be offered the option of talking with an African-American volunteer if one is available. Will the client be more comfortable? According to feedback we're getting, the answer is yes.

COLOR BLINDNESS IS BLINDNESS

It's common for white people to say, "I don't see color" when race is brought up, or to say to a person of color, "I don't see color when I look at you, we're all just human beings." The widespread belief is that if you're colorblind you're impartial, you treat everyone the same. That's good, isn't it? Isn't that what Dr.

Martin Luther King, Jr. meant when he said in his famous "I Have a Dream" speech that he longed for the day when people are judged by the content of their character, not the color of their skin?

Roberto Almanzán is another consultant I hired. Later he joined the crisis center staff and now is our cultural competency coordinator. He says, "I don't believe Dr. King meant that we should be oblivious to a person's skin color. I believe he was talking about not negatively judging someone based on the color of his or her skin. Often it's irritating to a person of color to hear someone say, 'I don't see color,' especially if it's said in a context where the speaker means that he or she doesn't discriminate on the basis of race. In the first place, it's unbelievable that one is not seen as African-American, Latino, Asian, or other person of color when oftentimes this is obvious. Secondly, most people of color want to be seen for who they are. When I hear someone say, 'I don't see color,' I understand that the speaker is attempting to convey an attitude of acceptance and equality. It makes me wonder, though, if the person has to ignore my ethnicity in order to accept and respect me. I want to be seen, accepted, and included for who I am, a Latino man. I'm proud of my ethnic and cultural identity."

He notes, "I've seen mothers 'shush' their children when one makes a comment or asks a question about someone's skin color. Why would a mother do this if what the child is referring to was not something that was shameful? Children are honest and direct. They haven't yet learned all of the things that we're not supposed to notice."

In 1968, after Dr. King was assassinated, a white schoolteacher in Iowa wanted to teach her class about racism, stereotyping, and discrimination. The exercise she developed was simple, yet the results were profound.

All the students in Jane Elliott's third-grad class were white. Elliott wanted them to experience what it felt like to be judged and discriminated against because of a physical characteristic that they couldn't change. She began her lesson by announcing that she had learned that blue-eyed people were smarter than brown-eyed people. Blue-eyed children were better behaved, learned faster, and listened better than those with brown eyes. She passed around large collars for all the brown-eyed children to wear so that they could be spotted from a distance. She gave blue-eyed children extra privileges and criticized the brown-eyed students, attributing any mistakes they made to their brown-eyed condition.

Brown-eyed students began to act as if the negative traits attributed to them were real. The blue-eyed students relished their extra privileges and joined the teacher in pointing out the negative traits of their brown-eyed classmates. The brown-eyed children became passive, distressed, anxious, and angry.

The next morning, Elliott announced to her class that she'd made a mistake. Actually, brown-eyed people were superior to blue-eyed people. She asked the brown-eyed people to remove their collars and give them to the blue-eyed students. Everything from the previous day was reversed. On this second day, blue-eyed children scored 25 to 35 percent lower on their spelling and mathematics tests than they scored on the previous day.

At the conclusion of two days of wearing collars and discriminating based on eye color, Elliott announced that no one was inferior or superior based on their eye color and that this was a lesson in how judging people based on the color of their skin or any other physical characteristic was unfair and racist. The children were elated to take off their collars and once again be included and appreciated by their classmates.

Elliott's "Brown Eyes/Blue Eyes" exercise became the subject of an award-winning film titled *A Class Divided*. The movie included a reunion of the students fourteen years later. Now adults, they talked about how powerful a lesson this was for them and how they felt like a family as a result of their common experience. The film also proved that racism is a learned behavior and not part of our genetic code.

Elliott continued teaching for a dozen years and used this exercise with each class she had. She also started using it with adults in organizational settings, with the same startling results. Today, she travels around the country speaking against discrimination.

TAKING THE RISK

Differences exist. The way to end racism isn't to deny differences but to recognize, understand, and appreciate them. But how do we do that? Where do we begin?

For executive directors, the first step is deciding to take the risk. Instituting multicultural practices is painful. It's a lot like therapy; you have to peel back layers to expose the problem. Ugly things come up that might seem better left alone, especially if an agency appears to be running smoothly. It takes strong commitment by agency leadership—the executive director and board—to institutionalize multicultural practices.

The next step is finding professional help. Effective cross-cultural trainers create a safe environment where individuals can examine their biases, become aware of their internalized misinformation, and develop perspectives that value diversity.

Each of us, without our conscious consent, has internalized misinformation about people who are different because of race, culture, age, gender, sexual orientation, physical ability, etc. This misinformation becomes evident in conscious and unconscious attitudes and behaviors that devalue and diminish people who are different. Just because someone has limited English-language proficiency, for instance, in no way reflects the person's intellectual capacity or ability to communicate effectively in his or her native tongue.

Similarly, we need to understand and accept that male-female roles in families vary significantly among cultures and ethnic groups. It's common in a counseling session with a white family, for instance, to ask, "Who wants to go first?" The same question to a Chinese family would be met with shock and disbelief. The father always goes first. Moreover, he makes all major decisions for the family.

A counselor who acts without knowing this would lose credibility in the eyes of each family member.

In our counseling, we strive to be nonjudgmental. This becomes challenging when talking with someone who's from a county where it's acceptable for parents to strike children and men to hit wives. Such behavior isn't appropriate here— moreover, it's illegal. Still, we have to be careful not to judge someone who grew up with different cultural standards.

Participants in cultural competency training learn from each other. More often than not it's the people of color who educate whites about things we never knew. For instance, the crisis center is situated in a mostly white, middle class area. Nights and weekends we're one of the few businesses that's open. When our African-American staff come to work then, it's not unusual for a police car to follow them into our parking lot and wait until they enter our front door, making sure they belong. I and other white staff were shocked to learn this. African-American staff were equally shocked that we didn't know it. "Welcome to our world," they said.

MEASURING CULTURAL COMPETENCY

Cultural competency is hard to measure. It's something that you continually strive for; you don't suddenly cross a threshold one day and are there. You're not culturally incompetent on Tuesday and culturally competent on Wednesday. You just keep moving a little farther along in the process. Every time we have a training, I realize how much more I don't know.

According to the "Cultural Competence Continuum" used by many groups around the country and articulated best by a social worker named Terry Cross, there are six levels of cultural competence. The levels apply equally to individuals and to organizations, although an individual within an organization may be at a different level—higher or lower—than the institution itself. Individuals and agencies need to assess where they are on the continuum, then plan effectively to move to higher levels.

The first and lowest level is cultural destructiveness. Agencies at this point have attitudes and practices that are destructive to cultures and, consequently, to individuals in the culture. The most extreme groups actively participate in cultural genocide. Nazi persecution of Jews is one example, white supremacy groups like the Ku Klux Klan is another.

The second level is cultural incapacity. Agencies don't intentionally seek to be culturally destructive; however, they lack the capacity to help minority clients or communities of color. Their attitudes are biased and based on the belief of racial superiority. They maintain a paternal attitude toward "lesser" races that includes discriminatory hiring practices, subtle messages to people of color that they're not valued or welcome, and generally lower expectations of minorities.

The third level is cultural blindness. This is where the crisis center was when I arrived. The expressed philosophy is to provide services that are unbiased.

All people are seen as being the same—in other words, culture and race don't matter. Agencies use a "one-size-fits-all" model, which is a really a model that's designed by and intended for whites. The belief is that if the system works as it should, everyone will be served equally. In practice, though, services become so ethnocentric that they're useless to all people of color except those who fit in easily with whites. Cultural strengths are ignored, assimilation is encouraged, and victims are blamed—oftentimes in subtle ways—for their problems.

A single mother, Latina, with young children, lives with her parents. According to white culture, she should work harder to become self-sufficient. In her culture, extended families are valued. Living with relatives is a plus, not a minus.

Consider the so-called Golden Rule: "Treat others the way you want to be treated." It works well among groups where everyone is from the same culture. It doesn't always work well, however, with diverse cultures. For example, you might believe that it's important to look at the person you're talking to. Yet in many Asian cultures, doing so can be disrespectful or even hostile. That's why a better principle is known as the Platinum Rule. The Platinum Rule says, "Treat others the way *they* want to be treated." It's a good corollary to the Golden Rule in our increasingly diverse world.

The fourth level on the continuum is cultural precompetence. For agencies, this means realizing weaknesses in providing services to racially, culturally, and linguistically diverse groups. Agencies genuinely desire to deliver quality services, and demonstrate a commitment to civil and human rights. Characteristics include hiring diverse staff, conducting needs assessments within diverse communities, improving aspects of service delivery for a specific ethnic or cultural group, and determining what the agency is capable of providing to minority clients and what it's unable to do.

The fifth level is cultural competence. Here, agencies accept and respect differences. Staff and volunteers have a clear understanding of the similarities and differences between racial and cultural groups, including subgroups. When major decisions are made, diverse communities are consulted. Personnel receive the support they need—cultural knowledge, multilingual interpreters, and translated materials—to work effectively cross-culturally.

The last level on the continuum is cultural proficiency. Agencies hold culture in high esteem. Characteristics include: (1) seeking to add to the knowledge base of culturally competent practice by conducting research, developing new treatment or interventions, and publishing and disseminating proven practices; (2) hiring staff and consultants who are specialists in cultural competency; and (3) actively advocating with and on behalf of individuals and families to support the design, implementation, and evaluation of culturally competent services and systems.

WHAT WE'VE LEARNED

Sometimes when it feels as if we're progressing slowly or not at all in becoming more culturally competent, as individuals and as an agency, the trainer asks staff to list the things that we've learned to this point. It's always a constructive exercise because it reminds us how far we've come, which invariably is farther than most people think. Here's a list that my staff developed a year into our training:

- I learned what it means to be white.
- I learned that other ethnic groups also experience racism (in addition to African-Americans).
- I learned (am learning) a common language to talk about diversity issues.
- I learned the difference between "Yes, but . . . " and "Yes, and . . . "
- I learned to appreciate my own culture more.
- I learned that our belief systems are deeply rooted, that each of us thinks our beliefs are right, and that when our beliefs are challenged it creates tension.

Another lesson was learned when the city manager of Orinda, one of the most affluent communities in Contra Costa County, proposed turning the city's old library, which had been replaced by a new $10-million structure, into a homeless shelter. The ensuing public debate pitted high-income, liberal-minded residents who welcomed the shelter against wealthy, conservative-minded residents who opposed it. Wire services across the country picked up the story. A series of hearings was held, attended by our homeless services manager, Minerva, and her assistant, Alella—both African-American women. Hundreds of people turned out, many of them in favor of the shelter, although their voices were lost in the din of opponents who were more vociferous. Most of the time, Minerva and Alella were the only people of color in the auditorium.

They were upset when the shelter was turned down, as was I, although what upset me more was something that I'd never considered before. In preparing for the hearings, Minerva and Alella deliberately dressed more like white people. They left much of their jewelry and their hair extensions at home. They knew that they'd be alone in the audience, even with other people from the crisis center present. I accepted this without thinking about it until afterward, when Minerva, matter-of-factly, explained to me and to other staff what it meant.

"The rest of you come into that big meeting room—or anywhere, for that matter—and you're all there. Nothing about you is missing. A lot of the time, though, I leave the best part of who I am—my ethnicity and culture—outside the door. People don't want to see it so I don't let them. They don't want to hear me talk the way African-American women talk, so I speak more like them. It don't make it right; it's just the way it is."

I thought about the times when I've spoken to all-black congregations. I didn't think beforehand about my attire or how I presented myself. I dressed and talked the same as always. Whereas a week before I was a white man in a white church, now I was a white man in a black church. The setting changed, but I stayed the same. As a member of the dominant culture, I didn't need to leave any part of me outside the door; all of me was there.

In 2004, I was asked to present a paper and lead a ninety-minute workshop on culturally competent crisis counseling at the annual conference of the American

Association of Suicidology. This is the national organization of crisis centers and suicide prevention researchers. Typically, about 700 people attend. I tried to back out of it, saying that as a white man whose agency was far from being culturally proficient, I wasn't an expert on the subject. In addition, the conference was in Miami, which is more culturally diverse than any community in Contra Costa County. It seemed misguided as well as inappropriate for me to talk about something that others were better suited to address.

The conference organizers were persistent, though, saying that crisis center directors around the country would be interested in hearing what my agency was doing. Moreover, even if I wasn't an expert, I'd developed some expertise in moving an agency down the road to cultural competency. Reluctantly, I agreed.

I asked staff, consultants, and other people whose opinions I valued to review the paper and Power Point presentation I developed. Everyone was enthusiastic, which gave me confidence that maybe it would be okay. I was asked to write a blurb on my workshop for the conference program. At least that's easy, I thought, and dashed off a brief description of some of the highlights. In particular, I focused on how cultural competency training was challenging some of our agency's long-standing clinical practices, such as whether we should hand off calls from non-white callers to non-white counselors. I didn't think to have anyone review what I'd written, I just e-mailed it to the person who was putting the program together. When it came out I showed it to Roberto, our trainer and cultural competency coordinator.

"What do you think?" I asked.

Roberto is kind-hearted. When he hesitated, I knew something was wrong.

"It's good," he said. "It's good, only—well, the best thing is to refer to people as what they are, not what they're not."

I looked at him, confused. "What do you mean?"

He pointed to my writing. "You talk about handing off calls from non-white callers to non-white counselors," he said, "as if being white is a standard that others are measured against. It'd be better to say handing off calls from people of color to volunteers of color. That way no one is compared to anyone else."

The mistake was so obvious that once it was pointed out, I couldn't believe I'd made it. "How could I be so dumb?" I said.

Roberto laid his hand on my shoulder. He'd been doing this work for more than twenty years, had been featured in the award-winning documentaries *The Color of Fear* and *Walking Each Other Home*, and had appeared on *Oprah* and *Donahue* to talk about diversity. He also was one of only two students in a graduating class of 750 at Garfield High School in East Los Angeles to attend a four-year college, as well as one of the first Latinos to graduate from Stanford.

"We're all learning," he said softly.

THE GIRAFFE AND THE ELEPHANT

There's a parable written by R. Roosevelt Thomas, another diversity consultant, concerning a giraffe and an elephant. A giraffe builds a beautiful new house with tall ceilings and doorways, high windows, and narrow hallways. The high windows let in lots of natural light and also ensure privacy, while the narrow hallways save valuable interior space. The house is so well designed that it wins a national award. Understandably, the giraffe is proud.

One day the giraffe sees an elephant walking by. The elephant serves with the giraffe on a parent-teacher committee. The giraffe likes the elephant and invites him in to see his house. The elephant is pleased; he likes the giraffe, too. When the elephant tries to enter, though, his body won't fit through the front door.

"That's okay," the giraffe says. "We made this door expandable to accommodate my woodworking equipment."

He releases several latches and the opening is widened. The elephant comes in, then finds that he can't go anywhere. The halls and interior doorways are too narrow.

The giraffe thinks for a minute. "We'll have to make you smaller," he says. He suggests that the elephant take dance classes to slim down.

The elephant knows that this isn't the answer. A house designed for a giraffe won't ever suit an elephant, not unless there are major structural changes.

The story is a metaphor for how white people like me design programs and services with our own culture in mind, thinking that they'll be appropriate for other cultures, too. The giraffe represents the dominant group. It's his house, his design, his rules. The elephant is genuinely welcome; however, the house wasn't built with elephants in mind.

The giraffe makes an effort to accommodate the elephant by enlarging the front door, but that's as far as he goes. He likes his house the way it is; after all, it won an award. His solution after that is to change the elephant because it's really the elephant's problem. If the elephant will just get skinnier, they can become friends.

No matter how much he exercises, though, the elephant will be an elephant. A house built for giraffes won't fit him, just like a house built for elephants isn't right for giraffes.

At the crisis center, we're learning that people, like animals, have different needs. Trying to serve African-Americans, Asians, and Latinos the same as whites doesn't work. We have to understand and appreciate the differences, and tailor our services accordingly. Only in this way can we create a home for all.

CHAPTER ELEVEN

Board Again: Shall We Dance?

When I was young, I liked to talk with my father about World War II. He was a lieutenant in the Army, responsible for dispatching trucks of food, clothing, supplies, and ammunition to the front. He was always a few miles away from the heaviest fighting and rarely carried a gun; still, artillery thundered in the sky and mortar shells burst around him.

I asked if he had any mementos from the war. He showed me a few medals, his dog tags, and several old uniforms. "Anything else?" I said.

He hesitated, then said that he'd brought home a German Luger that was given to him as a present by another soldier. My eyes opened wide. "Do you still have it?"

It was in the house, he said, but he didn't want to show it to me. The next time I was home alone I hunted for it. Within an hour I found it, under some clothes at the back of his closet. I held it in both hands. My heart was pounding with fascination and fear. I'd never seen or held a real gun before. It was small, black, made of metal, and surprisingly heavy—not at all like my toy guns.

I never told my father that I knew where he kept the gun. I never told him or anyone else how I fingered it and pretended to shoot someone—a burglar perhaps. When I put it back, I was careful to leave everything exactly as I had found it.

Within a few weeks I forgot about the gun. I think about it now, though, every time I hear about another suicide. Sixty percent of all suicides and 70 percent of all youth suicides are committed with a firearm. In nearly every instance, the gun was obtained at home. According to the national Centers for Disease Control, the risk of suicide is five times greater in homes that have a gun than in homes that don't. Every year in the United States, there are almost twice as many suicides by firearms as homicides by firearms.

Whenever someone calls our crisis lines—a parent, teacher, or friend—worried that a loved one is exhibiting suicidal tendencies, one of the first questions we ask is, "Is there a gun in the house?" More often than not the answer is yes, but . . .

"Yes, but it's hidden." "Yes, but it's locked up at all times." "Yes, but it's not loaded and the bullets are kept in a separate place."

This may not be enough. If someone—a boy especially—knows that there's a gun in the house, it's almost certain that he knows where it is. If it's locked up, he knows where the key is. Like me, he's held it and imagined shooting it. And if he can access the gun, then there's a good chance that he can find the bullets, even if they're stored elsewhere.

Adolescents tend to have lower self-esteem than adults. They're also more likely to be influenced by personal relationships and idealistic factors. When something goes wrong—they flunk a test, break up with a boyfriend or girlfriend, or are ostracized by peers—easy access to a loaded firearm can be fatal.

Eliminating the means reduces the risk. Get rid of the gun—before it's too late.

Spend a few minutes with Jim Hernandez and there's no doubt that he's been there. Born in Richmond, California to parents who were gang members. Joined a gang himself when he was fifteen. Lived the gang life until he was thirty. Shot and stabbed rival gang members (they lived, to his dismay). Saw his own brother murdered in a fight Jim started.

Today, Hernandez works as an anti-gang specialist, employed by school districts and the Concord Police Department. He hangs out in the streets and runs with current gangs the way he did when he was younger, but there's a difference. Now he helps youths escape the gang lifestyle.

"There are three rules in a gang," he says, ticking them off on his fingers. "Don't talk, don't trust, and don't feel. If you're immature and have low self-esteem, these rules keep you in the gang. They perpetuate the myth that the only way out is by dying, that if you try to walk away, someone will get you."

In fact, says Hernandez, the opposite is true. Stay in a gang and your life expectancy is short. What led Hernandez out of the gang was his brother's death. Determined to seek revenge, he came to realize that it wouldn't bring his brother back, it would just take him down an even darker road. The discovery changed him.

"People get caught up in the visible evidence of gangs," he says, "the colors, the names, the symbols. Crips in blue, the gang name or subset starting with M, the number 13 a symbol because M is the 13th letter of the alphabet. Bloods in red, gang names starting with N, using the symbol XIV because N is the 14th letter of the alphabet."

He shakes his head. "All of that can change. It's unpredictable. To make a difference, to get people out, you have to talk about feelings. I've had therapists tell me, 'I can't talk to these kids. I don't know what their life is like.' I tell them, 'You don't need to know what their life is like. Talk to them about how they feel.'"

When you do this, Hernandez says, the affectation, the hard face gang members put on, the pseudo-self disappears. In its place are depression, grief, loneliness, and fear. Deal with these and individuals will develop the maturity and self-esteem to get out.

It isn't easy. Hernandez has helped hundreds of youths give up gang life. At least ten teens he worked with died, though, killed in fights and payback retaliations.

"When you're young," Hernandez says, "the attraction of a gang, of belonging to a group, is strong even if you come from a family full of love. That's what people don't realize. They think gang members have dysfunctional homes. Many don't. The only dysfunction in their lives is the gang."

Maturity, perhaps developed through marriage and the starting of a family, more likely through the mentoring of an adult figure like Hernandez, changes that. The gang lifestyle becomes negative rather than positive. The myth that you can't walk away becomes false. A future exists.

Hernandez came to the crisis center as a client after his eleven-year-old son died in a playground accident. He completed counseling, then several years later returned and took the training to be a hotline volunteer. A few years later he became a grief counselor as well. Periodically, I talk with him about joining the crisis center's board of trustees. He has a lot to offer: former client; agency volunteer; anti-gang expert; police officer; Latino; plus he has a good way of thinking about life and expressing himself. He says he's honored, but the timing isn't right. There are too many things he wants to wrap up first.

In 2005 his life got even busier. In addition to mentoring dozens of youths, he was besieged by the media after it was learned that he was one of 199 individuals worldwide who'd been nominated for the year's Nobel Peace Prize.

"I suppose you really don't have time to join our board now," I said.

"No," he said. "And yet, I'd really like to. Let me see what I can work out."

I'm still waiting and he's still trying, which speaks to the patience that you have to have sometimes in order to develop a strong board. The best prospects usually are the busiest people. When they commit, they're willing to make changes in their lives in order to do a good job.

Successful boards are constantly evolving. As a result, board recruitment is critical. Many organizations recruit new board members using a shotgun approach. They ask multiple candidates to join the board in hopes that one or more will accept. A better strategy is sometimes called the rifle approach, where you zero in on specific candidates and court them through the recruitment process (shotguns fire a spray of pellets unlike rifles, which fire a single bullet, hence the terminology). In this way, agencies identify skills, talents, and resources needed on the board and discuss strategies for approaching key individuals who meet them. Rather than saying, for instance, "We need someone with marketing experience," the board development team says, "Susan Smith has the kind of marketing experience we need. How can we recruit her?"

Just as hiring good staff is one of the most important tasks of an executive director, so is recruiting good board members one of the most important responsibilities of a board. This is why the top people in the agency need to be on the board development team. They're best able to present the agency's goals and plans for achieving them, and they make the strongest impression on people who are being recruited. Typically, the team consists of the executive director, board chair, fund development director, and two to three other board members.

The process is fairly straightforward. First, the team assesses the agency's needs to determine the skills, perspectives, and clout desired by the board to achieve agency goals. Oftentimes, a matrix is used to plot these. Next, position profiles are developed. Similar to job descriptions for staff, the position profiles describe the expectations and responsibilities of each board slot. After that, a brief summary of the agency is prepared describing the history, mission, programs, finances, future plans, and anticipated outcomes of implementing these plans. This can be incorporated into subsequent marketing materials that are distributed more broadly.

The next step is to identify potential candidates and research them. Some people may be friends of the agency already, but that's not essential. Almost anyone can learn to fall in love with your agency if approached the right way. The key is to recruit leaders. Prospective candidates are contacted and, if interested, a meeting is arranged. Candidates are interviewed by the board development team to see if they match the agency's needs. At the same time, candidates have the opportunity to ask questions about the agency and responsibilities of board members to determine whether it's a good fit from their point of view.

A good strategy is to offer prospective candidates the opportunity to serve on a board committee first. This way they learn about the internal workings and culture of the agency while demonstrating their value as potential board members.

Before being nominated to the board, individuals may be invited to attend a board meeting. Some agencies are reluctant to do this because they worry that candidates will see that the board is less functional than portrayed, or they feel that it'll be awkward to turn down someone if he or she doesn't seem worthy. The first concern clearly isn't valid. Prospective candidates expect honest answers to their questions and will be turned off if they join a board that operates at a different level than what they were told. The second concern is legitimate; however, agencies have to put effectiveness ahead of kindness. It's worse to elect a less-than-ideal candidate to a board than it is to hurt someone's feelings. People get over hurt feelings, but a poor decision can haunt a nonprofit agency for years.

Early on in my tenure at the crisis center, Samuel was elected to the board. I wasn't enthusiastic about it, mainly because I didn't think he added any skills or perspectives that were lacking on the board, nor did he add diversity or financial capacity. He was committed to the agency's mission, though, to the point where he'd started training to answer hotline calls, so I reasoned that he wouldn't do any harm. Unfortunately, I was wrong.

A fair number of callers to any mental health hotline are manipulative. They try to play off one volunteer against another, and derive satisfaction in putting down others. If you understand the root of their psychoses, you make allowances. If not, the criticism can sting.

Oftentimes, a caller with a severe and persistent mental illness repeatedly expresses the same complaint, worry, or hurt. Counselors listen, try to be supportive, yet know at some point that the call isn't going anywhere. Their goal, then, is to end it.

"It sounds like we're going over the same things that we've talked about before," the counselor says. "I've provided all the help I can. Why don't you think about it, and maybe call back in a day or two if there's something new."

"What? You can't talk to me anymore?" the caller says. "Yesterday I talked with Joe, who had the courtesy to listen and he helped me a lot. You shouldn't be answering the phone with that kind of attitude. Who do you think you are, anyway?"

When Samuel started working the lines and callers said this to him, he responded immediately. "I'll tell you who I am; I'm a member of the board of trustees. I'm one of the people who make the rules. What do you say now?"

It was a clear breach of crisis center protocols. In the first place, counselors aren't supposed to disclose personal information about themselves. The focus of the call should be on the caller, not on the person answering the phone. Second, whether or not the counselor is on the board is irrelevant. It doesn't relate to a caller's problem in any way. Third, and most importantly, that kind of response undermines the caller's trust in the agency. It fails to provide comfort or assistance to the caller and, in all likelihood, escalates the caller's anxiety, anger, and paranoia. Granted, there are times when callers are so self-centered and illogical that the natural reaction, even for the most compassionate person, is to voice frustration. Hotline counselors must restrain themselves, however. They need to control the call and shouldn't take abuse; at the same time, the crisis center doesn't exist so that counselors can assert superiority over callers.

Clinical staff warned Samuel that this practice had to end. Before that even happened, though, another problem surfaced. Two young, attractive women on staff came into my office, closed the door, and said that Samuel was making uncomfortable comments to them. He told one woman that she "looked like a million bucks" but that she'd "look like five million bucks" if she wore pumps. He told the other woman when she was wearing a slitted skirt, "Finally you're showing some leg."

In other circumstances, Samuel's remarks might have seemed like innocent flirting; here they were inappropriate and violated the agency's personnel policies. I'd never had to deal with the issue of sexual harassment before, much less harassment by a board member. I asked both women what they wanted. They said that they wouldn't feel comfortable being alone with Samuel at the agency, but that all they wanted was for him to stop behaving that way. I asked each to give me a written statement, which they did, and I received permission to use their names in talking with Samuel about this.

Before Samuel and I met, I consulted with a lawyer. She said that my proposed course of action made sense and that I should document everything, which I was planning to do.

I told Samuel about the complaints and gave him a written summary. Neither of the women was identified, although he knew whom I was referring to. I said that his remarks violated our personnel policies, and even though he was a volunteer and wasn't bound to our personnel policies the way a paid employee was, as a board member his personal conduct should be at least as high as that of any staff.

"Being the executive director, I don't have authority over a member of the board," I said. "It's my responsibility to ensure a healthy, safe, and supportive environment, though, so I must insist that while you're here, you refrain from making comments of this nature. If you're unable to do so, and any other staff member or volunteer reports this to me, then I'll have to bring the matter to the attention of the board."

Samuel was contrite. He said that, in retrospect, he realized his remarks were inappropriate. He promised to cease immediately from making any further comments like this, and asked me to convey his apologies to the two women. He also promised to be more professional in the way he handled hotline calls. The matter was closed.

GOVERNORS AND SUPPORTERS

Typically, board members play a dual role. As governors, they protect the public interest by monitoring the agency's work, ensuring that the agency complies with legal and contractual requirements, and hiring and evaluating the executive director. As supporters, they raise money for the agency, contribute special skills (financial, legal, marketing, etc,), and serve as ambassadors to the community.

Oftentimes, the two roles conflict. When they're governors, board members stand above staff and are the ultimate boss. When they're supporters, they assist staff, serving as helpers. It's easy for these dual roles to create problems in an agency.

Jan Masaoka, former executive director of Compass Point, a nonprofit management center based in San Francisco, says, "Some boards become so excited about their roles as governors that they mistake governance for close supervision of management and begin meddling in minor management affairs. In other cases, as boards govern more, they shirk their support role. The challenge is to fulfill *both* roles, not simply switch from one to the other."

Masaoka cautions agencies to be leery of "the ideal board member." This is the person who's a generous donor and accomplished fundraiser, who has marketing savvy and political connections, who adds diversity, loves the agency, is liked by staff and other board members, and in general "fits in." The problem is that these qualities, which make someone an excellent supporter, don't translate into a good governor.

For instance, unless board members use the agency's services in some way, either as clients or as professionals who refer clients (case managers, social workers, clergy, etc.), they don't have independent knowledge to draw on. As a result, they rely on staff for information.

In addition, nonprofit agencies differ from large corporations and small businesses in fundamental ways, which board members may not realize. A company can discontinue an unprofitable product line or service and few people will care, yet if a child care center closes there are social consequences. Moreover, people in the for-profit world often are unfamiliar with fundraising costs, volunteer management, and the concept of governance by consensus.

Many executive directors don't want an active, governing board. "Supporters help the manager get the job done; governors often make the job harder," Masaoka says. "It is not in any manager's personal interest to make his or her job harder."

Nonprofit leaders rarely experience personal consequences as a result of poor governance. Even when an agency is hit by scandal or goes out of business with its mission unfulfilled, the careers and reputations of board members rarely are affected. The public quickly forgets anyone's role in the agency's demise, and the executive director usually is able to find another job. It's the community served by the agency that suffers.

The surprising thing is how well most boards govern in a crisis, even boards that have existed largely to rubber-stamp the recommendations of staff. Board members may have made a serious effort before, reading information sent to them, attending meetings, and participating in discussions. After a crisis, though, they go much further, meeting in emergency session, pouring over financial records, hiring outside investigators and analysts, and consulting donors and clients. No longer do they depend on staff for information. They realize that they need their own informants, and develop the sources.

The question is: If boards can govern effectively in a crisis, why can't they do it all the time? One reason is because board members tend to be busy people who aren't expected during normal times to put the needs of the agency above other interests, such as their careers and families. Most agencies limit the frequency and duration of board meetings and minimize other responsibilities of the board in order to reduce the demands on each person's time. If they didn't, many people might not be willing to serve.

Another reason, though, is because of a natural desire among people to avoid conflict. Boards that take their governance and oversight roles seriously ask uncomfortable questions. "Is a major reason why we're failing to meet financial goals because fundraising staff are less competent than they should be?" "Is the executive director over-compensated relative to leaders of similar agencies?" "If the agency's services are so important, how come none of my friends or neighbors has ever heard of them?"

During normal times, tension is considered bad and a smooth, working partnership among board and staff is considered good. Only during a crisis do board members ask tough questions. "In normal times," Jan Masaoka says, "boards need to learn how to use the authority they are willing to assert in times of crisis."

FIXING BROKEN BOARDS

The most common reason why a board is ineffective is because board roles are poorly defined and people receive insufficient training to do the job. An assumption is made that individuals know how to be board members when, in fact, they don't. Agencies provide minimal orientation and few opportunities for board members to develop needed skills. People are asked to raise money, for instance, when the agency lacks a fully-developed fundraising plan, hasn't carefully screened its prospects, doesn't have a solicitation strategy, and is still working on support materials like case statements and fact sheets. A consultant may be brought in to provide special training to board members with the idea that this will propel them to become successful fundraisers. It's like teaching someone to prepare an elegant meal, though, without providing the ingredients. Individuals may know what to do and be willing to do it; however, you're a long way from eating. Some important components are missing.

Fixing a broken board can be as simple as providing training, as straightforward as clarifying responsibilities and expectations, or as precise as formally evaluating each member annually to instill accountability. It can be as challenging as replacing or reinventing the current board system, or as revolutionary as changing the board and organizational culture. Florence Green, executive director of the California Association of Nonprofits (CAN), equates being a board member to being a parent.

"There are a million classes, books, workshops, and bits of advice passed on from those who have done it before us (and even from those who haven't!)," she says. "But in the end, most of us learn how to be a board member by being a board member. If we're lucky, we learn how to do it well. If we're unlucky, we don't—and the organization suffers."

She says that fixing a broken board requires openly acknowledging that the board is broken, breaking the cycle of bad governance as quickly as possible, establishing board orientation procedures, focusing attention on what needs to be done, and creating a culture that promotes effective board performance. Change can't be imposed from outside, it has to come from within the agency. Also, it doesn't happen overnight. New people may need to join the board to start the process or move it along.

One topic that's often discussed is term limits. Many agencies have limits for board members and believe wholeheartedly in their value. Typically, board members are elected to a three-year term and can serve two consecutive terms before they have to step down from the board. Other agencies don't have limits and would never consider implementing them.

The primary benefit of term limits is that they keep an agency fresh and dynamic. Oftentimes, the longer people serve on a board, the more rooted they are in the past and more resistant they are to change. New people bring new ideas, new perspectives, and new energy. They're less likely to develop cliques, more likely to have an open mind, and more likely to focus on the future.

Another benefit of term limits is that desirable candidates may be more willing to join the board if the commitment has an end date. Achievers have lots of things that they want to do in their lives. When they come into an agency, their goal is to understand it, improve it in some way, and move on. They don't see themselves tied to one cause or agency forever.

The argument against term limits is that they're arbitrary and can force key people to leave an agency before they're ready to part. No agency sets term limits on executive staff, so why restrict the tenures of board members who have learned their job, perform it well, and want to continue? Good leaders are hard to come by.

Proponents of term limits argue that valuable board members can be invited back after a year off the board, so the separation doesn't have to be permanent. My experience is that it might as well be. After a year's hiatus, effective board members lose the emotional attachment to an agency and find other things to do. Moreover, if term limits are such a good idea because they promote turnover, why circumvent them by allowing people to return?

To me, term limits are counterproductive if the board is functioning well, and needed if the board is dysfunctional. A functioning board has dedicated and talented people whose services it would lose after a period of time under term limits. A dysfunctional board, on the other hand, needs to transition "problem" people off the board (people who don't attend meetings, who don't contribute financially, who add nothing to board discussions, who have no special skills, who are contentious). Term limits is one way to do it.

At the crisis center, new board members are elected to a three-year term. At the end of it, the executive committee evaluates the person's performance. If he or she has done a good job and wants to continue, the committee recommends a second three-year term. Thereafter, active and valuable board members are elected to one-year terms. Individuals can serve an unlimited number of one-year terms; however, they're evaluated annually to make sure that they're still contributing. The pluses of this system, I've found, are that the agency continues to benefit from their expertise, and after six years board members are more comfortable making one-year commitments than three-year ones. It works for us.

OPERATING WITH INTEGRITY

The single most important quality of any board—and of any nonprofit executive—is to establish by example and attitude an atmosphere of integrity. Do this and most of the problems that plague dysfunctional agencies cease to exist. There still may be conflicts; however, everyone operates with the same goal: to make decisions that they believe are in the best interests of the agency.

One way that agencies institutionalize a culture of integrity and responsibility is to establish disclosure as a normal practice. Board members disclose when they have conflicts of interest and excuse themselves from the discussion and from voting.

It's standard operating procedure for agencies to have written conflict of interest policies in order to avoid both actual and perceived conflicts. Before or immediately after someone is elected to the board, he or she makes a written disclosure of interests and relationships that could result in a conflict of interest. It may be a simple declaration or a detailed accounting depending on the extent of the person's affiliations in the community and the breadth of the agency's influ-ence. The agency keeps it on file, and the information is updated throughout the person's tenure. Whenever there's a possibility that a board member or his or her business, close associates, or family could benefit from activities of the nonprofit, the disclosure is reviewed. If the agency plans major purchases, competitive bids are obtained to ensure that prices and services are comparable in the event that a board member participates in the bidding.

A common situation meriting disclosure is when two representatives of an agency—two employees or a board member and staff member—begin dating. The relationship may be in a formative stage; however, it potentially impacts the agency and should be brought to the attention of the executive director or, if the executive director is involved, to the executive committee of the board.

I neither encourage nor discourage office romances. It'd be hypocritical of me to discourage them because my wife and I had one. Neither of us expected it or had had a similar experience before; still, we fell in love on the job. While it'd be neater and cleaner from a managerial perspective if work relationships didn't become personal, it's hard to complain when two people find each other, especially if they've traveled a rocky road. In many respects, work offers the best opportunity to meet new people, and individuals who are attracted to the nonprofit sector tend to be compassionate and caring so it's natural that connections develop. I just try to be alert to them, and expect everyone to act professionally.

9/11

When terrorists attacked on September 11, 2001, I was just waking up. It was shortly after 6 A.M. California time, and my alarm clock sounded. It was tuned to an all-news radio station and a reporter at the scene was describing the disbelief, confusion, and horror of the first plane hitting the World Trade Center. No one knew how or why it happened. Then the second plane struck.

"Oh, my god," the reporter said. "There's another—oh, my god—another plane just hit the other tower."

Suzan and I jumped out of bed and raced to the TV. Within seconds we saw the now familiar, terrifying footage of commercial airliners, full of passengers, ramming into the twin towers, followed minutes later by the attack on the Pentagon and, an hour or so after that, the downing of the fourth airliner in Pennsylvania. The collapse of both towers, which no one ever imagined, and the agony of so many new deaths, were still ahead.

It was something that, along with millions of other Americans, we'll never forget. In the days, weeks, months, and now years that have passed since then, our lives have become divided. There was the period before 9/11 and the period after. It's not so different from my parents' generation in which the defining moment was Pearl Harbor. There was the period before the attack and the period after, the time of peace followed by the time of war. Granted, the circumstances were different. Few people second-guessed Franklin D. Roosevelt's decision to enter the war, either at the time or later in history. The target was clear, the reason obvious, the strategy well conceived. Nevertheless, for those who lived through it, the attack signaled a clear demarcation. You served in the military or you didn't. You saw action overseas or you didn't. You lost a loved one in the fighting or you didn't. Had it happened more recently, Pearl Harbor probably would be known today as 12/7.

Being 3,000 miles away, I didn't feel the same way about 9/11 as people living on the East Coast. I couldn't. Their everyday world was shattered. I felt terrible, but went to work and came home as usual. That didn't mean I was oblivious to the impact of 9/11, though. Far from it. The brother of one of my wife's business friends was a passenger on the Pennsylvania plane that crashed. A Contra Costa man also was on that flight, and he initiated the passenger revolt with the now immortal words, "Let's roll." Local police officers and firefighters exchanged their standard-issue headgear for New York Police Department and Fire Department of New York caps to honor those who fell and show their pride in being professionally related.

Two members of the crisis center board of trustees were directly impacted by 9/11. James was the western regional marketing manager of a financial firm that was headquartered at the World Trade Center. Forty-two of the top fifty officers of the company died, and all of its most important records were destroyed. In the blink of an eye, the company ceased to exist. Not only did James lose many close business associates, he suddenly was unemployed, with a wife and children to support.

The other board member, Melvin, worked for the San Francisco Bay Area Chapter of the American Red Cross. He grew up in New York and, following 9/11, was sent to Manhattan to assist with relief efforts there. I never saw him again. A month later, he sent me a short note formally resigning from the board. He apologized for not having had time to write sooner and said that, considering how much work there was to do, he'd probably be in New York "for several years, at least."

I was sorry to see him go. I had personally recruited Melvin to the board. In addition to his Red Cross experience, he had formerly worked for a large nonprofit agency dedicated to ending homelessness in New York City. He had a master's degree in public policy from Harvard, and an undergraduate degree from New York University. Also, he and James were the only African-Americans on our board at the time. The diversity and cultural competency they brought, in addition to their knowledge and expertise, were invaluable.

More than anything, I appreciated Melvin's attitude. He'd never been on a board, and was determined to do a good job. To this end, he did something that I've never had another board member do, before or since. He made appointments to meet with each of the crisis center's program managers to learn about their work. The meetings were scheduled on separate days so that he could focus his attention on one program at a time. At first staff were surprised and somewhat skeptical. I told them that Melvin wanted to know as much as he could about the crisis center so that he could make informed decisions on the board. Any reluctance people had at first to talk with him quickly disappeared. He was interested and engaging, asking the kinds of questions that staff loved to answer because it put their program in the best light possible. Afterward, they wanted to know why other board members weren't equally motivated to meet with them, and suggested that this be one of the steps in the board's orientation process. I agreed that it was a good idea, although I knew that the most I could do was suggest it. Board members had to take the initiative on their own.

After I received his note, I wrote back to Melvin and thanked him for writing, especially when his life was so busy. I expressed regret that he couldn't continue on our board, and wished him well. I also shared a few stories from our hotlines of people who had called and were grieving someone dead or missing, or afraid that more attacks were imminent, or just feeling sad in general. I told him how we approached these calls, and asked if he agreed with our strategy, which was intended to provide context for what had happened and comfort to callers whose anxiety levels were high.

The object of terrorism isn't to hurt a relatively small number of people. It's to promote fear and cause psychological damage to millions of others. The most effective way to paralyze a nation is to initiate random violence, violence that can't be predicted and, therefore, is hard to prevent. This is why the public isn't informed about bomb threats and other dangers thwarted every day by the police and Federal Bureau of Investigation.

That said, although we live in an age where terrorist acts seem more frequent and more deadly, they're still uncommon occurrences. It makes sense to be wary, yet people face greater risks to their health and safety every time they get in a car. We accept that risk, just as we accept the risk of an earthquake in California, hurricane in the Gulf Coast, or tornado in the Midwest, because if we didn't, our lives would be nonstop doom.

Admittedly, it's hard to put terrorism in perspective when we see graphic images of planes flying into buildings and buildings collapsing. What do we tell our children? That there are people in other parts of the world who don't like Americans? That they dislike us so intensely they're willing to kill us for no apparent reason and, in some instances, die themselves in the process?

With older children, parents can discuss U.S. influence abroad and the fact that, except for a small number of terrorist actions, the American mainland has never been attacked. Many people who live daily with the effects of war resent the United States for engaging in military conflicts abroad when foreign bombs have never exploded on our soil. While U.S. planes, ships, and land-based artillery unleash deadly assaults in the Middle East, soldiers' families are safe at home, thousands of miles from harm.

Young children need to be protected from excessive exposure to real-life horrors shown in the news. Still, children are entitled to the truth as we come to know it. Parents should encourage children to talk about their feelings, yet also recognize that it's okay not to have answers. Parents, like children, aren't experienced dealing with a tragedy as unique and unexpected as 9/11.

One thing that's critical is not to generalize. Terrorist acts are the work of a small group of people with a particular mission. Other people from the same culture or country shouldn't be held responsible, just as Japanese-Americans shouldn't have been held responsible for Pearl Harbor. They're as much victims as anyone else.

I don't know if Melvin ever received my letter. He probably moved a number of times the first few months he was in New York, from one temporary address to another. Even if he didn't move, it's unlikely that my letter was delivered because the city's postal system was immobilized. Either way, he never communicated with me again. Perhaps it was just as well. He had an important job to do, as did I, and our paths weren't likely to cross. Like so much else, his relationships with the crisis center and with me were casualties of 9/11.

CHAPTER TWELVE

Staff Again: Ringmaster of the Circus

I read an interview once with a man who worked many years in the nonprofit sector, then took a government job. When asked how it was going, he said that he enjoyed dealing with street paving companies. I thought he was joking, but he was serious.

"When street pavers come into my office," he said, "they tell me exactly what they'll do: they'll pave a specific number of miles, at a specific thickness, meeting specific standards, for a specific price. After years of dealing with the vagueness of public service agencies, it's a refreshing change."

It's true that those of us who aren't street pavers have a harder time measuring our work, especially if our focus is on preventing something from happening—abuse, neglect, drug use, violence, death. How does anyone truly measure a happier child, a long-term health strategy, a safer environment? The effects may not be visible for years—and then only after extensive studies.

In the field of suicide prevention, a person might think that a good way to gauge success is by the suicide rate. If it goes down, prevention efforts are working.

The problem is that outside factors like the economy have a major impact. There are always more suicides during a recession than during boom times. Also, suicide rates are flawed. If someone resides in one county and takes his or her life in another county, the death may be attributed to the second county.

It doesn't help that suicide is underreported. A driver who crashes into a tree, drives off a cliff, or runs into another vehicle may have fallen asleep at the wheel, lost control, or planned the accident—it's not always clear. Because of the stigma, as well as for insurance reasons, family members often exert strong pressure so that questionable deaths are ruled accidents rather than suicides.

We handle more than 1,000 suicide calls per year at the crisis center. Some callers are ideating (thinking about suicide), while others have a loaded gun or lethal dose of medication and serious intent. Will they follow through?

Suicide can be an impulsive act, especially among youth. It's important to buy time. That's why what matters most to us is the number of suicidal people who are still alive one month after calling us. A month can be forever.

By checking coroner's records, we know that everyone who called out hotlines last year expressing suicidal thoughts was still alive thirty days later. Is this precise and unquestionable? Not compared with a street paver's work. Is it meaningful? You bet.

It'd be nice if human suffering was as easy to measure as asphalt, and building hope was as tangible as building a road. That it's not doesn't bother me. The most important things in life—love, hope, faith, family, friends—can't be measured.

For years the crisis center provided grief counseling at schools and businesses following the death of a student or adult. Little did we know that one day we'd need the service ourselves.

In 2004 Judy, our crisis line manager of twenty years, died at age sixty-eight. Although she'd been battling cancer for months, it was in remission—or so all of us believed. She continued to work at the crisis center up until the end. On her deathbed she worried about holes in the next week's hotline schedule.

As a girl in Pittsburgh, Judy lived literally next door to TV's Mr. Rogers. Everybody's favorite make-believe neighbor was Judy's neighbor in real life. As an adult, she had a real estate license, a marriage and family therapy license, and two outside counseling practices. She also gave birth to four children in five years—once Judy set her mind on something, she didn't hesitate.

Wherever she and her children lived quickly became known as Mrs. Judy's Neighborhood. Everyone wanted to come to Judy's house. If Judy walked in to find her kids and their friends making a fort out of sheets in the living room, she'd say, "That looks like fun!" Then she'd go to the linen closet and get the sheets on the top shelf that the kids couldn't reach and suggest that the fort be extended into the dining room. Afterward, it would stay up for days, and the family would play games and sometimes eat meals inside it.

She never believed in curfews. "If it's nine o'clock and you're with the wrong people, come home," she advised her children. "On the other hand, if it's 2 A.M., you're having fun, and everything's okay, why not stay a little longer? Curfews are so arbitrary."

Similarly, she didn't understand the concept of grounding. "Why should I force a child to stay home if he or she doesn't want to? That sounds like punishment for me, not them."

"You can imagine how difficult it was for us," said Kathleen, the youngest of Judy's three daughters, at Judy's memorial service. "We had nothing to rebel against."

One could find Judy at the crisis center anytime—nights, weekends, it didn't matter. Her joyful spirit brightened our days, and her words of wisdom—affectionately called Judyisms—provided perspective. "Just breathe and know that things are as they should be," she'd say. "Stay present, trust the process, and the answers will come when they're meant to."

One of the hardest things I've ever done was speak at Judy's memorial service. More than 300 people attended, nearly all of them touched in a profound way by Judy's kindness.

I shared the story from my first staff meeting when I asked staff members to introduce themselves, turned to the person on my left—who happened to be Judy—to start and the first words out of her mouth were, "I don't do change."

People laughed. Judy was always happy with the way things were, yet adjusted easily to anything.

One year I couldn't afford to give raises to staff, and the next year I could only afford 2 to 3 percent raises. I called Judy into my office, said how much I valued her dedication to the crisis center and how much I respected her as a person, and apologized that the best I was able to do was give her a 3 percent raise. Embarrassed, I handed her a sheet of paper showing her current salary and the new salary.

Judy looked at the paper and her eyes got wide. "I've never made so much money in my life!" she said. The next week she made a personal donation to the crisis center in the amount of her entire raise.

I concluded my remarks quickly, trying to get through before breaking down. "It hurts to say good-bye," I said. "At the same time, we're grateful for all of the opportunities we had to say hello—and so much more. Our lives are ever richer because we now carry a part of Judy with us."

Judy's daughter, Kathleen, was last. Kathleen told about their fortresses made from sheets and of her first driving lessons (Judy was an impatient driver; if a light stayed red too long and no one was around, she bolted through). Kathleen also told of recent years, of Judy playing on the floor with her grandchildren and of the time that Judy disappeared while all of them were at a park. Family members found her a half hour later gleefully going down a slide with a bunch of children she'd just met.

They were wonderful stories, and wonderful memories. Through it all we heard Judy saying, "Miss me, and let me go." That was easier said than done. The Monday after she died was the first day in all my years at the crisis center that I didn't want to come to work. Throughout the week, volunteers pulled into our parking lot and couldn't bring themselves to get out of their cars. A pall hung over the agency. No one wanted to erase Judy's name from our in/out board. People wore lime green clothing because that was Judy's favorite color.

Without Judy, the workplace was different. Some volunteers offered to take additional shifts as a tribute to her. Others lost interest and stopped volunteering. Staff snapped at each other, angered by little things that masked a deeper hurt and angry at Judy for leading all of us to think that she was healthier than she was. A week before her death, bedridden and weighing next to nothing, Judy said to me, "Don't give my job away. I'm coming back." I wanted desperately to believe it, denying what I knew to be true.

Near the end, Judy said that she wanted donations made in her memory to fund an appreciation event for agency volunteers.

"I want the volunteers to have a big party on me," she said.

So many donations were received that we had funding for volunteer parties for several years. Donors' names filled a full page in our newsletter. One donor ordered a tile in Judy's memory for our Wall of Caring, which is a large display of specially-inscribed clay tiles that adorns our lobby. The tile said simply, "She who dies helping the most people wins."

Shortly after Judy died, three program managers left. One was in tears because she didn't want to go, but her husband had accepted a job in New York. The second had a sudden opportunity to move to Colorado and be near grandchildren. The third wasn't able to function effectively in Judy's absence and decided to resign.

Their departures added to the overall malaise; at the same time they presented opportunities. It was odd; for nearly three years there hadn't been a single vacancy at any level. Now in the course of a few months there were four, and all were important positions. Moreover, they totaled fifty years of experience at the crisis center. That was a lot to lose.

The belief among most funders as well as the general public is that low turnover is good. If the staff is stable, programs and administration usually are stable. This is reassuring to people who have invested or are considering investing in an agency.

Low turnover can be as bad as high turnover, though, albeit in a different way. High turnover usually indicates management problems. People are hired and either don't work out, which calls into question the judgment of the person doing the hiring, or quit because the job, the agency, or the internal culture is different than what they were led to believe. Low turnover implies general satisfaction among staff—people aren't actively looking for work elsewhere—but the downside is that staff can stagnate. People look at things the same old way. New employees, in contrast, bring new ideas and new energy. They make the workplace alive and vibrant. What you gain by having the same people in the same jobs is consistency. People know what to do and what to expect from others. What you lose is vitality. People aren't as compelled to question longstanding practices. No one suggests new ways of delivering services. New personalities aren't introduced into the mix.

It took eighteen long months before all of the changes at the crisis center were completed. There were moments every day when each of us—staff and volunteers—was reminded of Judy, and we laughed or grew quiet based on the memory. Gradually, the melancholy wore off, replaced by a renewed sense of optimism. New staff came on board. A record number of people enrolled in our next hotline and grief counseling training classes. New program opportunities surfaced. Things were beginning to look up.

AN UNEXPECTED WINDFALL

A month after Judy died, we received an unexpected windfall. A U.S. district court judge phoned me to say that the crisis center was a potential beneficiary in a class action lawsuit that was close to being settled after ten years of litigation. As part of the settlement, about thirty nonprofit agencies, including the crisis center, had the opportunity to receive a charitable donation. The judge asked each agency to submit a single-page description of what we would do with a hypothetical gift of $50,000.

Several weeks later, representatives from each agency were invited to court. When we arrived, the judge said that we'd be given three minutes to answer two questions: What is the single greatest accomplishment in your agency's history, and what will be your greatest accomplishment in the next ten years?

I said that the crisis center's biggest accomplishment was always being there. Twenty-four hours a day, 365 days a year, for more than forty years, people in the community could count on us; they weren't alone. Despite budget cuts, agency moves, power outages, deaths, and more, we'd always answered the call. Tens of thousands of people had been helped.

Regarding the second question, I said, "The easy, flip answer is to say that in ten years our greatest accomplishment will be that we're still answering the call. Considering how hard it is for any nonprofit agency to survive today, much less operate around the clock, that would be an accomplishment. Frankly, though, it's not enough."

I described the crisis center's current work in making our services more culturally competent. In ten years, I said, our twenty-four-hour hotlines, grief counseling program, and other services will be valued as highly by African-Americans, Asians, and Latinos as they are today by whites. I mentioned a couple of specific things we were doing, then time was up.

A few weeks later, I received the judge's ruling. As a preamble to the disposition of funds, she wrote, "While these charities serve what some would describe as society's wrong—poverty, abuse, illness, crime—they are also a sign of what is right with our community. These charities feed our hungry, educate our children, shelter our elderly, aid people in crisis, serve as an example of what community service is, and bring hope to all. The Court believes that distribution of the settlement funds will facilitate that hope."

It was the next three sentences, though, that really moved me. They explained that the crisis center would receive $100,000 per year for three years. At least 25 percent was stipulated to further the development of our multicultural services, "a goal which the Court found to be both well-thought out and particularly useful in our diverse community."

It was the crisis center's largest gift ever. I was overwhelmed with gratitude. I also wondered whether Judy was looking after us.

CONFLICT MANAGEMENT

Whenever two or more people are together, the potential exists for conflict. Strong agencies have mechanisms for dealing with it effectively, while agencies that don't deal well with conflict can be torn apart by it. If conflict isn't managed, coalitions form. People have their own interests and feel separate from other parts of the agency. Individuals become isolated and believe that they have to fend for themselves because others can't be counted on. Productivity and job satisfaction diminish. Employees don't cooperate, share resources, or work together for common goals. There's less problem solving; after all, why help solve someone else's problem when he or she won't help solve yours?

When conflict is managed, employees are motivated. Individuals feel part of a group that values and supports them. People cooperate to attain agency goals. Change is accepted. Employees are more likely to identify problems, bring them to the attention of others, offer solutions, and work to implement them.

Conflict management is minimizing the negative effects such as anger, stress, hurt feelings, resentment, grudges, and blame. The first step is to cool down. Stop the action and decide what you want and what you need. They may be different things. Take deep breaths. It's easier to assess a situation and your options when you're calm and composed.

The next step is to define the problem. Understand the other person's perspective by asking open-ended questions, listening actively, showing empathy, using "I" messages ("I think" rather than "You may think . . . "), stating your feelings and needs, and being direct. Conflicts can be resolved most effectively when people understand each other's point of view and, especially, the other person's feelings.

After that, strive for a solution. Be flexible and willing to negotiate. If what you're doing isn't working, try something else.

In one of our agency's workshops on conflict management, I had a disagreement with the crisis center's grief counseling director. Roberto, our trainer, used the opportunity to model effective conflict management skills.

At that time, Susie had been in the position for more than twenty-five years. She was widely recognized as one of the foremost death educators in the country. I considered her passionate, knowledgeable, dependable, organized, resourceful, and efficient. She also was protective of her program and didn't want to talk about any deficiencies it might have, no matter how small. This was a source of frustration to me. She eagerly jumped into conversations about how other programs could be improved, often offering good advice, but was quick to cut off dialog when suggestions were made regarding the grief counseling program. One day, during staff training, it happened again.

Roberto asked staff to suggest a real-life conflict that people could role-play to practice effective conflict management skills. I thought of a conflict that had happened recently in our grief counseling program between a female client and Susie. The woman's husband had died several years earlier and, because she never adequately addressed her grief, she wanted to join our support group that was starting for people who had lost spouses and partners. Susie admitted her, which proved to be a mistake. The woman would interrupt other group members, make dismissive remarks, and try constantly to bring the conversation back to her grief, ignoring the needs of everyone else. After the first night, Susie took her aside and told her that if she wasn't able to be more respectful of others, she'd have to leave. The woman didn't understand, thought the group was there to support her, and felt rejected by people whom she believed should have been more compassionate.

If anything, the situation became even worse the second night. During a break, Susie told the woman that she was being disruptive and needed to go. The woman refused. There was a brief exchange of words, Susie threatened to call the police, and the woman stormed out. The following day, Susie told me about it because she thought I might receive a complaint from the woman.

"I think this is a relevant scenario to role-play," I said. "It's easy to understand the points of view of both people. There's no real middle ground so consensus is unlikely, which makes it a richer subject to explore than one where the solution is clear-cut. Moreover, it's the type of situation that can occur in any of our programs, so all of us can relate to it."

Susie disagreed. "There's nothing to discuss," she said. "It was a one-time incident and I handled it. End of story."

"Just because it's over doesn't mean we can't discuss it," I said. "We're looking for an example of a real-life conflict, and this seems appropriate." I added, "No one's going to second-guess your actions if that's what worries you."

Susie started to respond, but Roberto stopped her. "Can you tell John what you just heard him say?" he said.

Susie paraphrased my remarks. She was a good listener and accurately synthesized what I'd said. After she finished, Roberto asked me whether what Susie heard me say was what I thought I'd said.

"Yes," I replied.

Roberto nodded to Susie and she said why she thought my suggestion was a poor one. "We discuss specific clients and cases in supervision all the time; however, I'm not comfortable talking about a client or former client with the whole staff. It's not because of confidentiality; no one else knows enough to be able to identify this particular woman. It just doesn't feel right. There are lots of other things we can talk about. If you want to talk about a client, talk about someone we don't know, like someone who calls the homeless hotline and we're not able to help them."

I knew that Roberto was going to ask me to repeat what Susie said. Even so, once she started talking I couldn't wait for her to finish so that I could respond. In my eagerness to rebut her I didn't listen fully, and I didn't do a good job capturing her comments.

Roberto asked Susie whether I'd heard what she'd said. "Some of it," she replied.

"What didn't he hear?"

"I don't think he heard the first part, about not wanting to share the circumstances of a specific client with everyone on staff."

Roberto nodded. "Can you tell that part to John again?"

Susie did. This time I listened and repeated her comments accurately.

We continued in that vein. I acknowledged the importance of client confidentiality and the fact that this happened only once. My real concern was that every time someone mentioned anything having to do with the grief counseling program, Susie didn't want to hear it—unless it was praise.

Susie repeated what I said, admitting that she was protective of her program. She didn't distinguish between being appropriately protective and overly protective, which I noted when I reiterated what she said. We left it at that, knowing that we needed to continue the conversation, but outside a staff meeting.

Roberto asked us how we felt. Susie said that it was awkward for her to argue with her boss. "I want to keep working here," she said.

I said that it was awkward for me, too, in part because I was the boss. "I was conscious of not wanting to use my position of power to dictate the outcome," I said.

Other staff commented on the way Roberto facilitated the dialog. He prompted both of us to focus on what was being said, to reflect, to summarize, and to appreciate each other's willingness to work on this issue. Afterward, I knew that I would handle conflict differently in the future.

BARBARA AND PEG

One of the biggest sources of conflict at the crisis center seemed, on the face of it, inconsequential. It was our dog policy.

It wouldn't occur to most agencies to allow dogs. Some people are allergic to them, others are afraid of them, and a few just don't like them. Even dog lovers can be surprised when they walk into an office and suddenly are confronted by a dog.

Because the crisis center operates twenty-four hours a day, people work nights and weekends. For them, dogs offer protection and security, especially after hours. Dogs also offer therapeutic benefits. Some teens in our youth grief groups have a hard time opening up to peers or to adult counselors, but melt in a minute when a dog is present. A dog-friendly agency also feels welcoming in general, less like an office and more like a home.

The crisis center had always permitted dogs, and most of the time volunteers and staff appreciated it. The only real problem was Peg, Barbara's dog.

Before she came to the crisis center, Barbara was a teacher in a tough, inner-city high school. Educated and also street smart, she cared about her students and could handle virtually anything they threw at her. Dealing with school administrators was another matter, though. Barbara wasn't one to do things by the book, and her independence irritated people higher up. Finally, she decided to try something else. Because she was a night owl, preferring to sleep in the afternoon and then only for three or four hours, she was interested in our job announcement seeking someone to answer crisis calls from midnight to 8 A.M. every day.

It proved to be a perfect fit. Barbara could use her experiences and natural empathy to provide counseling and support, there was minimal supervision, and the late-night solitude between phone calls gave her opportunities to think fondly of her husband, Bob, who had died several years earlier. The latter was important because arthritis and carpal tunnel syndrome had stopped her from doing scrimshawing, a favorite hobby. On occasion, when coerced, she'd bring in samples of her work, which were extraordinary—museum quality.

Shortly after she started at the crisis center, Barbara decided to run for city council of a local municipality. She was upset about a variety of issues and determined that the best way to influence the outcome was to have a say in the vote. She'd never run for elective office before, and some people were put off by her casual attire and earthy manner, which was direct, without tact, and often profane. Others found her lack of pretense refreshing. She said what she believed regardless of the audience. With the help of friends who campaigned for her, Barbara won.

For the next twelve years—six terms—she served on the council. She also worked full-time at the crisis center. She'd finish her hotline shift in the morning, then go off and do city work. It was a grueling schedule, especially for someone getting on in years. Her biggest comfort was her dog, a three-legged white terrier named Peg that Barbara had rescued.

Peg loved coming to work with Barbara, and Barbara loving having her there. Despite her small size, Peg was an effective watchdog, scaring away potential intruders and once making such a ruckus that when Barbara went to investigate, she saw burglars fleeing the office next door. In addition, early-morning visitors to the crisis center were taken with the mangy, orphaned, three-legged dog that, like many of our callers, had been saved.

Peg had the run of the agency, and exercised territorial control. Barbara didn't see a problem with this, even when Peg would charge another dog coming in our front door. Peg yapped but didn't bite, Barbara said, and more often than not targeted dogs that were much bigger. Even if this was true—and no one was certain that it was—it was unnerving to hear Peg barking wildly. Several volunteers who were in the habit of bringing their dogs to the agency stopped doing so.

Then there was issue of Peg's grooming, or lack thereof. Any oblique references to Peg's matted hair, smell, or periodic fleas failed to register with Barbara.

What really brought things to a head was that as Barbara slowed down, she took Peg on walks less often until, between the lack of exercise, Peg's need to claim her territory, and her increasingly uncontrollable bowel movements that came with age, Peg started leaving small "surprises" inside our offices. Barbara paid hundreds of dollars to have all the carpets deep cleaned, but it wasn't enough. The practice had to end.

The challenge was that Barbara was so wedded to Peg that if Peg was banned from the agency, Barbara said she'd quit and we didn't have anyone to replace her. Her ability to handle suicide calls without backup, vast knowledge of our chronic callers, and willingness to work hours that no one else wanted to, were invaluable. Every time Barbara and I talked, she was contrite, apologizing for Peg's indiscretions, paying for damages, and promising that the problems would end. Unfortunately, they didn't.

The longer this continued, the more agitated staff became. "Do something," they implored me. I felt trapped. Either dogs were allowed, at least after-hours, in which case Peg could continue to be disruptive, or they were banned altogether, to the dismay of people who appreciated their company. It didn't help that the individuals agitating most for a ban weren't hotline staff and therefore wouldn't have to work overnights if Barbara left.

Eventually, I had no choice. I informed Barbara and several volunteers who were in the habit of bringing dogs to the crisis center that their pets no longer were welcomed. Barbara was upset, but didn't quit. Instead, she asked if it'd be all right for her to bring a small kennel, leave it outside our back door, which opens onto a communal courtyard, and put Peg there while Barbara worked. Peg was old, in declining health, and Barbara was afraid to leave her home unattended.

Technically, that complied with our new policy. Against my better judgment, I said okay. Little did I know what it'd lead to. A few weeks later I learned that Barbara had started to work outside at night. With the back door to the crisis center wide open, and the full contents of the agency exposed, she ran long phone cords from our hotline room out the door so that she could sit on a chair next to Peg in the kennel and answer calls on multiple lines. She didn't have access to the many resources in the room; however, she'd worked at the crisis center long enough not to need them; they were in her head.

I was horrified. And steaming. The only saving grace was that nothing bad had happened. With no one else around between midnight and 8 A.M., confidentiality hadn't been breached and neither Barbara nor the crisis center had been harmed. We'd been lucky.

I asked Barbara's supervisor to talk with her rather than talked with Barbara myself. I was afraid that I'd say something I'd regret, invalidating Barbara's many years of exemplary service by focusing on this one ill-advised and character-istically headstrong act. In my mind I replayed remnants of a conversation that Barbara had told me about recently. The caller was a seventeen-year-old girl whose mother was ranting in the background. The girl had three younger siblings and was expected to care for them without any help, much less appreciation, from her mother.

"All I want is for her to say thank you sometimes," the caller told Barbara. "I don't expect a medal; I'd just like her to notice."

"What do you think it'd take for that to happen?" Barbara said.

The girl hesitated. "I'd have to leave," she said. "I've done it before. I leave for a few days, then come back and she cares, but only for a little while."

Barbara was tempted to ask her where she went, but that was another conver-sation. If the call went the way Barbara wanted it to, the girl wouldn't need to run away.

"Is that what you want to do now?" Barbara asked.

"No," the girl said. "I want to be here for my sisters and brother."

Barbara was impressed. The caller was more mature than most seventeen-year-olds.

"You sound like you've had to grow up fast," Barbara said, "be a responsi-ble adult when you're still a teenager. That can't be easy. Could you have this conversation with your mother? It sounds like you're ready for it."

"I'm ready," the girl replied. "But she isn't."

"Could you have it anyway? What do you have to lose?"

The girl considered this. "Nothing, I guess."

They talked a little longer. Barbara's last words seemed especially wise. "Take a deep breath," she said, "and start your life."

With her supervisor, Barbara didn't offer any excuses. That wasn't her way. Peg was old, in poor health, and Barbara just wanted to be with her.

As it turned out, Peg died a few months later. Her last weeks I allowed Barbara to put Peg's kennel in the men's bathroom opposite the hotline room. It didn't matter to anyone else; the issue had been decided. It mattered to Barbara, though, who was grateful.

Afterward, the crisis center stopped being a dog-friendly agency. I was sad about that; however, I was glad to have the issue behind us.

ENVIRONMENT OF TRUST

Retaining good employees is as challenging as retaining good volunteers. People who are experienced, talented, and hardworking can go anywhere.

Though nonprofit agencies usually can't compete with government or the private sector in terms of salaries, pensions, benefits, or stock options, there are other ways that we can maintain our workforces. One of them is to create an environment of trust. People are shown in words and deeds that the agency trusts them. For volunteers, this means giving them things like Internet access and the authority to make decisions if staff aren't immediately available. For employees, it's allowing them to set their own schedules, giving them an agency charge card, being generous with vacations and sick leave, and providing options for health care. Employee evaluations provide another opportunity for managers to demonstrate trust. I like to use evaluations as a forum for supervisors to assess the performance of people who work under them and for employees to assess whether their supervisors are providing appropriate support, guidance, and coaching. It's a two-way dialog that works only if employees trust the supervisor to accept constructive criticism the same way that the supervisor expects employees to.

At the crisis center, I developed a three-part evaluation form. In the first part, the supervisor rates the employee in a variety of categories—planning and organizing skills, perseverance and resiliency, motivation, judgment, teamwork, written communication, verbal communication, job knowledge, and cultural competency. The other two parts are completed by the employee. One is a self-evaluation in the same categories, as well as a statement of two goals for the coming year. The second is an evaluation of the supervisor. Each part has a four-level rating system based on whether the employee is fully achieving expectations, nearly achieving expectations, needs improvement, or is performing unacceptably.

I make it clear to employees that the expectations for each position are different. The development director and finance manager both may be rated "fully achieves expectations" in the area of written communication, for instance, but this doesn't mean that their writing skills are comparable. In the former, the ability to write well is critical and anyone in the position is expected to be a good writer. In the latter, there's little writing and the standard is lower.

One thing virtually every employee discovers in doing a self-evaluation is that writing a thoughtful, constructive performance review is hard. Employees who don't supervise anyone develop an understanding of what's involved in doing reviews when they have to do their own. They learn to appreciate the time and effort required of supervisors to be honest, fair, complimentary, tough, and thorough in an assessment, even if they disagree with portions of it. It's a good lesson in seeing things from another person's perspective.

MINERVA

At the crisis center, one of the persons whose perspective continues to enlighten me is Minerva, our homeless services manager. Her life has been filled with a seemingly endless string of tragedies—family members and close friends murdered, robbed, killed in accidents, incarcerated, institutionalized with mental disorders, found dead by suicide. For several years Minerva herself was a drug addict and homeless. Strung out, she couldn't care for her kids, and Children's Protective Services removed them from her custody.

It was then that Minerva vowed to turn her life around. She went through detox, then completed rehab. Clean of drugs, she got her children back. She also rekindled a deep, spiritual fire by becoming active in a local church. In addition, she went through training and started volunteering as a substance abuse counselor at a local treatment center.

After taking so many big steps, the next step—finding a job—should have been easy. It wasn't. No one wanted to hire a middle-aged, heavyset, African-American woman with a criminal record for drug dealing and little work experience. Even McDonald's rejected her.

Minerva didn't hide any facts of her life when she interviewed with me. She was open and honest about her past. She also was proud of how far she'd come since hitting rock bottom. She told me that she had three goals—to be hired by the crisis center, to be promoted one day to a managerial position, and to earn enough money so that at some point she could buy a house for herself and her children.

I was impressed by her comeback, her plan, and her positive attitude. I was even more impressed by her heart, though. It was clear that she cared deeply about others and would do anything she could to get people back on their feet.

I hired Minerva as an assistant in our homeless services program, answering calls on the crisis center's twenty-four-hour homeless hotline. From the moment she started, she was incredible. Callers knew instantly that her empathy was genuine and that at some point she'd been where they were. They trusted her with intimate details of their lives, realizing that the more information she had, the more she could help them. They also knew that they couldn't browbeat, cajole, manipulate, intimidate, or deceive her. She was street smart and had tried every tactic herself at one time when she was trying to access services. Other crisis center counselors, including licensed staff with many years of experience, listened to her talk on the phone in awe.

"I got you a bed in a shelter," she'd say to a caller, "but you got to show up. Don't you go playing games with me, saying you be there, then deciding you don't want to. If I make this appointment for you, I don't want to hear no excuses later 'bout how you couldn't get there or you didn't like the case manager they give you so you up and split. No way, none of that—understand? I got lots of people wanting beds tonight, and if you not serious 'bout getting off the street and into some kind of program, I don't got time for you and no one else does neither. I just want to be clear 'bout that."

People loved her. She was the best kind of friend, someone who cared but wasn't fooled, who listened to a litany of injustices and half-truths with compassion and understanding, then cut through them like a razor blade to the raw truth. Few others in their lives played that role.

After she'd worked at the crisis center several months, Minerva visited an adult shelter in Concord. It was one of the largest shelters in the county, although she hadn't stayed in it when she was homeless. Since she placed callers there, she wanted to see what it was like. A resident greeted her at the front door.

"Can I help you?" he asked.

"I'm Minerva," she said. "From the homeless hotline."

His eyes widened. "Oh, my god," he said. He let her in, then turned and shouted to people behind him. "Hey, everyone. It's Minerva! It's Minerva!"

It was like a fire alarm. People poured out of rooms, calling to others, "Hurry up, Minerva's here." "Minerva's here, from the hotline." "I can't believe it—Minerva!"

Two dozen people gathered in the main room. The first thing they did was to give her a standing ovation. At last they were meeting the person behind the phone. Tears streamed down Minerva's face. She knew she'd found her calling.

One winter a San Francisco TV station did a story on homelessness in the Bay Area. The reporter interviewed Minerva, then me. Afterward, he wanted to film a few visuals to accompany the story. He asked Minerva to pretend that she was having a conversation with a homeless caller. The sound would be off, so her voice wouldn't be recorded; however, she needed to be speaking so that it looked real. Minerva immediately picked up the phone.

"Homeless hotline," she said. After a few seconds, she nodded. "Okay, let me get this straight. You say you in the hospital now and they want to release you but you don't got no place to go?" She paused. "Who told you that?" Another pause. "Honey, if you ain't sick no more they going to release you. They ain't running no hotel." She seemed to listen for a good twenty seconds. Then she said, "What you want me to do? I want to help you but you got to want to help youself. I know—" She stopped as if interrupted. "I know you want to stay there but you can't. Not unless you sick and you don't sound sick to me. Here's what I can do. I can—"

"Cut," said the reporter. Minerva immediately laid down the phone.

I stared at her in amazement. "I can't believe you made that up on the spur of the moment," I said. "Even the pauses sounded authentic."

She smiled. "I have conversations like that all the time. Sometimes I know what someone's going to tell me before they know it themselves. There are only so many stories, you know, and I've probably heard 'em all."

"Anytime you want to go into acting," the reporter said, "give me a call."

In 2003, Minerva was named Woman of the Year by a local city. At the awards ceremony I introduced her, then she spoke. She hadn't prepared a speech, but she knew what she wanted to say. She told her personal story, about her drug use and rehabilitation, about her attempts to find employment and her work at the crisis center, and about her three goals.

"I want everyone here to know that I made it," she said. "I got hired, and after a few years I was promoted to program manager, and earlier this year I bought me a house."

She raised her fist triumphantly. The audience cheered.

"I also went back," Minerva said, "to the McDonald's where the manager said he couldn't hire me. He was still there and I showed him my business card with my name and title. 'Look,' I told him. 'You did me a favor when you turned me down for a job here.' He looked at the card, then at me. 'I remember you,' he said. 'I'm glad things worked out.'"

In 2007 Minerva celebrated her tenth year at the crisis center. She has no plans to leave, and I have no plans to let her go. County departments continually offer her jobs, but she turns them down. They weren't around when she needed them.

One of our core tenets at the crisis center is: Don't give up on people; miracles happen every day. It's a driving principle of our work. Minerva is living proof of it.

CHAPTER THIRTEEN

Major Gifts: "Dear God, Please Make Dean . . . "

Most people are familiar with the movie *It's a Wonderful Life*. Made long ago by legendary director Frank Capra, it's on TV every holiday season.

In the movie, George Bailey (played by Jimmy Stewart) laments the failure of his business and his unrealized dreams. Christmas Eve he's ready to jump from a bridge when Clarence, his guardian angel, appears seemingly needing to be rescued himself. Through Clarence, George comes to see positives in his life—his family and friends, people in town who depend on him—and finds reasons to live.

Some people think the movie is trite, but I like it. Yes, its message parallels our work at the crisis center. Yes, our counselors act as guardian angels sometimes. Mostly, though, I like it because I'm a sucker for happy endings. When lovers ultimately find each other, or when the underdog comes out on top, or when right prevails, I feel glad.

You might think that the hardest part about answering crisis calls is saying the right thing to someone who's distressed. Or it's staying upbeat after listening to people's pain. Or, it's talking with someone whose problems seem unsolvable.

All are tough, but oftentimes the hardest part is not knowing what happens afterward. It's not knowing how the story ends.

A teenage boy calls our crisis lines. His girlfriend is pregnant and their parents want the youths never to see each other again. They love each other, though, and can't imagine the thought of being separated. What complicates the situation is that both are straight-A students who recorded near-perfect scores on their SAT exams. They have scholarships to Ivy League colleges. Now, instead of facing secure futures, they have big decisions to make and are scared.

We listen without judging, explore options, and provide resource information based on what the caller—not us—thinks is best. He thanks us, then hangs up.

Sometimes people call back later and tell us what happened. This caller doesn't.

Several years have passed. We can't help but wonder: Did she have the baby? Are they still together? In school?

We'll never know the answers. We have to accept that. We just trust that they made the right choices—and hope they have a wonderful life.

When fundraisers get together and tell stories, they're often stories about major donors—their quirks, lifestyles, and odd ways in which they've been solicited or responded to being solicited.

The most unusual story I've ever heard concerns the most unusual donor I've ever met. Her name was Margaret Lesher. Her death in 1997 at the age of sixty-five was the subject of mainstream and tabloid news for weeks. The *New York Times* covered it, as did *Vanity Fair*, *Hard Copy*, and the *Today* show. When she died, Contra Costa County lost its biggest and most glamorous philanthropist, a woman who loved expensive clothing, jewelry, and cosmetic surgery (which she was quite public about), and also loved to give large sums of money to a variety of charitable causes, giving that her heirs continue today through the Lesher Foundation.

To understand the story, it's important to know a little about Margaret's life. Born in Texas, she moved to California with her first husband and their four children, all girls. When the marriage ended, she worked a succession of clerical jobs to support her daughters and herself. Several years later, she met Dean Lesher. He was seventy years of age (she was thirty-nine), a graduate of Harvard Law School, and a highly successful newspaper publisher. His first wife had died, his four children were grown and, like Margaret, he was lonely.

Their marriage lasted twenty years, until Dean's death at age ninety in 1993. By all accounts, both were happy. Their union provided Margaret immediate social standing and riches she never could have imagined. He, in turn, found an attractive companion with an engaging sense of humor, flamboyant style, and deep spirituality. Together, they became the most powerful and influential couple in the area, as well as the most generous. Almost every local agency that launched any kind of fundraising campaign turned to the Leshers for the lead gift, and more often than not they gave it.

I met Margaret and Dean on numerous occasions, although I'm sure they never knew my name. Then Margaret, a born-again Christian who at one time recorded a number of gospel songs, and Dean, who wasn't known to be religious but acquiesced to Margaret on such matters, donated $250,000 to the local Christian broadcasting station. In appreciation, the station let her host a weekly, half-hour television talk show. Several months after Dean died—an event that was front-page news in every local paper, including ones he didn't own (the governor of California attended the service)—her producer called me asking if I'd be her guest. I'm not a fan of Christian television; however, I jumped at the chance to address a large audience, as well as have a one-on-one conversation with Margaret.

Because I'd never watched the show, I didn't know what to expect. I didn't know, for instance, that in the past she'd described each of her surgical procedures to the audience. She assumed that people were interested—and they probably were.

When I arrived, I was ushered through a backstage door into a large warehouse that housed half a dozen sets for the station's various shows. I looked for Margaret, but the only woman I saw was a redhead on the most distant set. She was bathed in spotlight, wearing a clingy burgundy dress that accentuated her curves, and giving directions to several stagehands. From where I was she looked to be in her thirties, although all I could see was her shoulder-length, perfectly styled auburn hair and svelte figure. All of the other sets were empty, so I gravitated toward the woman. When I was close enough to see her face I realized, with a shock, that it was Margaret. Her face was unlined and flawlessly made up. She had a huge diamond ring and an equally impressive necklace. She was sixty-three at the time.

She came over, introduced herself, and showed me the fax that I'd sent, at her producer's request. "These are the questions you want me to ask you, right?" she said.

I looked at the sheet and nodded. "Yes."

"Okay," she said. Then to no one in particular she announced, "We're ready to go."

I was led to the guest's chair and fitted with a small microphone. Margaret told a technician to soften the lighting further, then she asked the cameraman whether the backdrop—a bookcase lined with real-looking leather-bound classics—appeared too busy. "It's fine," he said.

"How's my face?" she said. "Are there any shadows?"

He looked through the camera. "Perfect," he said.

It was a strange interview. She kept my printed questions on her lap, just out of view of the camera, and went right down the list. We didn't interact; she just waited for me to finish talking, then asked the next question. When the interview was over, she extended her hand, we shook, then she turned and walked off the set.

One didn't get many chances with Margaret Lesher, and I felt like I'd just blown mine. She continued to support my agency, but I got no closer to her.

In contrast, the staff and board of a local domestic violence agency were resourceful and adaptable in dealing with her, and it paid big dividends. One time, the agency was in the final stages of a campaign to raise money for a new shelter. Even after a big push, however, it was $200,000 short. In desperation, the executive director and the president of the board made an appointment to talk with Margaret. She and Dean already had contributed the first and largest gift to the campaign, yet a final, big gift was still needed. The appointment was at noon at Margaret's estate. The two women were met by her butler, who informed them that Margaret was in bed.

"Is she sick?" they asked.

"Oh, no," the butler said. "She's expecting you."

He led them to her bedroom where Margaret was, indeed, lying down. After the butler closed the door behind him, Margaret said, "Do you know why I'm in bed?"

The two women looked at each other, then at her. "No," they said.

"Because I just had liposuction!" Margaret exclaimed, and she threw off the bedcovers to show them the results of her latest surgery.

The president and executive director hardly blinked, knowing that, with Margaret, they needed to be ready for anything. They told her why they'd come; the agency needed $200,000 to pay the remaining costs of the new shelter.

Margaret looked at them aghast. "I don't have that kind of money," she said. She thought for a moment, then said, "What we need to do is pray."

She insisted that the two women kneel down beside her, facing the bed. Then Margaret clasped her hands and bowed her head. "Dear God," she said, "please make Dean see the light and give the shelter $200,000." She was serious.

Several days later the agency received a short note from Dean Lesher. With it was a check; Margaret's prayer had been answered.

SECURING MAJOR GIFTS

I never participated directly in a face-to-face solicitation of the Leshers. When I was a development director, though, I did research on them and provided information that resulted in a gift of $150,000. It was my first experience with major gift fundraising, and even though my role was small, the result was exciting. Someone asked for a lot of money and they gave it—how great!

Many nonprofit agencies avoid face-to-face solicitation. I understand; my agency doesn't do it nearly as much as we should. Neither the thrill of acquiring a major gift nor the knowledge that we can put a new gift to good use makes me welcome the process. And I'm not alone. The biggest problem with major gift fundraising, as any consultant will tell you, isn't getting people to give. It's getting people to ask. Any agency, no matter how small, has at least one or two prospects, starting with the board. Finding people who are willing to ask is much harder. Fear of rejection is the biggest reason—what if I ask and they say no?

Consultants have a ready answer. "Don't take it personally. They're not rejecting you, they're rejecting the idea, and they could have any number of reasons for doing so."

I know that's true; still, I don't want to be turned down. If an agency does its homework, that's less likely to happen; however, there are no guarantees. The right person can ask for the right amount at the right time and still the donor can decline. So why do face-to-face solicitations? And what, exactly, constitutes a major gift?

It's important to understand why individuals are solicited. There are three reasons. Number one: that's where the money is. In a typical year, Americans donate more than $200 billion to charity, and nearly 90 percent comes from individuals. Focusing an agency's fundraising efforts on corporations, foundations, and government, which make up the remaining 10 percent, doesn't make sense.

Number two: Individual donations, by and large, provide unrestricted income. Grants and other revenues tend to be designated by the funder for a specific purpose. What agencies need most is income that's discretionary, that can be used in a variety of ways depending on the agency's needs. Few individuals specify how their money is to be spent, thus individual donations offer more flexibility than income from other sources.

Number three: Many individuals increase their giving over time. Donors who value the agency often give more frequently and more generously, especially when cultivated. This isn't true of corporations, foundations, and government. In fact, it's often quite the opposite. A multiyear grant is front-loaded so that the payout is biggest the first year and lower each succeeding year. A government contract ends and isn't renewed because priorities have changed or money isn't available. At best, funding from other sources remains constant. This is a worse-case scenario when raising money from individuals.

Because individuals are the best source of funding, and because the most effective fundraising is personal, face-to-face solicitation is the best way to raise major gifts. Robert Zimmerman, a fundraising consultant in my area, explains it like this: "If you want to get milk from a cow, you don't send the cow a letter. You go to the source and squeeze."

The definition of a major gift—one that's solicited face-to-face—depends on the agency. For small agencies, $500 might be a major gift. For the crisis center, it's $5,000. For a large nonprofit, it could be $50,000. For theatrical companies, hospitals, and universities, it may be $1 million or more. The bottom line is that a major gift is whatever amount an agency feels is a sufficient payoff for all of the hard work, time, and energy needed to secure it.

The biggest difference between major gifts and annual gifts is that major gifts are larger. That's obvious. Another important difference, though, is that with major gifts the focus is always on the donor's needs while with annual gifts the emphasis, as often as not, is on the agency's needs. A third key difference is that the sequence of events for major gifts—the ask, the negotiation, and the close—can require multiple face-to-face meetings over a period of months while with annual gifts they all happen simultaneously.

Depending on the authority, there are anywhere from three to seventeen steps in major gift fundraising. My personal belief is that those who subscribe to ten or more steps are soliciting much bigger gifts than I am. I'm not that sophisticated, so I choose to break it down into four steps: prospect research, donor cultivation, the ask, and the thank you.

PROSPECT RESEARCH

The first step is to identify prospective donors and determine whether they have the will and the means to give. It's possible to change someone's will, but not his or her means. Knowing the person's will helps you gauge how much work is ahead of you, while knowing the person's means helps you separate people who are top prospects from people who aren't. The way you determine a person's will and means is to collect and assess information on his or her capacity, interests, values, and relationships.

Capacity is the person's financial ability to give. Knowing it involves learning his or her salary, investments, real estate holdings, and other assets. Much of this information is easily available. Google is great for researching major donor prospects. So are these web sites: donorseries.com, lexis-nexis.com, wealthengine.com, opensecrets.org, and fundrace.org.

One resource I recommend highly is a real estate search service. This is an online listing of all residential and commercial properties on file in a county's tax assessor's office. You can enter someone's name and see all of the property that he or she owns locally with all of the relevant details—address, lot size, square footage, date of purchase, and sales price. The first time I used it was when my agency received a sizable donation from a woman who'd never donated before. I looked her up and learned that she owned a large shopping center.

Researching the capacity of donors also includes researching their giving history to your agency and others. In addition to internal records, I encourage board members, staff, volunteers, and friends to collect annual reports, programs, and newsletters from other agencies in order to gather information on people's giving elsewhere.

All of this is necessary to establish a gift target, which is the amount you're going to ask someone to give. If you don't have a goal, then you don't have an ask.

Researching the interests of prospects helps you identify giving opportunities that appeal to them. Someone who is older or is providing for an elderly parent may be most interested in services for seniors, for example. Someone with young children may be most supportive of an agency's education programs. A major donor in my area, who used to own the Oakland A's baseball team, loves sports and hunting so much that he paid for the cost of the football and soccer fields at a local university, the construction of a large athletic club where boys are taught boxing and wrestling, and the preservation of hundreds of acres of prime marshland that are a refuge to wild ducks. Collect as much information as you can about a person's family, business, civic activities, faith, education, hobbies, and social circles. Know whether your prospect bases decisions on solid information such as cost benefit analyses or on warm fuzzies such as client testimonials.

Also learn about an individual's values. What are the person's needs, priorities, and lifestyle? Knowing what's important to your prospect, then demonstrating how your agency can perpetuate these values long after the person's death, is central to major gift solicitation.

The final and, in many respects, most critical piece is determining who has good, strong relationships with the prospect. The closer someone is, the more success he or she will have cultivating, contacting, and soliciting the person. You also have to look at the role of the prospect's spouse or partner. Most couples today make decisions jointly, so meeting with one person and not the other could delay or even undermine your chances of securing the gift. This wasn't the case when the domestic violence agency solicited Margaret Lesher; however, the solicitors knew this. They also knew enough about her values and lifestyle not to be shocked when she displayed the effects of her surgery, or when she asked them to kneel and pray. As uncomfortable as it might have been for the solicitors, they never forgot why they were there: to get the gift.

Prospect research is a lot of work, and there are no shortcuts. Every potential donor requires a unique, individual strategy of solicitation.

DONOR CULTIVATION

Donor cultivation is the process of building a bond between the individual and your agency. The goal is to increase the person's interest by inviting him or her to tour your facility and attend a special event, by sending news clips and other information on the agency, and by thanking the person often and imaginatively for past donations.

Once it's determined that someone is ready to be solicited, the next step is to make the appointment. Don't mislead the prospect by implying that there's any other purpose of the meeting. Just say it like it is.

"I'd like to talk with you about making a special gift to the crisis center, a gift that will preserve our life-affirming services for future generations while offering you the opportunity to build a legacy."

Why would a prospect be willing to meet, knowing that you're going to ask for a gift? First, he or she has a need. Giving is a meaningful experience that makes something good happen in the life of the donor, in the life of the agency, and in the lives of people served by the agency. Second, the prospect isn't being asked by just anyone, he or she is being asked by a family member, friend, or business acquaintance. This makes it hard to say no. Third, the prospect is interested and invested in the agency because of the cultivation work that's been done. He or she has donated before, received appropriate recognition, attended agency events, met agency leaders, and seen agency clients being helped.

It's also important to remember that in all likelihood this isn't the first time that the donor has been approached about making a major gift. People who have the means and will to give are solicited by many causes. In some sense they even expect it because they know that major gifts are the only way that libraries get built, shows get produced, open space gets preserved, museums and galleries get new collections, and a whole range of health and social services get delivered in the community.

THE ASK

Everything leads up to the ask. When donors agree to meet, they know that the reason is to solicit a gift. They know when the meeting is, where it is, and who's going to be asking. The only thing that's unknown to them is the amount.

Major gifts are stretch gifts where people are asked to give above their usual level for a special reason—to support a new project, an expanded service, a capital campaign, or an endowment. After establishing rapport and summarizing the donor's experiences with the agency, the solicitor transitions to the question. It can be framed a number of ways, depending on who's doing the asking. Ideally, the solicitor already has donated or pledged an amount equal to what the prospect is being asked to give. Then the solicitor can say, "Will you join me in giving at this level?"

Another way to ask is to present a giving pyramid showing the desired number of donations at varying levels. If the prospect is being targeted for a $50,000 gift, the solicitor points to the section of the pyramid for $50,000 donations and says, "We need three gifts at this level. I think if you were first, others would follow. Can you go this high?"

Depending on the need, the ask can be presented as a pledge to be paid over several years. Alternatively, if someone hesitates, a "bookends" strategy can be used in which the person is asked to give $25,000 now and $25,000 at the end of the campaign.

There are no magic words. The only rule is that you need to indicate a specific amount or range of money you want.

Almost always the solicitation is done by a two-person team. One person knows the prospect and is expected to do the ask, while the second person typically is the president or executive director of the agency and answers questions related to the agency's work and how it'll use the money. It behooves both members of the team to be clear about their roles well in advance of the meeting. At the same time, the person not designated to do the ask needs to be ready to jump in if the solicitor gets cold feet.

My very first ask long ago was of a board member. It was predetermined that the president of the board was going to solicit the gift and I would support him. At the critical moment, though, the president couldn't bring himself to ask the question. Instead, he changed the topic of conversation. The prospect was confused. He knew he was being propositioned for a major gift and appreciated directness. I stepped in.

"Would you be willing to consider a gift of $10,000?" I said. "I know it's a lot of money, but it'll be a big help."

The president breathed a sigh of relief. Even the prospect seemed to relax. The amount was higher than he'd expected, but at least it'd been voiced. Now he could respond.

"I need to think about it," he said. "I'll let you know in a few days."

According to many fundraisers, that's the best result possible. The amount isn't so low that the prospect says yes right away, or so high as to be totally out of the question. His hesitancy indicated that we'd set the right target gift for him.

"That's fine," I said. "Is there anything else we can tell you that'll help you decide?"

"No," he said. "I just need to think about it."

Several days later he called me to say that he was going to give $10,000. I grinned from ear to ear. It was a heady experience to have my first ask be a textbook case.

There's an adage in sales that the person who talks first after a big question is asked loses. It's true in major gift fundraising. If, after asking for a gift, the solicitor becomes uncomfortable by the silence and starts to speak before the donor responds, he or she risks losing the donation. There's no reason to clarify the ask or apologize for the amount until the donor speaks. If something isn't clear or the amount is too high, donors will say so. Most have been in this situation before. They're capable of expressing themselves and don't need help from anyone. Once you make the ask, it's essential to be silent. One of three things will happen: the person says some version of "yes," some version of "no," or some version of "maybe." Listen carefully, understand what you're hearing, then negotiate. Fundraising consultant Kim Klein offers the best advice I've ever heard on this.

When donors say, "Yes, I can do that," Klein says, they mean, "Yes, I can do that." Be appreciative, but not too excited; after all, you want them to think that you've handled gifts this size before. When donors say, "That's a lot of money," they mean, "Do you know that that's a lot of money?" Assure them that this is as big a gift for the agency to receive as it is for them to give. When donors say, "I don't think I can go that high," you're on your way to some kind of gift. Tell them you don't need it all at once, would they like to pay over time? Alternatively, ask them what they feel comfortable giving. When donors say, "I need to talk it over with my husband/wife/partner," they may need to consult with someone else—or they may have a concern that they're reluctant to raise. Tell them that you understand; it's a big decision. What will the other person want to know? When donors say, "Why are you spending so much money on rent?" or whatever, they mean, "Are you really operating as efficiently as you say?" Acknowledge the objection and address it. For example, the cost of a building may be high because it's important for the agency to be downtown. When donors say, "What if you don't raise all of the money you need?" they mean, "I don't want to be the only fool who gives." Respond by saying that you're well on your way to meeting your goal, and have more donors to ask. Worse-case, the start would be delayed a little if all the money doesn't come in, although that's not anticipated.

PLANNED GIVING

About 40 percent of adults in America have a will. Of these, only 8 percent include money for charities. This means that nonprofit agencies have two goals: (1) convince people who are leaving money to charity to add your agency, and (2) convince the 60 percent of people who don't have a will to get one and include your agency. Adding an agency to a will is easy. It's called a codicil and is a simple amendment to the original document. Convincing individuals to get a will can be accomplished by sponsoring an estate-planning seminar. The focus is educating people on the value of a will so that their assets don't end up in probate after they die. The opportunity of leaving something for charity is presented, but not emphasized. It's up to the donor to pursue it if interested.

Of the small percentage of people who have wills and are planning to leave money to charity, the vast majority of gifts are bequests, meaning that they're revocable. Donors can change their mind at any time. Consequently, even if a charity is named as a beneficiary, money isn't guaranteed until a donor dies and his or her last will is revealed. Even so, it makes sense for most nonprofits to pursue bequests rather than irrevocable gifts. The reason why is because bequests are easier to solicit. Donors are more likely to agree to a bequest because it's not binding until their deaths. Charities can take solace in the fact that most people don't change their wills very often.

The majority of donors who have wills and aren't planning to leave any of their estate to charity say that they want to make sure that their children and grandchildren are taken care of. This is understandable and is the biggest obstacle that nonprofit agencies face when soliciting bequests. It's easy to deal with, however.

Says Kim Klein, "We leave our children many things. One of the things we leave them is a good example. It's possible to provide for those you care about and also give something to charity, to help others. After all, no one can live this life alone."

THE THANK YOU

Once a major gift commitment has been made, thank donors in ways that meet their needs. Every donor wants some form of recognition, whether it's public praise or private acknowledgement that the gift is going to make a difference.

A number of years ago, a food bank I know of launched a $5-million capital campaign to build a state-of-the-art food distribution center. The board president was a pear farmer who wanted to lead the campaign. Development staff were wary because his biggest gift to date had been $1,500—not nearly enough to set the standard for a successful, multimillion-dollar fundraising effort. When they met with him, though, he surprised everyone by pledging $150,000. He made another significant gift at the end of the campaign to ensure that the goal was reached. In between, he successfully solicited other major gifts.

His leadership, hard work, and generosity proved invaluable and the agency wanted to thank him in a special way. The problem was how. Like many farmers, he lived simply. Putting on a necktie to talk with corporate donors was a big adjustment for him. He also wasn't comfortable being singled out for special recognition. Moreover, money was important to him; he didn't like to see it wasted.

The agency decided to honor him with a relatively inexpensive yet tasteful and fitting gift—a glass paperweight in the shape of a pear. It was specially ordered and custom made. Because the agency knew him, knew his values and needs, it was absolutely perfect. He loved it. He said he'd give it a special place in his home, meaning that it continues to serve today as a reminder of his important role in making something good happen in his community.

A CULTURE OF GIVING

Whenever there's a major disaster in the world—a tsunami in Indonesia, an earthquake in Pakistan, a terrorist bombing in London or Madrid—Americans open their pocketbooks. It doesn't matter how many thousands of miles away the victims are, people in this country give. When the disaster involves Americans—be it Oklahoma City, 9/11, or Hurricane Katrina—we give even more. We may not know anyone in the area, and we may never have been there ourselves, still, we want to help.

Foreigners believe that Americans are generous because we're rich. It's true that our standard of living is high, yet countries in Scandinavia, Europe, and Asia have comparable standards of living but people there don't feel as compelled to contribute. The difference is that giving is a cultural norm in the United States. From the early days of European settlers to the Founding Fathers and up to the present, our nation has been built on a frontier mentality of individualism and community self-reliance. People have taken solace in religion, which teaches one the importance of sharing and looking after those who're unable to care for themselves. Individuals haven't waited to see whether others were going to lend support; rather, they've immediately lent it themselves.

It's not just the rich in this country who give. Far from it. People like Bill Gates and Warren Buffett may make headlines because their giving is so great; however, in any year three out of four Americans contribute to charity. Low-income people, as a group, tend to donate a larger percentage of their income than those who are affluent. If agencies could exist on $20 donations alone, they'd do all of their prospecting in poor neighborhoods.

It takes a lot of $20 donations to equal one $10,000 donation, though, which is why major donors are solicited. Although they give a smaller percentage of their wealth, each gift has greater impact because of its size.

People outside the nonprofit sector oftentimes are horrified to learn how sophisticated fundraising is in general, and major gift fundraising in particular. They believe, or assume, or want to think that giving is a simple process in which people learn about a need and naturally are motivated to support it. It'd be nice if it happened this way, but it doesn't. There are many worthy causes, and charities that are reactive rather than proactive in their fundraising end up at the back of the line. Even after a disaster, successful fundraising is deliberate and strategic.

One reason why people are upset by fundraising tactics is because of the taboo that exists in much of America around money. Along with politics, sex, and religion, talking about money is frowned upon, at least in white society (African-Americans that I know tell me it's a common topic in their culture).

"The net effect of these taboos about discussing money," says Kim Klein, "is that money takes on the air of being both mysterious and bad. The hidden message is that good people don't deal with money except insofar as they must in order to live. Many people, misquoting the Bible, say, 'Money is the root of all evil.' In fact, Paul's statement to the Phillippians in the New Testament is, 'Love of money is the root of all evil.' Money, itself, has no good or evil qualities. It is not a moral substance."

Any fundraiser who believes that money is taboo should consider a different profession. Learning about money—about how to raise it and manage it effectively—is essential not only to the success of an agency's fundraising efforts but to the success of the agency itself.

One thing many people don't realize is that the relationship between a major donor and a charitable organization almost always is deeper and more personal than the relationship between other donors and the agency. Over lunches, meetings in the donor's home, and special events, an executive director and perhaps one or two board members come to know major donors fairly well, and vice versa. A bond develops, based on mutual trust and respect. I've had major donors tell me about going through drug rehab, the challenges of caring for a family member who's mentally ill, and the suicide of a loved one—things that they don't mention to everyone, and sometimes not even to friends and coworkers.

All of this makes the cultivation of major donors interesting, but does nothing, I've found, to reduce the dread I feel sometimes leading up to a new solicitation. This dread is based less on being rejected—I know that when donors say no, it's not personal—than it is on losing a donation I've been counting on. The only thing that lessens this fear isn't, surprisingly, success. Rather, it's having more prospects to ask, knowing that each one doesn't have to say yes. A few gifts, if they're the right size, are enough.

STRANGER IN A STRANGE LAND

Many years ago the president of Stanford University flew to England to solicit a huge gift from one of the wealthiest men in the country. For weeks leading up to the trip, staff tried to brief the president, but he was always too busy. "We need to talk about the case statement," they said. "We need to review the donor's giving history, business interests, art collection, and personal life."

The president scoffed. "Just get me on the plane," he said. "I'll take care of the rest."

"He's only giving you 30 minutes," staff said. "Don't you want to do a mock ask to make sure you don't run over?"

"Waste of time," the president said. "I know what to do."

A driver picked up the president at his London hotel and drove him miles out into the British countryside, to the donor's estate. It was massive, encompassing hundreds of acres. The main house had dozens of rooms—bedrooms, sitting rooms, game rooms, libraries, a large dining hall, ballroom and, at the far end, the donor's private office. Surrounding the mansion on all sides were elegant grounds—terraced lawns, fountains, gazebos, and gardens. Beyond these were horse trails, fox runs and, still part of the estate, distant woods and streams.

The doorman led the president on a brisk walk through a labyrinth of hallways to the donor's office. When they arrived, the president was out of breath. The donor was seated at his desk. He glanced at his watch, and invited the president to sit.

The president sat down awkwardly in an armchair, wiped his brow, and remarked that just getting from the main door to the donor's office presented quite a workout. The donor remained silent. Impatient with small talk, he folded his arms, prepared to listen.

For the next twenty minutes, the president described the university's current campaign—the need, the fundraising goal, the strategy designed to achieve it, and the campaign's relevance to Stanford's future. He said that the campaign was in its critical, formative stage and leadership gifts were being sought. He emphasized the importance of these gifts in setting the tone for a successful fundraising effort, and said he hoped that the university could count on the donor to provide a milestone gift. The donor said relatively little.

It was time for the ask. Development staff and the campaign committee had worked out a number. It was enormous, especially for the time. They had every reason to believe that the donor could afford it, although it represented a significant stretch. The donor was unlikely to say yes outright, and might even be stunned by the university's audacity.

The president hesitated. The donor's silence unnerved him. The president was used to being the one in charge, who sat behind the desk, who made the decisions. Here, he was clearly subordinate. The size and grandeur of the donor's estate, the distance that the president had traveled to get there, and the long, vigorous walk were intimidating, though not nearly as intimidating as the man's taciturn personality. The president couldn't bring himself to do the one thing that he'd come all this way to do: namely, ask for a specific amount of money. Instead, he began reiterating elements of the case and dynamics of the campaign. The donor listened for another ten minutes, then the phone on his desk rang. He picked it up, and after a few seconds put his hand over the receiver and said, "Excuse me, I have to take this call. Would you mind waiting outside?"

The president, surprised, mumbled no, that was fine. The donor motioned to him to take his briefcase and close the door behind him.

In a dark-paneled alcove outside the office, the president reviewed the meeting in his mind. It wasn't going the way he wanted it to; then again, this donor was more challenging than others he'd solicited. The president could appreciate a man who didn't waste words. He vowed to go back in, make the ask, listen to the response, deal with it, and be done.

He expected the door to open any minute. After a quarter of an hour, he tried the handle. The door was locked. He knocked, timidly at first, then more aggressively. There was no response.

Unsure what to do, the president found a door that led outside. The office had windows that looked out on a flower garden, and the president thought that he could attract the donor's attention from there. He felt a little silly calling through a window; however, he prided himself on being a man of action and this was the only action that came to mind.

There was no corresponding shout from within. When he got close enough to see through the glass, he realized that no one was there. The office was empty.

"His call probably just ended," the president thought. "Now he's looking for me."

The president chided himself for being impatient, as well as for getting freshly-turned dirt from the garden on his newly-polished shoes. He retraced his steps to the door that led him outside. It was locked. He pounded on it with his fist, but no one seemed to hear. That didn't make sense; surely the donor was inside. He tried other doors. They, too, were locked.

It took at least twenty minutes before the president, circling the grounds, arrived once again at the main door. Sometime during that long, embarrassing walk his shoulders slumped, his pace slowed, and he realized the awful truth: his meeting was over. When the doorman told him that the donor had left to catch a flight to the continent, it became clear. There would be no leadership gift. The president's inability to ask at the crucial time had doomed everything.

I heard this story in a workshop on major gift solicitation. The presenter had been a development officer at Stanford long after the president in the story had retired. It was continually retold, he maintained, to development officers, university trustees, and subsequent presidents to remind them of one thing: without an ask, you don't have a gift.

I think of the story virtually every time people at the crisis center solicit a major donor. It's comical to imagine someone as powerful and commanding as the president of a top university locked out, frantically trying doors, utterly humiliated. It's also scary. If that can happen to him, something even worse can happen to people who aren't as powerful and commanding, people like me. Not that major donors don't cancel appointments, or decline requests to meet, or say no. That's always going to happen. I can't change that. What I can do, though, is make sure to ask when I have the chance. I just remember the president. If nothing else, I want to be able to exit a room the same way I enter it—with dignity.

CHAPTER FOURTEEN

Financial Management: A Home for the Rolls

During my college years I worked summers at a family camp in the Sierras for alumni of the University of California. A month into my first summer, I was running on a mountain road, stepped on a sharp rock, and broke a small, metatarsal bone on the outside of my foot. It was the first and only time I've ever broken a bone, and I was miserable. I was sent home to recuperate and couldn't wait to heal and return.

A soft-spoken man named Norm was hired to fill in for me temporarily. He made the most of his one-month opportunity by falling in love with Francie, the pretty, dark-haired woman who ran the camp store. A few years later, they married.

We weren't close friends and I wasn't invited to the wedding. Nevertheless, when our paths crossed later, they thanked me for bringing them together.

"What do you mean?" I asked.

"Well," Francie said, "if you hadn't hurt your foot, Norm and I might not have met."

I smiled. Since they were in love, it seemed okay to take a little of the credit.

Soon after that I lost track of Norm and Francie. Somewhere in the back of my mind, though, I held onto the belief that they were still together, still happy, and this made me happy, too.

Years later I learned by chance the real story. They divorced long ago after having a daughter. More recently, Norm took his life.

For weeks after hearing this I reviewed my role in their misfortune. If only I hadn't broken my foot, I thought, Norm might be alive today. Francie might not be a single mother. A little girl might not be growing up with the pain of a father who killed himself.

It was foolish of me to think this way. After all, I hardly knew Norm or Francie. I didn't make them fall in love, or out of love, or cause anything that followed. Still, I was consumed by guilt.

The experience helped me better understand the feelings of people we counsel, especially people who have lost loved ones to suicide. The self-recriminations—on top of the grief—can be overwhelming. The only thing that really helps is talking with someone who's been there, who knows and cares and isn't afraid to say that beating yourself up—as natural as that seems—accomplishes nothing.

I wish it were as easy for people to heal from grief as from a broken bone. I also wish, sometimes, it were as easy to get rid of guilt as it is to assume it.

Once, when I was staying at a large hotel, I took a wrong turn and ended up walking into a convention center, which was attached to the hotel. I started to turn around and retrace my steps when I noticed an open set of double doors in front of me and an audience of several hundred people inside. It was midday, everyone had just finished lunch, and all eyes were focused on the front of the room, which I couldn't quite see. Someone was introducing the guest speaker, then there was polite applause. I ambled over to the doorway to get a better look. It was a mixed group of men and women, dressed in business attire. I had no idea who they were or what the speaker would be discussing, but many speakers start out with some sort of amusing anecdote and I wondered whether this one would. He did.

Back in the days of J.D. Rockefeller, the speaker said, a man came into Rockefeller's bank and wanted to borrow $100. The clerk nodded—this was a typical transaction at the time—and asked what the man planned to put up as collateral.

"My car," the man said, and he pointed to a glistening white Rolls Royce parked in front of the bank. He added that he'd pay back the loan in a month.

The clerk excused himself and went into Rockefeller's office. He said that there was a customer who wanted to borrow $100 and put up a Rolls Royce as collateral.

"Okay," Rockefeller said, "But when he comes back to get his car, tell him I want to see him."

A month later the man returned, paid back the loan and $6 worth of interest, and was ushered into Rockefeller's office.

"I'm curious," Rockefeller said. "Why'd you put up such an expensive car on a $100 loan?"

"Well," the man said, "my wife and I were taking a trip. We debated about where we should store our car and knew that for $6 your bank would take good care of it."

The audience erupted in laughter. I laughed, too. The couple's pecuniary motives and ingenuity were comical. What really hit home with me, though, was that nonprofit agencies have to be this careful with our money. We have to get the most out of every dollar we have.

FINANCIAL INDICATORS

Managing an agency's day-to-day finances is one of the most important responsibilities of an executive director. Overseeing an agency's financial management is one of the most important responsibilities of the board. Although I'm not good about managing personal finances (fortunately, my wife handles this), I pay scrupulous attention to my agency's financial position. For one thing, the crisis center's services depend on it. For another thing, donors have invested in our work and I want to make sure that they get the best value possible. If I fail to make the most of my own finances, so be it. Wasting someone else's money, though, is unforgivable.

Good financial management gives donors and the community confidence in an agency. Poor financial management jeopardizes everything that the agency does. Continually, operating close to the edge burns out donors, staff, and volunteers alike.

There are five primary indicators of an agency's financial health. They are: (1) the ability to produce regular financial statements in a timely manner, (2) the ability to produce annual, audited financial statements, (3) the presence of operating reserves, (4) the absence of operating deficits, and (5) low debt to equity ratios.

At a minimum, financial statements should include a balance sheet, an income statement, and a budget comparison. Many also include a cash flow analysis and breakdown of current grants. Bank statements may be attached as verification of financial activity, although they aren't included with the rest of the statement when copies are provided to funders since they contain account information that needs to be guarded.

The balance sheet is a snapshot of the agency's overall financial position at a point in time (usually the end of a month). It's a summary of the agency's assets and liabilities, of what the agency owns and what it owes. To be honest, I pay little attention to it since the crisis center's assets—our building, equipment, small endowment, and minor stock holdings—change relatively little month to month. It's valuable, though, for new board members, funders, and others who are seeing this information for the first time.

The income statement provides a picture of the agency's income and expenses over a period of time (usually the fiscal year to date). It shows what the agency has collected in revenues and what it has spent in operating and administrative costs, usually in detail by dozens of individual line items. In any given month, there may be considerable variations depending on the timing of income and payment of expenses. The important thing is that, overall, the agency takes in as much money as it pays out, if not more.

One consideration is whether the income statement reflects actual or accrued income. Actual income is money in hand. Accrued income is money that has been promised—and the agency may have billed for it—but it hasn't been received yet. Either method is acceptable. Using actual figures is preferred if there is some doubt as to whether income that has been promised will be received. Accruing income, which is what the crisis center does, presents a truer picture of the agency's financial position because the bottom line isn't distorted positively or negatively by a single event. A $12,000 grant, for instance, paid at one time but covering a period of twelve months, is booked in its entirety on the balance sheet but the funding is accrued on the income statement in increments of $1,000 per month. Similarly, a government funder may be slow to process payment, especially at the start of a fiscal year. This would look serious if actual rather than accrued figures were reported.

Whichever method is used—actual or accrual—agencies should adopt a formal revenue recognition policy that describes how income is booked. This policy is then applied consistently across the board. Accounting problems at Enron occurred when company executives started fudging when income was received and expenses were incurred. A good revenue recognition policy leaves no room for interpretation—or exceptions.

Budget comparisons track the flow of money in and out of the agency—again by line item—relative to budgeted projections. While my finance manager is most concerned with our income and cash flow statements because he wants to make sure we have enough money to pay bills, my primary interest is how revenues and expenses are doing compared with our budget. This helps me determine whether we need to step up fundraising efforts or reign in costs to maintain a positive balance.

At most agencies, some revenue sources are seasonal. Individual donations may be low during the summer, for example, and high during the holidays. I keep these variations in mind so that budget comparisons are meaningful. It wouldn't make sense to take our annual projection for individual donations and simply divide it by twelve for monthly reports. Instead, the budget reflects the ebb and flow of donations depending on the time of year.

All agencies should be able to produce monthly financial statements by the fifteenth day of the following month. Large agencies with lots of accounts and assets to manage might take a little longer, and small agencies with few resources and a manual bookkeeping system might be able to get by with quarterly statements. In general, though, agencies should generate a complete financial statement two weeks after the closeout of the previous month. A prompt turnaround is necessary to deal effectively with any serious problem that develops.

Nonprofit agencies with gross annual incomes of $25,000 or more are required by law to file a Federal 990 form with the Internal Revenue Service every year. This form contains information on the agency's finances and programs and is available free to the public through Guide Star and other Internet sites. Usually it's completed by an outside certified public accountant who has been hired by the agency to conduct a full audit. The audit provides an impartial examination of the agency's books and a fair representation of the nonprofit's financial situation. Any irregularities in the agency's accounting practices are noted in the management letter, which accompanies the audit and is addressed to the board. It behooves an agency to work closely with the auditor to get the cleanest audit possible, as well as take all necessary steps to address any exceptions noted in the management letter. This doesn't mean coercing the auditor or hiding information. Despite a few highly-publicized exceptions, auditors are scrupulous. They're hired to provide an accurate, objective study of the client's finances and determine whether the client is operating according to generally accepted accounting practices. They're not hired to find evidence of wrongdoing. Auditors present the facts and leave it to others to interpret them.

It's appropriate, even advisable, for the president, treasurer, or executive director to respond in writing to the management letter if there are things in it that the agency feels need an explanation. For example, the auditor may note in his or her findings that the person who prepares agency checks for signature also handles agency deposits, and recommend that these responsibilities be performed by different people. The agency may have such a small staff, however, that this isn't possible. In its response, the agency can acknowledge the wisdom of separating these functions and say that one of the disadvantages of being a lean operation is that it doesn't have this luxury. The agency's letter is added to the management letter at the end of the audit.

MORE IS LESS

Every nonprofit agency needs to have money in reserve to deal with temporary shortfalls in funding. Grants can be delayed, contracts can be misplaced, and individual donations can be sluggish depending on the season, the appeal, and the current state of the economy. If an agency has insufficient savings, it can't cover payroll, rent, utilities, and other operating costs.

The accepted rule of thumb is that an agency should have, at a minimum, reserves totaling three to six months of its operating budget, and preferably a year's worth. This means that if the agency receives no money during that period of time, it can still pay all of its bills. Having less indicates potential cash flow problems.

Having too much money in reserve also is cause for concern, however. A small number of nonprofit agencies are so adept at raising money that they stockpile large amounts of cash and other assets primarily because they can. One agency in my area, Guide Dogs for the Blind, has more than $200 million in reserves—ten times its annual operating budget. Even so, the agency continues to mail thousands of solicitation letters annually. To me, this is unconscionable. Most donors give because they want people to be helped, animals to be rescued, or the environment to be saved *today*—not because they want a charity to sit on their money for decades.

One reason why the American Red Cross has received unfavorable publicity in recent years is because of its practice of banking donations from one tragedy to help fund the next one. It makes sense to store resources for a rainy day, especially if your work involves mobilizing a large number of people and a sizable amount of equipment quickly when all hell breaks loose. At the same time, donors who give to support victims of the Oklahoma City bombing, 9/11, Hurricane Katrina, tornadoes, earthquakes, and tsunamis aren't happy when they hear that millions of dollars are sitting idly in savings accounts while needy people are unserved. If this is how you operate, donors should be educated about it *before they give*. No one should learn it after the fact.

Contrast the Red Cross model with Doctors Without Borders, the physician-run relief agency headquartered in France that received the 1999 Nobel Peace Prize. Within days after the December 2004 tsunami struck Southeast Asia, killing more than 150,000 people, representatives of Doctors Without Borders instructed the media to stop encouraging people to send donations. The organization already had more money than it needed to do its work there, and additional money wouldn't assist tsunami victims.

Most agencies temporarily stop fundraising once they reach their goal; however, they don't turn off the spigot. Money continues to pour in and the agency gladly accepts it. This was the first instance I knew of where a relief organization deliberately and repeatedly told donors not to give because it wasn't needed—and only days after the tragedy, when donors around the world were just starting to respond. I've always been a supporter of Doctors Without Borders, and this made me more of one.

AVOIDING DEBT

Few nonprofit agencies are well endowed. More common is the situation where an agency is operating at a deficit.

Short-term, relatively small deficits are manageable. If the agency has reserves that aren't restricted, they can cover it. Alternatively, a line of credit can be activated.

Ongoing, large deficits require immediate action, however. They erode an agency's assets and, if unaddressed, lead to bankruptcy.

Determining an agency's ratio of debt to equity is a critical factor in assessing the agency's fiscal health. The goal is to have little or no debt and lots of equity. This means that the agency doesn't need to borrow money to pay ongoing costs. Some borrowing may be necessary, especially if the agency is financing the purchase of property or equipment. Excess debt can hinder the agency in fulfilling its mission, though. As a rule, agencies shouldn't spend more than 10 percent of their budget servicing debt, and preferably less.

THE FISCAL CYCLE

Every nonprofit agency is required to have a fiscal year, which is defined in the agency's incorporation papers. Sometimes it's January 1st to December 31st, coinciding with the calendar year. Many agencies choose a different period, mainly because closing out a fiscal year can be time-consuming and people don't want to do it right after the holidays. Most common is July 1st to June 30th.

Whatever twelve-month period is used, it's best if agencies line up everything else accordingly. For the board, this means that officers (president, vice president, secretary, and treasurer) start and end their time in office consistent with the fiscal year so that they're accountable for what happens during that period. I think it's a good idea for the terms of *all* board members—officers and those who are at large—to coincide with the fiscal year for the same reason, although I understand the thinking of agencies whose board terms end one year, two years, or three years from the month that the person was elected. Staggering terms this way makes it easier to build a succession plan because you don't have a large number of people rotating off the board at the same time. The same objective can be accomplished in other ways, however.

For the staff, the fiscal year becomes the basis for setting goals, evaluating job performances, and determining salary increases. Program objectives, funding, and personnel decisions are tied to the same timeframe.

Every fiscal year starts with the development and approval by the board of an agency budget. Done well, budgeting is more than simply deciding how much income you anticipate receiving and how it's going to be spent. It's about deciding who you want to serve and how you want to serve them. What outcomes are most important? How much money are you going to spend on each outcome? How will you know whether an outcome has been achieved, and how will you measure success relative to the investment?

I wish that public entities, in particular, engaged in this kind of thinking more often, especially when budget cuts have to be made. Rather than mandating a 5 or 10 percent across-the-board cut, as is often the case, government leaders should decide how to produce the value citizens want with the limited money available. How much is kindergarten to grade twelve education worth relative to health care, transportation improvements, or public safety? What's more important, keeping a homeless shelter open or maintaining deputy positions in the sheriff's department? Should we lay off people in the county assessor's office, recognizing that it may impede revenue collection, or reduce immunization services in local health clinics? Budgeting is all about making choices. What continues and what ends? Which services are sustained and which are cut?

TWO BOTTOM LINES

I'd been directing nonprofit agencies for more than twenty years before I attended my first workshop in financial management. I thought I had a pretty good idea how to read financial reports and, more importantly, how to manage an agency's money effectively. I enrolled in the workshop mainly because it was in the middle of an all-day conference and there were no other workshops at the time that interested me.

The workshop proved to be eye opening, but not in the way I'd imagined. The presenter made financial management seem incredibly complicated. First off, she used acronyms that many of us in the audience had never heard of—SOFP, SOFE, SOA, BSOA. When people asked what they stood for she seemed perturbed, as if she thought she was teaching a graduate class in accounting and had ended up with remedial students by mistake. Okay, so most of us didn't know that she was referring to the statement of financial position (SOFP), the statement of financial expense (SOFE), the statement of activity (SOA), and the budgeted statement of activity (BSOA). We had different names for them. Then she gave us a large packet of financial documents for a fictitious agency, each document precise, meticulously prepared, and more layered than any nonprofit report I'd ever seen. It was far more information than necessary.

It takes a little work to understand a financial statement, but it's not much different than a personal checking account. Moreover, the questions one asks when managing a nonprofit agency are similar to the questions of a head of household:

- Do we have enough money to pay our bills?
- Are our fundraising efforts effective?
- Are we on track with our financial plan?
- How are our programs performing financially?
- Do we have sufficient reserves?

I prepare a single-page summary for board members of each month's financial statement. It's divided into three sections. The first section describes our cash position—the total amount of restricted and unrestricted income we have and how many months of our operating budget this equates to. The second section describes finances for the month—whether we finished up or down, if there were any unusual revenues or expenses, and compares revenues and expenses to the budget. The third section duplicates the second section but is for the fiscal year to date.

In my experience, most board members aren't interested in details of an agency's financial position. They joined the board because they support the agency's programs and services. All they want to know about finances is whether there's anything that they should be concerned about.

The main thing everyone—executive directors, board members, staff, volunteers, and donors—needs to understand is that nonprofit agencies have two bottom lines. One is the agency's mission. Who is served, how often, and in what way? Agencies measure the quantitative and qualitative impact of their services on individuals and on the community. The second bottom line is profitability. Are direct and indirect costs covered? Is there any surplus?

There's inherent tension between the two. Few activities have high mission impact and also high profitability. Invariably there's a trade-off. An agency starts or expands a program, knowing that the benefit—furthering its mission—will be offset by the cost—a decline in profits. The same agency may organize a new, special event, which brings in additional revenue—good for the financial picture—yet requires staff participation and diverts people from programs—bad for the mission.

Both bottom lines are necessary. Neither, by itself, is sufficient. Striking a balance between them is the essence of good nonprofit management.

WHAT'S APPROPRIATE OVERHEAD?

It's common for donors to ask what percentage of an agency's budget is spent on direct services (programs) and what percentage is spent on administration and fundraising (overhead). The conventional wisdom is that the more money an agency spends on programs and the less it spends on overhead, the better. Some watchdog groups rate agencies this way, giving high scores when 90 percent or more of an agency's operating budget is spent on direct services and low scores when overhead constitutes 40 percent or more of the budget. This information is important and can help guide someone's giving; however, it also can fail to tell the whole story.

Consider the case of the crisis center's hotlines and grief counseling programs. Because volunteers provide much of the service, a larger proportion of our budget is spent on administrative expenses. We don't need to spend as much money on programs because of the savings derived from using volunteers.

Habitat for Humanity spends 23 percent of its budget on fundraising. Compare that with Girl Scouts, which spends 1 percent of its budget on fundraising. Is Girl Scouts more efficient in raising money than Habitat? On paper, yes. In real life, no. Habitat doesn't include in its budget the value of donated labor—a major component of the charity. If it did, then the percentage devoted to fundraising would drop considerably. Girl Scouts, meanwhile, derives nearly half its revenues from membership dues, an income source that's easy to manage. Moreover, when it does fundraise, Girl Scouts has a built-in base of donors and doesn't need to solicit cold prospects like Habitat does, which is an expensive form of fundraising.

The point is, just because a charity says that it has a low overhead rate doesn't mean it's more cost-effective than another charity with a higher rate. What's more important is knowing the number of people served and the level of service relative to the number of staff and the amount of money spent. Even more important is knowing the impact the charity is making on the community. With this information, which admittedly is harder to obtain than a simple financial rating—although it often appears in some form on an agency's web site—a prospective donor can make an informed decision.

One piece of financial information that no donor, public or private, individual or foundation, ever asks is: What's the ratio of your highest salary to your lowest? This amazes me because I think it's a critical question. In recent years, much has been made of the fact that the average salary of chief executive officers of large companies in the United States has grown exponentially, to the point where it's now 430 times that of their lowest-paid worker. To understand what this means, if the lowest-paid employee earns $24,000 per year, the CEO's salary is more than $10 million. Nonprofit agencies have much smaller budgets, obviously, and the salaries of top staff pale in comparison. Nevertheless, much of an agency's culture can be determined by knowing the answer to this question. Is the executive director's salary ten times that of the lowest-paid employee? By for-profit standards this is extremely modest, yet in a sector where staff tend to be treated more as equals, and there's greater parity between management and line staff in terms of compensation, one person earns $24,000 while another person makes $240,000. That's still a big difference, and can't help but influence working relationships. A better goal, to my mind, is a salary structure where the highest salary is no more than five times that of the lowest salary. The executive director still earns considerably more; however, if he or she wants a raise, other salaries have to be raised, too. At the crisis center, my salary is two-and-a-half times the salary of my lowest-paid employee. I'm proud of that. Maybe one day a funder will ask about it.

REGULATION AND ACCOUNTABILITY

According to the National Council of Nonprofit Associations, one "cannot help but be impressed by the number and complexity of regulatory and reporting requirements nonprofits must fulfill in addition to their missions." The council lists dozens of documents that nonprofit agencies have to submit from the time that agencies are established and continuing through annual filings. Here are a few:

Establishment
- Articles of incorporation (file with state)
- Bylaws (state)
- Employer identification number (Federal)
- Taxpayer identification number (state)
- Tax-exempt status (Federal)
- Property tax exemption (state)
- Trademark or service mark registration (Federal and state)
- Charitable solicitation registration (state and local)

Annual Filings
- Form 990 (Federal)
- Form 990-T (for taxable unrelated business income) (Federal)
- Employment tax returns (W-2, W-3, etc.) (Federal)
- Lobbying reports (Federal and state)
- Charitable solicitation reports (state)

Ongoing Compliance
- Audit (Federal or state)
- Worker's compensation coverage (state)
- Unemployment compensation coverage (state)
- Copyright protection (Federal)
- Articles of incorporation update, including name change (state)
- Nonprofit bulk postage rate (Federal)
- Health Insurance Portability and Accountability Act (HIPAA) (Federal)
- Medicare and Medicaid contracts (Federal)
- Drug-Free Workplace Act (Federal)
- Patriot Act list for employees (Federal)
- Motor vehicle registration and insurance (state)
- Youth work permits (state)
- Licenses for nonprofit day care centers (state)
- Lobbyist registration (state)
- Regulation of professional fundraisers (state)
- Conflict of interest laws (state)
- Oversight of charitable trusts and protection of charitable assets (state)

- Anti-fraud enforcement (state)
- Merger (Federal and state)
- Dissolution (Federal and state)
- Health and safety codes; food handling and sanitation (local)
- Real estate assessments (local)
- Probate court for charitable bequests (local)

In 2002, in response to corporate scandals at Enron, WorldCom, Tyco, and elsewhere, Congress passed the Sarbanes-Oxley Act. Named after Senator Paul Sarbanes (a Democrat from Maryland) and Representative Michael Oxley (a Republican from Ohio), it requires all publicly traded companies to follow tougher standards in governance in order to build public trust. Nonprofits weren't targeted for reform; however, it makes sense for us to comply.

Many agencies, the crisis center included, already followed most of the provisions of the act before it became law. We didn't need to be told, for instance, that we should conduct an annual audit, that the auditor should be selected by a committee of the board rather than by the chief executive officer, or that the full board should review and approve the audit results. We were already doing this. We didn't need to be told that we should have a conflict of interest policy, or that the board should approve the salaries and benefits of the executive director and chief financial officer, or that the board should review all financial statements after the executive director and chief financial officer sign off on them. This was standard operating procedure. We didn't need to be told that board members shouldn't be paid for serving on the board or that the agency shouldn't provide personal loans to directors and executives. Neither crossed our minds.

Sarbanes-Oxley also provides whistle-blower protection by requiring businesses to investigate employee complaints and correct any problems or explain why corrections aren't necessary—something every businesses, nonprofit and for-profit, should do as a matter of course. In addition, businesses are instructed to stop document shredding if an official investigation is underway or likely—another obvious and prudent practice.

In California, the Nonprofit Integrity Act (SB 1262) was passed and became law on January 1, 2005. It requires all nonprofit agencies registered with the state attorney general to meet certain accountability standards consistent with Sarbanes-Oxley. Nonprofits with gross revenues of over $2 million, not counting government funding, have additional requirements. Some executive directors welcome the oversight, recognizing that every nonprofit agency is affected when one acts improperly and becomes front-page news. Increased accountability roots out problem agencies and boosts public trust in the sector as whole. Other executive directors are more leery. They worry that this is could be the first of many measures to regulate nonprofits closely, and will lead agencies to become bureaucratic and infertile. If that happens, the leanness and creativity that the community values so highly will be lost.

SHOW ME THE MONEY

In dark moments, I ask myself why anyone would want to manage a nonprofit agency. Workloads are high, salaries tend to be low, and public confidence wanes whenever a well-known agency such as the Red Cross, United Way, or Goodwill slips up. While state and Federal governments can push their liabilities into the future and build deficits, nonprofit agencies can't. While the private sector can falsify profits or declare bankruptcy, nonprofits can't. We continually have to operate within our means, something that's hard to do when the means keep diminishing and the demand for our services keeps rising.

One of the biggest frustrations is that dollars don't always follow success. A nonprofit agency that's meeting an important community need efficiently and effectively can still go out of business. In fact, many do. Donors don't know about it, or if they know they don't care. Impassioned pleas from board members and staff—no matter how articulate, how compelling, or how desperate—fail to save the service.

Conversely, in some communities there are one or more charities whose programs have significantly less impact than portrayed, whose boards play virtually no governing role, whose staffs turn over constantly because of morale problems, whose leaders neither collaborate nor cooperate with others, that nevertheless enjoy positive name recognition and raise lots of money. Their success derives largely from who's associated with the agency (celebrities, politicians, and corporate leaders), the marketing skills of top executives, and the agency's past reputation. Since it doesn't serve any nonprofit to publicly criticize another (both end up tarred), executive directors of other agencies can only hope that these "star" charities fade rather than implode. This way all nonprofits don't suffer from the fallout.

A different kind of frustration, one that seems specific to the nonprofit sector, is the continual challenge of doing more with less. When times are tough, nonprofit agencies are expected to cut their budgets and serve more people simultaneously. That's pretty amazing when you think about it. No one expects a hospital to reduce staffing, then see more patients. No one expects a school to lay off teachers, then enroll more students. No one expects a retailer to terminate sales people, then generate greater sales.

When cuts occur in hospitals, schools, businesses, and elsewhere, the best anyone hopes for is to provide nearly the same level of service to nearly the same number of people. This is a big accomplishment in itself. It's not enough for charities, though. When government cuts funding for health and social services, nonprofit agencies are expected to fill the void even though government cuts our funding, too. When businesses impose large-scale layoffs, local charities are expected to serve those newly out of work, even though corporate giving to charities is cut as well. When individuals tire of frequent requests for money, the number of people needing services grows anyway, leaving us to help them and deal with fewer donations, too.

The problem, I think, is that for a long time now those of us in the nonprofit sector have fostered the belief that we can keep expanding services while reducing costs. With employees who are motivated by good work rather than good salaries, and scores of volunteers who give their time generously, we've continually increased our efficiency and effectiveness. The problem is that this can't go on forever. One day we have to do less with less.

Several times in recent years, I've received a call from our county mental health director. She has to make a number of budget cuts and one of them is terminating the contract that the crisis center has had for thirty years to operate the county's twenty-four-hour suicide hotline.

"I hope you'll be able to continue the service anyway," she says. "Unfortunately, your contract is a luxury that the county can't afford right now."

What she means is that suicide prevention isn't a mandated service. Counties aren't required to provide it, and they don't receive state or Federal funding for it. When budget cuts have to be made, mandated services like law enforcement, fire fighting, courts, and jails are protected. It's the nonmandated services—homeless shelters, domestic violence programs, prenatal health care, sexual assault counseling, suicide prevention, and more, services that are provided largely by volunteers and are valued highly by the public—that end up being cut. Ironically, at the exact moment when the mental health director once called me with this news, volunteers in our hotline room were engaged in a desperate—and successful—effort to save a suicidal caller's life. Some luxury.

One thing we tell individuals who call out hotlines is that as hard as it may be to believe at the moment, today's problems can diminish in importance and even disappear someday. Just as good times don't last forever, bad times don't last forever, either.

Each time our hotline contract has been threatened, I've responded immediately. Although it's been presented to me as a done deal, that county funding is going to end, I've never accepted it that way. I've set up media interviews, mobilized advocacy teams, activated phone trees and e-mail alerts, spoken to church groups and service clubs, and met individually with every elected official who might be able to influence the decision in our favor. So far, the crisis center's contract continues to be renewed. The fact that it represents one-tenth of 1 percent of the county mental health department's budget is part of it. The fact that county funding is matched three-to-one by other sources, and that $100,000 in volunteer hours is devoted to the service also helps. In addition, our hotline saves the county an estimated $5 million per year in emergency hospitalizations, police action, and other costs. What makes the biggest difference, though, is that people can't imagine living in an area that lacks such an essential, safety-net service. A member of the county board of supervisors, whose own father died by suicide years earlier in another part of the country, went on record as saying, "If this service had been available to my father, he might be alive today." No one could argue with him.

Standing up for our contract has been a lot of work. For weeks, sometimes, I've done little else. At night I come home emotionally exhausted. By the end of budget hearings I'm drained. I've never considered it wasted time, though. While I've invested countless hours fighting something I'd rather not fight, the result is always worth it, not just in the continuation of county funding and the services it makes possible, but in increased public awareness of the crisis center and the growing legion of supporters who appreciate what the agency does.

One day our funding may be so secure that I don't have to worry about it anymore. Every executive director has this wish. Somehow, I doubt that that day will ever really come, though. It rarely does.

CHAPTER FIFTEEN

Advocacy: Gateway to Change

The *Reuters* news service was one of the few to report it. That's too bad; it deserved broader press.

For a few moments, the only sounds heard in the chambers of the United States Senate were the sobs of a grieving father. Gordon Smith, a Republican from Oregon, was introducing youth suicide prevention legislation named after his dead son.

"He saw only despair ahead and felt only pain in the present," Smith said, "pain and despair so potent that he sought suicide as a release."

Garrett Lee Smith killed himself in his college apartment a day before his twenty-second birthday. He'd battled learning disorders, dyslexia, and bipolar disorder for years.

When Senator Smith started speaking, the room was nearly empty. He went on anyway. "There's no owner's manual to help you bury a child," he said, "especially when the cause is suicide."

Peers who weren't there heard about Smith's testimony. One by one, they made their way to the chambers. Senator Pete Domenici (Republican-New Mexico), whose daughter is mentally ill, had gone home early; however, he rushed back to the Senate to sympathize and lend support.

After Smith finished, colleagues embraced him. Senator Harry Reid (Democrat-Nevada) recalled attending Garrett Smith's funeral and hearing everyone talk openly about suicide. It was a revelation. After Reid's father shot himself, Reid said he was too ashamed to talk about it for years. Senator Don Nickles (Republican-Oklahoma) rarely discusses his father's suicide but said, "It's a lot of pain."

Annually, 30,000 Americans die by suicide. This is the equivalent of 9/11 happening almost every month. It's also the equivalent of a major airliner filled with passengers crashing every two days. By comparison, there are 18,000 homicides annually in the United States. One wouldn't know it from reading a newspaper or watching *CNN*, but there are far more suicides in this country than murders.

Four thousand of the 30,000 people who die annually by suicide are youths. Suicide is the third leading cause of death for people age ten to twenty-four. Smith's bill, the Garrett Lee Smith Act, is providing funding to help reduce and prevent youth suicide. It's a good start, but more is needed.

As I'm writing this, the war in Iraq has gone on more than four years. Nearly 4,000 Americans have died, as well as countless Iraqi soldiers and civilians. During the same period, over 120,000 Americans have died by suicide. They haven't had flag-draped coffins. Only family members and friends know their names.

As a country, we grieve each war casualty. As individuals, we grieve each suicide.

For a year, moviemaker Eric Steel secretly filmed people jumping to their deaths from the Golden Gate Bridge. His work brought attention to the fact that the bridge is the strongest suicide magnet in the world. It also may lead—at long last—to a suicide barrier.

There are more than 1,300 reasons why a safety railing is needed, each one compelling. That's the number of documented suicides since the bridge first opened in 1937. The real number undoubtedly is higher since the bodies of some victims are never recovered, so their deaths can't be confirmed. Naturally, it doesn't include all of the children, spouses, partners, parents, siblings, friends, and other loved ones left to mourn the people who have jumped.

Against this number there are three reasons cited why a railing shouldn't be constructed. The first one is cost. A suicide barrier costs money. Of course it does. It also costs money to put airbags in cars, design child-proof caps for medicines, and have lifeguards at beaches, but no one complains. These actions save lives.

The second argument against a railing is aesthetics. The Golden Gate Bridge is beautiful and a suicide barrier will mar it. Well, guess what? There's nothing beautiful about a body lying broken on the rocks, that didn't make the water (people who jump from the north end sometimes don't leap far enough). There's nothing beautiful about taking a walk on the bridge and seeing someone hurtle to a gruesome death.

And it is gruesome. A body falling 200 feet reaches a speed of seventy-five miles per hour, hitting the water like concrete. Bones are crushed, vertebrae snap, lungs burst. Many people don't die immediately; instead there's internal bleeding, they plunge deeply, and drown—their final few seconds terrifying and painful.

Many of the designs for a suicide barrier use flexible steel rods that are so thin, they'd be invisible from shore. You couldn't see them unless you were on the bridge, and if you were they wouldn't block your view of San Francisco, the Pacific Ocean, or the Marin hills. They'd just block someone from jumping. The idea behind them is that if someone tries to climb up, the top folds back into the person, making it virtually impossible to surmount.

Before 2003, the Prince Edward Viaduct in Toronto was the site of nearly 500 fatal jumps. Then $4 million was spent on a "luminous veil" of stainless steel rods constructed above the railing. The number of suicides dropped to zero. Moreover, the safety barrier received the Canadian national engineering award for design elegance. Aesthetics were actually *improved*.

The third argument against a barrier is that suicidal people are so intent on killing themselves that if one means is closed to them, they'll find another. Individuals— including some bridge officials—use this argument as an alternative to appearing cheap or lacking in compassion. "If a barrier truly prevented suicides," they say, "I'd be in favor of it. But if people really want to die, nothing can stop them, so why bother?"

This belief in the inevitability of suicide is contradicted by the facts. According to a 1978 study by Dr. Richard Seidon, a professor at U.C. Berkeley, of 515 people who were stopped from jumping off the Golden Gate Bridge between 1937 and 1971, 94 percent were either still alive twenty years later or had died by means other than suicide.

To date, twenty-six people have jumped and lived. Only one of the twenty-six subsequently died by suicide. Kevin Hines is the last survivor. He hurtled over the side in 2001.

"As soon as I jumped, I wanted to live," Hines says. Eighteen years old at the time, depressed, and fighting personal demons, Hines broke his back in the attempt but he was lucky; not only did he live but he was able to walk again.

Ken Baldwin, another survivor, was twenty-eight in 1985 when he jumped after telling his wife that he'd be home late. "I still see my hands coming off the railing," he told a *New Yorker* reporter. "I instantly realized that everything in my life that I'd thought was unfixable was totally fixable—except for having just jumped."

When a suicide barrier was erected on the Empire State Building, suicidal people didn't walk across the street to the RCA Building (now the Rockefeller Center) and jump. It didn't have the same attraction. The biggest impact on the suicide rate in California was when a three-day waiting period for buying a gun went into effect across the state. Over night, the suicide rate dropped almost in half.

The Golden Gate Bridge wasn't always the world's leading suicide location. The Duomo in Italy, Eiffel Tower in Paris, Empire State Building in New York, Sydney Harbor Bridge in Australia, St. Peter's Basilica in Rome, Arroyo Seco Bridge in Pasadena, California, and Mt. Mihara, a volcano in Japan, rivaled it for that distinction. Eventually, barriers were erected at all of these other sites, though, and suicide attempts ended. The main reason why the Golden Gate Bridge is a magnet is because jumping off from there is easy. The bridge has a pedestrian walkway open year-round to the public with a guardrail that's only four feet high. Hoist yourself over it and in the blink of an eye you're gone. One local psychologist describes such easy access as the equivalent of living in a house where a loaded gun is permanently placed on the kitchen table.

Eve Meyer, executive director of San Francisco Suicide Prevention, says, "If three or four golden retrievers jumped off the bridge, a safety railing would be erected immediately. The public would demand it. Because it's lonely, troubled, depressed people who are taking their lives, no one seems too concerned."

Another way to look at the issue, she says, is to imagine that the Golden Gate Bridge doesn't exist. A pagan god comes to San Francisco and says, "I'll build you the most beautiful bridge imaginable. People will come from near and far to see it. It'll be one of the wonders of the world. In return, you have to sacrifice 30 people a year. Do you accept it?"

A suicide railing is overdue. With it, all of us can enjoy a magnificent span and know that the tragedies associated with it have ended.

BECOMING AN ADVOCATE

I didn't know much about suicide before I came to the crisis center. I hadn't thought about the need for a safety railing on the Golden Gate Bridge, or about the effects of suicide contagion, where one suicide leads to repeated, imitative behavior (common among youth), or about the pros and cons of physician-assisted suicide.

My knowledge was limited; however, I learned quickly. As I did, my attitude changed. No longer did I consider suicide solely an individual's problem; society also is to blame. Little or nothing is done to restrict access to means. Many tall buildings lack suicide barriers. People can buy a firearm with little or no waiting period. Over-the-counter medications like Tylenol, which can be fatal if swallowed in large quantities, are sold in bulk here (in England, these medications are sold in "blister packs" that require consumers to press a tab with their thumb to remove each individual tablet).

Also, too few people are properly trained in suicide prevention. In most states, physicians, psychologists, therapists, counselors, and clinical social workers aren't required to take any suicide training to receive or maintain professional licenses, even though they may have frequent contact with suicidal people. The same is true for police officers, firefighters, and other first responders. Teachers and coaches seldom receive instruction in recognizing suicide warnings signs, assessing risk, or responding effectively.

Several years ago I was asked by a local service club to speak to the group. "We want to hear about the crisis center's services," the president of the club told me, "but in particular we'd like to hear about your work preventing youth suicides."

"Sure," I said. "Is there a particular reason why you're interested in youth suicide?"

He paused, then told me the story. He'd been driving along College Avenue in Berkeley when he saw something out of the corner of his eye that didn't register on his consciousness. He drove several more blocks, then realized that what he'd seen was someone jump out of a dormitory window. He turned around, went back, and by the time he got out of his car there was a group of people standing around the body of a young woman. She was lying face down, dead. Someone rolled her over and the president of the service club let out a gasp. She was a Berkeley student who'd received a scholarship from the club. It turned out that she was failing her chemistry class and was so ashamed of letting down everyone who'd supported her that she considered suicide the only way out. Little did she know that in that one tragic moment she changed the lives of everyone who knew her forever.

We place such high expectations on our children sometimes, wanting the best for them. It's unfortunate when that's all they feel, the pressure to excel, and not the love behind the expectations, which is forgiving.

That's why I'm now an advocate. Advocacy is speaking up, drawing attention to an important problem, and building support for a solution. It can include many short-term activities aimed to reach a long-term vision, and incorporate a variety of strategies and approaches. The scale can be relatively small, such as seeking to transform the internal culture of an organization, or huge, such as altering an entire community or system. Advocacy is the process of people participating in the formulation of decisions that affect their lives.

There's another word for advocacy: lobbying. Many people think of lobbyists as high-paid guns for hire who have little integrity and few scruples. In this context they confuse lobbying with campaigning. Campaign lobbyists work for a political candidate or party and have one goal—to see their person or party victorious in an election. Nonpartisan lobbyists, or advocates, on the other hand, have a different agenda—to bring about change.

The distinction is critical because some charities mistakenly believe that they can't lobby. They avoid becoming advocates—even on their own issue—because they consider it illegal. In fact, lobbying is perfectly legal as long as a charity follows the rules. The key rule is being nonpartisan. Nonpartisan means being nonpolitical. Charities can't engage in any activities that are intended to help or hurt the chances of a candidate or group of candidates in an election. A candidate is defined as someone who has publicly announced that he or she is running for office or someone who's being promoted publicly to enter a race.

It's actually pretty simple. A charity can't endorse a political candidate or let a candidate use its space for a political function. No one in the agency can write a letter of support for a candidate on agency letterhead, make agency donations to candidates or parties, or participate in a political campaign as a representative of a nonprofit organization. Employees can't use agency time, phones, or computers for campaign-related work, including e-mailing friends and inviting them to political events outside office hours. Violate any of these and the Internal Revenue Service can revoke an agency's tax-exempt status and levy a fine.

That said, there's a lot that nonprofit agencies *can* do. They can organize get-out-the-vote drives and target their efforts on disadvantaged or excluded groups as long as they remain nonpartisan. They can host forums for candidates to speak on different issues and publish voter guides with this information if they include candidates from all parties and don't do any rating of candidates. Staff, board members, volunteers, and clients can work on campaigns, endorse candidates, and even run for political office themselves providing it's clear that they're acting as individuals and not as representatives of the agency.

Activities designed to present issues to the public and to elected officials who make public policy also are permitted. So, too, is lobbying elected representatives in their official legislative capacity during an election. Since the survival of many nonprofit services depends, at least in part, on influencing local, state, or Federal representatives to take positions that are in a charity's best interests, lobbying is an important part of any agency's work.

As an executive director, I'm always aware of how far I can go in making a case for or against something I believe in. One consideration, as mentioned previously, is whether it's legal. I would never want to do anything that put the crisis center's tax-exempt status in jeopardy. Another consideration, which is nearly as important, is that I would never want to take a public position on an issue if I didn't have the full backing of everyone at the crisis center. After all, executive directors represent more than just themselves; we represent all who are connected with our cause. We have to lead and inspire, but we can't dictate or abuse our power. I feel that an important part of my job is to convey messages to the community that emphasize the crisis center's life-affirming mission. It's not appropriate for me, though, to turn my position into a soapbox for airing personal opinions.

TURNING FACTS INTO EMOTIONS

In being an advocate, I always started with the facts. While facts are subject to interpretation, their existence is difficult to deny, especially if the source is credible. In England, for instance, the suicide rate went down dramatically after natural gas was introduced. It replaced a more toxic gas that had become a popular way for people to kill themselves. A person might not consider this cause and effect, and believe that the change in home fuel had no impact on the suicide rate. That's subject to debate. What can't be disputed is that the two events occurred simultaneously. That's a fact. Knowing it, most people would conclude that there's a relationship between the two.

The next step is to put a human face on facts. Facts, by themselves, are cold. They move us intellectually, but not emotionally. As soon as they're linked to an individual, though, they produce a visceral response. This response is what advocates count on to energize others to join their side. It's why victims have so much power, be they 9/11 widows and children, parents of soldiers killed in Iraq, or mothers against drunk driving. Once people are emotionally invested in an issue, their mind follows.

The challenge for an agency is to provide a human face without taking advantage of its clients. Trotting out someone with a heartfelt story merely because it serves the agency's needs is wrong. I've been to countless budget hearings where nonprofit agencies whose funding is being threatened have organized a parade of speakers to testify on their behalf, all of them helped in one way or another by the agency. Their words have impact, largely because there's genuine emotion behind them. Battered women who've escaped abusive spouses, foster care children who found a loving home, frail elderly who depend on a daily meals program for food and companionship—how can anyone not be moved by what they have to say? Many times their testimony has the desired effect—the cut is rescinded, funding is restored. A small part of me believes that the agency has lost as much as it's gained, however, by using its clients this way.

At the crisis center, we use client stories in direct mail appeals, grants, and newsletters because of their evocative power. Each time they appear there's a disclaimer, though, noting that people's names and some of their characteristics have been changed to protect identities. Obviously, it's impossible to do this in live settings, which is why we don't ask clients to speak publicly on our behalf. A few have anyway, long after they recovered from whatever trauma brought them to the crisis center. When it's happened, I've been grateful, but also uncomfortable. I wish it was possible to have the same effect without "outing" them.

One option is to use volunteers. Ours are bright, articulate, compassionate, skilled, and dedicated to the crisis center's mission. When they give public testimony about calls they've answered or clients they've counseled, always careful to disguise any identifying characteristics in order to protect confidentiality, the room invariably becomes quiet. They don't embellish the story because they don't need to; the facts themselves and the inherent emotion behind the telling are enough. Added to this is the realization in everyone's mind that volunteers are a self-selecting group. They don't have to give their time. No one pays them and no one rewards them, except with a few words of appreciation. They volunteer for the simplest and purest reason—because they want to help.

Even using volunteers can be tricky, though. I'm always conflicted about asking our volunteers to publicly identify themselves for two reasons. First, some of our hotline callers try to stalk our volunteers. It's not a dangerous kind of stalking; instead, the callers are so lonely and in need of human connection that they gravitate to anyone who has a kind voice and shows interest in their lives. All they want is a relationship. Unfortunately, we can't provide it; that's not our role. Making public the full name of a volunteer and—even worse—showing the person's face just increases the risk.

The second reason is because, in an odd way, having volunteers speak on behalf of the crisis center may discourage people from calling us. Suppose you're a parent and just discover that your oldest son is using drugs. You don't know whether to confront him or what to say; communication hasn't been good between the two of you lately. You're too ashamed to confide in friends or coworkers, and may not believe that they'll be much help anyway. You want to call the crisis center for advice, only you know that your next-door neighbor volunteers there. Suppose he or she answers the phone?

INTERNAL ADVOCACY

The biggest difference between experienced and first-time executive directors is the degree to which the former change the internal culture of their agencies. Experienced directors assess an agency's culture and alter it if necessary. Inexperienced directors are less aware, usually too overwhelmed by the variety of job responsibilities and the challenge of shared governance that epitomizes the nonprofit sector to notice whether anything needs changing.

As I've noted elsewhere, when I started at the crisis center only one board member and one part-time staff member were persons of color. Almost none of the agency's 200-plus volunteers were African-American, Asian, or Latino. Few staff, board members, or volunteers seemed aware of the discrepancy, or concerned by it.

All of us, as individuals, are drawn to people like ourselves. Growing up, that's who the members of our family are, and as we grow older it's usually who we choose as friends and neighbors. We're most comfortable interacting with people like us because we understand them, share many of the same experiences, and tend to have similar values. There's nothing wrong with this; however, it insulates us from people whose age, gender, ethnicity, culture, religion, social position, economic status, or sexual orientation is different than our own. Because they're different, because it takes some effort to understand them whereas it's relatively easy to understand people like ourselves, we may not try. The irony is that, among members of our cultural or ethnic group, we tend to emphasize the similarities between us and minimize the differences, while among members of other cultural or ethnic groups we emphasize the differences and minimize the similarities.

The best way to begin transforming the internal culture of an agency is to bring in people whose allegiance is to the future, not the past. In my first few months I had the opportunity to hire four new employees who added different perspectives and experiences.

Rocio was from Peru, with a college degree in business. Since coming to the United States ten years earlier, she'd only been able to find part-time clerical work and had to supplement her income by working as a waitress in a Mexican restaurant. She became the crisis center's first full-time office manager.

George was a former football player who still liked to lift weights. Homeless when he was younger, he'd worked in several shelters before coming to the crisis center. In his free time he coached youth football teams. For vacation, he traveled to amusement parks all over the country and rode roller coasters. When I asked him why, he said, "Because that's the only place I know of where a 300-pound black man can scream at the top of his lungs and no one's scared." He was hired to answer our homeless hotline.

Brian was our youngest staff person. Only three years out of college, he already was an experienced hotline volunteer and grief counselor. Charismatic and irreverent, he could be counted on to make a clever quip about anything that seemed stodgy or routine. He was the perfect tonic for someone who was feeling down— and the perfect antidote for an agency that had become set in its ways. I was glad to have him as our education coordinator.

Minerva was a former drug addict who hit bottom, then turned her life around. She'd been clean for several years; however, she had been unable to find work because of past convictions for drug-related offenses. At the time that she applied to the crisis center, she was volunteering at a detox program, gaining experience as a case manager. I knew she'd be perfect working with George in our homeless services program, and I was right.

I didn't make a point of saying that three of the four new hires were persons of color, but it was impossible for others not to notice. My message was clear: the crisis center is going to start looking like the broader community we want to serve.

Despite the vibrancy of a diverse workplace, there's still a tendency for staff to hire people like themselves. I understand this. As executive director, though, I can't let it happen.

Mary manages our resource database. It's a huge job keeping everything current—2,500 resource listings, each with more than forty fields of data, each listing searchable by 1,600 keywords and 1,300 taxonomy codes, and each included in one or more of a half-dozen specialized print publications. Several years ago, when her assistant left, Mary conducted interviews for a new assistant. The goal, in her mind, was to find someone whose skills matched her own. This wasn't easy because Mary worked in the computer industry twenty-five years. She could write code in multiple programming languages, taught classes in a variety of software applications, and was happiest when presented with a technical challenge that required ingenuity and persistence. Moreover, she was hardworking, meticulous, and highly motivated. Several candidates had excellent qualifications in her mind, and she was excited by the prospect of hiring one.

"Are any of the top candidates people of color?" I asked.

"No," Mary said, "but they're all really sophisticated computer users. Any one of them would be great—and would relieve a lot of my workload."

"Are any of the second-tier candidates people of color?"

Mary grimaced. "One is Filipino. She's young and somewhat knowledgeable, though nowhere near the level of some of the others."

"Could she do the job?"

"Barely," Mary said. "I'd have to spend a lot of time training her, and I don't know whether she'd stick around long enough to make it worthwhile."

There's a danger in not allowing managers to hire their own employees. When it's their choice, managers do everything they can to help a new person succeed. When it's not their decision, though, they can be less supportive.

"It's really hard to hire licensed clinicians who are people of color," I said. "There aren't many to begin with, and the few who are can pretty much write their own ticket. The same is true with fundraisers. It's not a profession that other ethnicities are drawn to. Computer people are different, though. There's a lot of diversity in the field. That's why in filling this position it's difficult for me to justify hiring someone who's white."

Mary started to respond, but I wasn't finished. "I know you're backlogged now," I said, "and feel that you need someone to assist you who can hit the ground running. I appreciate that. If I was in your position, I'd probably feel the same way.

From where I'm sitting, though, this is what I see: There's nothing mystical about the work; it's technical and the person has to be attentive to detail, but anyone with good basic skills who's smart can learn to do it. Someone who isn't Filipino, though, can never learn what that's like. That makes Liezl an asset in a way that the other candidates aren't."

Mary understood my point, but she wasn't happy. Having to tell people whom she considered more qualified that they weren't chosen was upsetting. Fortunately, Liezl proved to be a quick study. Within days she knew many of the nuances of our database. She also learned how to program our phone system—something no one else on staff had mastered, saving us hundreds of dollars in service charges that formerly we paid to an outside vendor. That she stayed only two years before taking a higher-paying job with a tech company didn't make me regret hiring her. She added an important point of view while she was at the crisis center.

Not every person of color I've hired has worked out. Far from it. Nor has every white person. There have been failures, a few of them spectacular, made worse because I was slow to admit it. When it's clear to everyone except the boss that someone isn't pulling his or her weight, morale suffers. If the employee is a person of color, whites believe that the agency accepts lower standards for minorities and don't accord multicultural staff the respect they deserve.

Hiring diverse staff is only the beginning, though. An agency also has to:

- Include multicultural values in its mission and vision statements.
- Have a diverse board.
- Recruit and retain diverse volunteers.
- Incorporate cultural competency standards into job descriptions, performance evaluations, and personnel policies.
- Collect information on the ethnicity of clients in order to assess the sensitivity and appropriateness of services they receive.
- Provide services to clients in their primary language.
- Develop multilingual program materials and feature multicultural people in agency brochures, newsletters, posters, web sites, etc.
- Establish a process for receiving feedback from people of color (exit interviews, for example, when multicultural staff and volunteers leave the agency).
- Decorate agency offices with multicultural artwork.
- Develop working relationships with other agencies that serve multicultural clients.

All of these require someone championing the cause—the higher up, the better. They don't just happen on their own.

In 2005, the American Association of Suicidology in Washington, DC, which oversees the work of suicide prevention centers throughout the United States, began revising its certification standards. When I received a draft, I could barely contain my frustration. Despite umpteen pages of detailed criteria governing every other facet of crisis counseling, there wasn't a single reference to cultural competency. When I called the national office about this, the person in charge of certification apologized for the omission and invited me to write language for a cultural competency section to be added to the standards. I was a little taken aback, uncertain whether I was qualified to do this. Still, I barely hesitated. How many times does one have the opportunity to define criteria that affect a nation-wide service? I consulted with Roberto, our cultural competency coordinator, then submitted my recommendation. The review committee approved it. Today cultural competency is one of the criterion by which all crisis centers are judged. A few of my colleagues aren't pleased because it means additional work for them, but I couldn't be happier. Like it or not, all crisis centers will provide even better service in the future as a result.

IMMIGRATION

Having written and spoken about the value of diversity, I was nevertheless caught off guard when a longtime friend, a superior court judge, asked my opinion on immigration. It was right after Mexicans in California staged a one-day work stoppage to protest new, harsher treatment for illegal immigrants. The event reminded me of the movie *A Day Without a Mexican*. In it, the economy of Los Angeles and, by extension, all of California, comes crashing to a halt because everyone of Mexican descent vanishes for twenty-four hours. Without day laborers, child care workers, restaurant staff, landscapers, auto mechanics, maids, fruit pickers, and dozens of other low-paid yet essential service people, the infrastructure of the state collapses.

Immigration is such a complex issue, however, that when my friend asked my opinion, I just rolled my eyes. We don't have enough housing, classrooms, health care, jobs, and other essentials to support a limitless stream of people into this country. Yet where do we draw the line? At one time, virtually all of us were immigrants. Except for Native Americans, our ancestors arrived here from other lands drawn by dreams of prosperity. My father and his family came through Ellis Island from England. My mother's family came through Ellis Island from Norway. Once here, both clans worked hard and assimilated into the prevailing culture, in New York and North Dakota, respectively. Why should others be denied the opportunities that my ancestors—and later my family—had?

The thing that makes me most uneasy about the immigration debate is that it smacks of privilege. Once people are admitted into an exclusive group, be it a private college, fraternal order, social group, county club, association, or community, they advocate for tougher entrance requirements. They're in; now they want to keep others out—especially people who don't look like them, talk like them, think like them, or act like them. In the same way, immigration seems to me like a deliberate attempt to protect the rights of people who once were on the outside and now are on the inside. Erecting barriers to prevent individuals from entering the country illegally, or deporting people if they surmount the barriers, results in minimizing contact with individuals who are different and, some might think, inferior.

Roberto turned the current controversy over immigration into an enlightening, two-step exercise with staff. Imagine that the worst effects of global warming take place, he said. Polar ice caps melt, the oceans surge, and huge currents of water wash over much of California. Whole communities are wiped out. People panic and flee to Mexico. Within days millions of Americans have crossed the border, homeless. They overwhelm the capacity of local officials and relief agencies to feed, clothe, and house them all. In desperation, the Mexican government closes the border, refusing to let anymore Americans into the country. Families who try to enter are turned back. Children and adults either die or are left to suffer from hunger and exposure. The president of Mexico goes on international television to say that his heart and the hearts of his countrymen go out to the victims; however, the government has to take care of its own people first. It can't use money from Mexican taxpayers to help needy Americans when many of its own citizens live in poverty, without clean water, adequate health care, or sufficient educational opportunities.

Roberto paused to let all of that sink in. Everyone was silent. Now imagine that you're among those trying to escape, he said. Your whole family is in your car, you have little money, everyone has only one change of clothes. A few miles away lies a better life, the kind of life you've dreamed about for you and your children. At the border you're met by a group of guards and armed civilians who show no respect for you or have any compassion for what you've experienced. All they see is a carload of poor, dirty people whose skin is a different color, who speak a different language. All they're concerned about is keeping you out, protecting what they have. Your entry is blocked and you're told in harsh words to go back where you came from. How do you feel?

Predictably, this produced strong reactions from staff about the importance of helping others, regardless of nationality. Crisis center counselors are used to putting other people's needs ahead of their own, so this wasn't surprising. When Roberto asked us how long we thought this obligation should last, however, and whether Mexico should set limits on its assistance given finite resources, opinions were divided. When you can't help everyone, how do you decide who has priority—children or adults, women or men, skilled professionals or mothers, people who are able bodied or people who can pay their own way, those who came first or those who are most in need?

Now add cultural biases. All of us tend to be ethnocentric, believing that our own culture and its social rules—the way we speak, our perspectives, our values—are superior to other cultures. Without being conscious of it, we may be hesitant to help people whose culture is different than our own. We think they're lacking, less able, ultimately less deserving. Even Americans who are in favor of strong, impenetrable borders don't seem to worry about Canadian, European, or Scandinavian immigrants. It's the thought of more people coming into the United States from Central America, South America, the Middle East, and Far East that has immigration vigilantes in an uproar. Who has priority—Caucasians or Latinos? Asians or African-Americans? Christians or Jews?

For the second step in the training, Roberto told us to imagine that twenty years have passed. Some Americans have moved back, yet hundreds of thousands remain in Mexico. A small percentage are fully assimilated into Mexican culture; however, many still live on the periphery. They haven't learned the language, so they have a hard time finding work and being self-sufficient. Because of linguistic and cultural barriers, they're also unable to access health care and other services. The Mexican government decides to start cultural competency trainings for native health and social workers so that they can better serve Americans in their midst. After all, displaced Americans form a significant portion of the population. To understand their needs, the government convenes all of us to serve as a focus group. Our task is to provide information on what it's like to be American. What do we tell them?

Staff rebelled at this assumption. "We're all individuals," they said. "There's no way that a small group of us can speak on behalf of everyone in America."

Roberto considered this. "Haven't we convened focus groups of African-Americans and Latinos to inform us as we try to make crisis center services more culturally sensitive and appropriate?" he said. "No one thought that was foolish. Why is this different?"

No one had an answer. Roberto was right.

When we tried to articulate what it means to be American from a cultural perspective, though, we were challenged. The United States is a melting pot of different races, cultures, and religions. The one commonality is a belief in the American dream. Yet what justification is there to deny that dream to others? Because one's ancestors arrived first? Because they came from predominantly white cultures—British, Irish, Italian, French, Polish, Nordic—that are more tolerated?

There are twelve million illegal immigrants in the United States today. Many more are knocking at the door. I don't know whether we should let them in; but locking them out seems wrong.

Robert Frost said, "Good fences make good neighbors." There's truth in that; however, as I grapple in my mind with the problem of immigration, I don't think the same thing can be said about walls—especially thick, high walls topped by barbed wire that run for hundreds of miles, separating people. One of the highlights of recent history was when the Berlin Wall came down. Citizens everywhere rejoiced.

I don't want to live behind a wall, nor do I think that others should have to live in front of one. There must be a better way—I just wish I knew what it was.

MEETING THE ARCHDRUID

Few nonprofit advocates have been more vocal over a longer period of time and reached a larger number of people than the late David Brower. Famed mountain climber and inveterate hiker, he was for many years widely considered the foremost environmentalist in the country. The first executive director of the Sierra Club, and later a board member—until he resigned in protest because he thought that the club had become too compromising in its strategies—Brower subsequently founded two other nonprofit agencies, Friends of the Earth and the Earth Island Institute. He also was the main character in John McPhee's classic work, *Encounters with the Archdruid*.

A druid is a prophet and Brower was that, portending doom unless people took care to tread lightly on the planet. Like all prophets, he had his share of flaws (one of them was that he accepted with little argument vestiges of man—buildings, roads, bridges, trains, tunnels, etc.—that preceded him, decrying only those developments that occurred after his birth). Nevertheless, he inspired, challenged, motivated, irritated, led, pushed, denounced, and praised a great many people, some of whom were instrumental in seeing that his vision of environmental stewardship was implemented, at least in part.

I only met Brower once, for the briefest moment. It was memorable, though. In 1978, three graduate students and I were renting a professor's house high up in the Berkeley hills. The professor was on a two-year sabbatical and we hoped that he'd never return. It was a spectacular house, rustic and full of windows, looking out on San Francisco Bay. The entire wall facing the bay was louvered and opened up onto a deck. Past the deck was a wooded ravine with a creek and narrow trail that led a quarter mile down to a residential area. From there it was a ten-minute walk to campus and Berkeley shops. It was so secluded that the only house besides ours that was visible, other than those in the distance, shared a long, steep, S-shaped driveway with us. It was the modest residence of an older man named Alfred Peet, the founder and president of Mr. Peet's Coffee.

One day late in the afternoon, at the end of summer, I walked up the trail to the house. Sunlight filtered through the trees, and the creek was reduced to a trickle. When I emerged at the house I saw a trim, fit, gray-haired man wearing shorts and hiking boots standing in our yard. The sight of him caused me to stop in my tracks. Other than Mr. Peet, I'd never seen a soul around the property.

His back was to me and he was holding a hose. I cleared my throat so that he knew I was there. He didn't move right away. When he did turn, he wasn't the least bit surprised to see me. On the contrary, he seemed slightly perturbed that I was interrupting his work.

It was David Brower. I recognized him immediately. I knew that he lived in the area, though not exactly where.

"Can I help you?" I said.

"No," he said. "I was just passing by and thought your plants looked a little thirsty."

I nodded dumbly. Not knowing what else to say I said, "Thanks."

He gave a little half-wave, then turned back and continued watering.

That was it. Nearly thirty years later, though, I still remember. "I was just passing by and thought your plants looked a little thirsty." Passing by *there*? No one passed by that house. Most of our friends couldn't even find it. I hardly ever saw anyone on the trail, and then only on the lower section. I wondered how many other times Brower had stopped somewhere during his travels and been moved to act like that.

It's one thing to say that something should be done; it's another thing to take responsibility for doing it. I could only shake my head in amazement. *That's* an advocate.

CHAPTER SIXTEEN

Ending Up: Where the Heart Is

Recently I came across a poem, by Linda Ellis, titled "The Dash." In it, a man speaks at the funeral of his friend. He refers to the dates on her tombstone, to the date of her birth, which was a joyous occasion, and to the date of her death, which everyone is now grieving. What matters most of all, he says, is not those dates, not the beginning or the end, but the dash between them.

"That dash represents all the time she spent alive on earth," the man says. "Now only those who loved her know what that little line is worth."

He goes on to say that it doesn't matter "how much we own, the cars, the house, the cash. What matters is how we live and love and how we spend our dash."

At the crisis center, we have more opportunities than most people to learn how fragile life is. Every day we answer calls from people who are abused, depressed, suicidal. Every week we provide face-to-face counseling to children and adults who are mourning the death of a loved one. Every year we meet with thousands of students at middle schools and high schools to talk about the stress and pressures they feel.

We hear about people's ups and downs, about their lives—about their dash. We listen to their problems, discuss options, and provide emotional support. Most importantly, we convey hope. If there was a time when things weren't so bad, do you remember how you felt then, we ask. With support, and perhaps with counseling, you may be able to feel that way again, sooner than you think.

The child who died can't come to life, the love who left may never return, and the test that was flunked or car that crashed or job that was lost can't be changed. Still, a new relationship, job, or interest might be just around the corner.

Our message, which we relay in countless ways to people in despair, is: Don't give up too early. Miracles happen every day. Even "small" miracles—a child's laugh, a summer sunset—can lift one's spirit.

If people give themselves a chance, oftentimes they find, years down the road, that their dash has become more than a small line between two dates. It's become a lifetime.

Many people gravitate to the nonprofit sector because they want to help others and feel good about the work they're doing. They have a passion for the agency's mission and a desire to make their communities better places to live. All too often, though, once they become executive directors they experience burnout, usually because of concerns about agency finances. After a few years worrying every day about making payroll, paying rent, replacing old, worn-out equipment, and just keeping the lights on, they realize that their passion for the agency's mission is secondary to operational challenges. The job begins to lose much of its allure.

According to several studies, the majority of executive directors stay in their jobs for four years. After this relatively short tenure, they pursue other careers, sometimes with foundations, sometimes as consultants, oftentimes with for-profit companies.

I don't doubt it. At the same time, many people I know are the exception. I belong to an association of nonprofit executive directors called the Contractors Alliance. There are twenty-five of us, representing the biggest agencies in our area, and we meet monthly to discuss issues of common concern. Over the years people have come and gone, although in general the turnover has been low. Half the members have been executive directors for at least ten years. Five have directed their current agencies for twenty-five years or more. I served as president of the Alliance, while also running the crisis center, for as many years—four—as the average executive director stays in the sector.

Perhaps our group isn't representative. After all, it takes longer to get to the top of a large agency, the pay is better, and the geographic area where we work—the San Francisco Bay Area—is highly prized. Maybe it's not surprising that people here are more likely to stay in their current position. Then again, virtually every meeting of the Alliance is dominated by conversations about money, followed by exclamations of frustration, anxiety, and fear. As a group, we never lack vision or ideas about how to improve our community. What we lack is funding to keep essential services going.

The thing most likely to keep executive directors awake at night is financial worries. If your agency is well funded now, you worry about what you're going to do next year when a large grant ends, a major donor moves away, or the biggest giver on your board terms out. If you're not well funded, you worry about how you're going to pay new bills and which staff you might have to lay off. The pressure never ends.

At one point in an Alliance meeting, after everyone had belabored the latest round of county budget cuts and all of us were feeling low, someone asked, "So why are we all here?" The person meant why were all of us still in the sector, still directing our agencies, still trying to stretch every dollar as far as possible, enduring the headaches it produces?

There were a few shrugs. "Beats me," one person said.

"Someone has to fight the good fight," another person muttered.

"Because I'm too young to retire," said a third person, to a few laughs.

The real reason for me, and I think for my colleagues, is because there's nothing else we'd rather be doing. Yes, it'd be nice to direct an agency that's so well endowed one doesn't have to worry about funding. I'd love to be able to sign a stack of checks and not think about where the money is coming from to pay for everything, or be able to give my staff raises that reflect their true worth, or be able to replace old furniture and office equipment long before they wear out or break down. At the same time, it's fulfilling to drive around a community and see the results of your labors, the child care center you helped develop, the food bank you grew, the soup kitchen where you served meals, the homeless shelter you've supported, the crisis center you built. Each is a source of pride.

ORANGES AND MUSHROOMS

In 1980, when I got my first nonprofit job, the personal computer was still a dream for most people. Typewriters were used for all written work, spreadsheets were maintained by hand, databases consisted of card files that, in their most advanced state, were on microfiche, newsletters were printed on mimeograph machines, and CDs, DVDs, scanners, faxes, cell phones, laser printers, PDAs, and digital cameras were among the many things that didn't exist yet. It was a different world.

The food bank where I worked didn't own a forklift. Everything was loaded and unloaded by hand. One of my most vivid memories is driving an old flatbed truck to a packing plant near Sacramento, setting it up under a chute, and watching the truck fill with oranges. Then back at the food bank, I and other workers would position empty field bins around the truck, lift up the stake sides, and get out of the way as oranges flew into the bins. Many bounced off the rims or missed altogether and rolled to far corners of the warehouse or out the front door. I scrambled after them, wanting to make sure that I tracked them down before neighboring vehicles ran over them or I discovered them, weeks later, misshapen and moldy under pallets of food.

Once a week I drove the flatbed to a S.B. Thomas English Muffin warehouse on the Peninsula. First I stopped by Discovery House, though, a local drug rehab program, and recruited a couple of volunteers. They helped me stack racks of muffins to the top of the stake sides. No one was sophisticated enough in those days to use tarps, so on the way back the muffins that were exposed would sail off the truck, a fact I was never fully aware of until I arrived at the food bank and saw how many were missing. Miraculously, no one ever stopped me or gave me a ticket. I don't know if I was just lucky or if other motorists and local police saw the food bank's name on the truck and were forgiving.

One Friday I picked up a load of milk and yogurt from a new dairy, excited by the possibility that the food bank would have a steady stream of dairy donations. I delivered it the same day to local food pantries thinking there'd be more, only to learn on Monday that the dairy had burned to the ground over the weekend.

Later there were truckloads of U.S. Department of Agriculture cheese—thousands of them—delivered regularly to food banks across the country. The cheese was surplus, the result of a national price support program that paid (and continues to pay) dairy farmers for unsold products. There were also military rations—MREs (Meals Ready to Eat)—that were donated following the Persian Gulf War. My sympathies for the soldiers increased with every shipment.

The people I worked with at that time were equally memorable. Harry, a driver, made a written list that he kept with him at all times of the characteristics he required in a mate. Included were such things as the exact length, color, and cut of her hair. The list was three pages long. The only thing longer would have been a list of Harry's neuroses. One Halloween he bought a big pumpkin and carved it with a circular saw. Really. He considered a knife too slow and too much work.

Vivian was in a training program, and her warehouse position was funded by the Federal government. Her previous job was working on the assembly line of an electronics company that went out of business. She loved doing the same thing repeatedly, and regretted that the food bank didn't offer her this experience. I regretted it, too, every time I had to give her a new task.

Bud was hired with funding from the local Area Agency on Aging. A candy vendor in the Chicago burlesque house Dillinger's in the late 1920s, he spoke colorfully of his life, and freely shared his opinions. On a high-priced call girl: "Just goes to show you: if I'd been born the right sex, I could make a million dollars. I got the right attitude." On a corrupt politician: "He's so crooked that when he dies, they'll have to screw him into the ground—he won't go in straight." On Dean Lesher, probably the wealthiest man in Contra Costa County and publisher of the *Contra Costa Times*: "If I had his money, I'd throw mine away."

Dominick was the agency's most faithful volunteer. Retired, living on Social Security, a small pension, and income from a house he rented out, he worked every day in the warehouse. Then on weekends he drove to Reno to gamble. One Monday morning I asked him how he'd done. He shrugged. "I went up in a $5,000 car," he said, "and came back in a $200,000 bus."

Perhaps the most memorable person of all was Nicholas, another warehouse volunteer. Shortly after he arrived in the United States from Russia at the age of seventy, he came across a vacant lot where wild mushrooms were growing. He couldn't believe it; in Russia, wild mushrooms were picked and eaten on the spot. He didn't know what kind of mushrooms these were; moreover, he knew that some varieties were poisonous. Nevertheless, he filled his pockets with mushrooms, took them home, and boiled them. Then he sat down at the dinner table, the plate of mushrooms in front of him, and commanded his wife, Luba, to sit across from him with the phone book opened to the page of emergency phone numbers. This way, if he started to get sick she could summon help immediately.

MORE THAN A PAYCHECK

When I started at the crisis center, Margie was the part-time office manager. She only worked in the afternoon because in the morning she was studying to be a paralegal aide. She was highly skilled on the computer, and adept at running a business office. I regretted that she couldn't work more hours, and knew that someday I'd lose her altogether. Still, I couldn't blame her for wanting to earn more money and have a "real" career.

After she graduated, Margie was hired by the legal department of a large bank. While she was teary-eyed to say good-by to everyone at the crisis center, she also was excited to put her education to work and enjoy the benefits of a higher salary, bigger office, and increased opportunities for advancement. I wished her well.

Several months later she called me to ask if I knew whether any nonprofit agency was looking to hire an office manager. I was surprised. "What happened at the bank?" I asked.

"I can't work there," she said. "People don't care about each other, much less about individuals they don't know. All they care about is collecting a paycheck."

Her experience wasn't unusual, I think. Most working adults spend at least eight hours a day surrounded by coworkers. If these people are self-centered, insecure, power hungry, or boring, there's no joy in being there. You're just putting in time. No matter how big your salary is, each day is long, frequently stressful, and ultimately depressing. Weekends and holidays offer the only relief.

In the nonprofit sector, salaries may be low, however everything else—especially job satisfaction—tends to be high. The workplace is filled with people who are compassionate, loving, connected, upbeat, committed, interesting, and generous. Few are there for the money; in fact, many are volunteers.

Equally important, every nonprofit job is directly or closely related to helping someone in a tangible way. You're not making or selling products that people don't need. You're not managing accounts or inventories for the primary purpose of seeing them grow. You're not moving information around, or trying to increase demand for your services, or worrying about what your competitors are doing. You're just trying to make a small, meaningful difference in the lives of a few people you start out not knowing anything about and oftentimes come to care a great deal for.

One of our volunteers at the crisis center is named Loree. She's in her seventies and has worked on our hotlines and been a grief counselor for more than two decades. Several years ago, she counseled a twelve-year-old boy whose grandfather died. The two, grandfather and grandson, had been unusually close, and after the elder's death the boy became withdrawn, sullen, and uncommunicative. He and Loree met once a week. Most of the time he said relatively little, no matter how hard Loree tried to get him to open up. After several months, she feared that he'd continue to hold his sadness inside him for a long time.

One day the boy asked Loree if she'd go on a bike ride with him. Without hesitation, she said yes. She dusted off an old bike that had belonged to one of her children who were now grown, and the two set off along a bike trail near the boy's home. During the ride, all of the emotions that the boy had held in check since his grandfather's death poured out. It was a breakthrough that happened only because Loree was flexible, willing to meet him where he was, physically and psychologically.

In 2003 another volunteer, nicknamed Jug, took a call from the youngest person we've ever counseled on our hotlines—three years old. Forty years in operation, more than one million crisis calls answered, and we provided support for the first time to someone born in the new millennium. It was a sobering moment. The little girl was hysterical after police had left her home following a domestic violence complaint. When the girl's mother couldn't calm her down, the mother called us. Jug answered and the mother explained the situation.

"Will you talk with my daughter?" she said.

It was a tremendous act of faith for a mother to entrust her young daughter's emotional state to the care of a stranger. At the same time, Jug wondered what he could say to a three-year-old girl. One thing that distinguishes crisis center volunteers, though, is their ability to think and respond in the moment. Jug had been doing this work as long as Loree, and like her he didn't hesitate.

"Of course," he told the mother.

When the mother passed the phone to her daughter, Jug heard the sobbing of a young child. "I'm Joe," he said gently. "What's your name?" (Jug, like other volunteers with unusual first names, uses a pseudonym on our lines.)

The girl's crying turned to sniffles. "Penny," she said. Her voice was barely audible.

"Penny, that's a pretty name," Jug said. "Do you have a grandfather, Penny?"

Penny didn't reply. In the background Jug heard her mother say, "You have to speak into the phone, honey. He can't see you moving your head."

"Uh hunh," Penny said. Jug wasn't sure whether this was a yes or a no until Penny added, "He's nice."

"That's good," Jug said. "That's good. I want you to think of me like your grandfather, Penny. Can you do that?"

Penny couldn't see Jug's white hair and twinkling eyes, but she didn't need to. His voice was calm and soothing. "Okay," Penny said. She wasn't crying anymore.

"Your grandfather cares about you a lot, doesn't he?"

"Uh hunh," Penny said.

"I care about you, too," Jug said. "It sounds like you're feeling better. Anytime you feel like you need you talk with someone, though, you ask your mommy to call this number, okay?"

"Okay," Penny said.

"Do you want to put your mommy back on the phone?"

Jug checked with the mother to make sure everything was okay. When she hung up, he sighed deeply. It was impossible to know whether Penny or her mother would need our services again. So much can happen in a lifetime. At least they knew that the crisis center could be trusted, and that we were there for them.

WHY I DO IT

I've managed nonprofit agencies for more than twenty-five years. Every year has been different. Not harder, although some years have been harder than others. Just different. In addition to funding challenges, board transitions, staff changes, program developments, capital purchases, system upgrades, volunteer turnover, political elections, demographic shifts, societal influences, and emerging community needs, all of which demand thought and careful planning to address effectively, there are new laws and regulations to learn governing everything from nonprofit lobbying to financial recordkeeping.

Though many programs and services continue to disappear from the landscape, new ones keep springing up. They're started because a small group of people—or sometimes just one person—is bothered enough by an injustice, a disparity, or an unmet need that they're motivated to do something about it.

The spirit that exists in America of wanting to help others is truly amazing. It's the reason why so many nonprofit agencies exist here. In many other countries, there's little charitable activity outside of the church.

The vast majority of people in the United States over the age of twenty—and many who are younger—volunteer somewhere during the year or give money to a charitable cause. Millions do both. Anyone who thinks that Americans are lazy, uncaring, or concerned only about themselves need spend just a few minutes at a nonprofit agency to feel his or her spirits lifted. No one is there for the money. No one is there because they have to be. No one believes that he or she is better than the people being helped—just more fortunate.

Yes, the United States is a country of stunning wealth that's often squandered in frivolous and self-centered ways. Yes, there are times when our nation's leaders take actions that make me feel disgusted and ashamed. Yes, I grieve the effects of inequalities, be they based on race, religion, age, gender, income, sexual orientation, culture, physical abilities, mental abilities, or class, which keep people from reaching their potential. The societal cost, on top of the personal, emotional toll, is too large to measure.

At the same time, I'm thankful to be where I am. The nonprofit sector is one of the most creative sectors in America. New ideas are born, pursued tenaciously, and turned into reality with incredible frequency.

The work is gratifying and meaningful. There's enormous satisfaction in being able to change lives and, in some instances, whole communities.

The people are compassionate and resilient. In tough times, they work even harder because the nonprofit sector has the most dedicated workforce in the country. Against great odds, with inadequate resources, they achieve what others consider to be impossible—day after day after day.

It's an honor to be part of it.

Index

About the Author

JOHN BATESON has directed nonprofit agencies for twenty-seven years. In 1996, he was named a Community Hero by United Way and chosen to carry the Olympic torch. For the past eleven years, he's been Executive Director of the Contra Costa Crisis Center in Walnut Creek, California. He and his wife, Suzan, also a nonprofit executive, have four children.